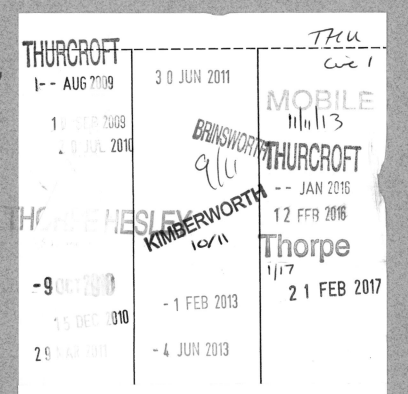

FLIGHTPATH
TO MURDER

In September 1944 an Allied fighter pilot force-lands his damaged aircraft deep inside hostile territory. He survives but minutes later his life is brutally ended.

Ten months on and the Allied forces occupying Hitler's defeated Fatherland have to re-establish order from chaos and ruin. Deemed essential is the bringing to justice of those who perpetrated war atrocities, to 'pursue them to the uttermost ends of the earth' and 'deliver them to their accusers in order that justice may be done'.

In July 1945 Allied war-crimes investigators exhume the body of an airman. The visible and ghastly damage suggests foul play. Identification proves problematic and an investigation opens to piece together the last moments of the pilot's life. What was the cause of death? Who was responsible? Was it a war crime?

Flightpath to Murder relates the comprehensive investigation surrounding the murder using testimony from those involved and the investigating officers, and from official documentation. Steve Darlow tells the pilot's story, beginning in a distant country, through to the fateful day; and the stories of the men held accountable for the killing. He asks what turned them into killers and why a man described as 'a tender father who as a good Christian disliked every violent action' became a killer in cold blood?

Flightpath to Murder records the hitherto untold story of a journey to barbarism and the terrible consequences that befall individuals who venture along that path. It opens an important new chapter in the telling of the 1939–45 air war and its effect on individual lives.

FLIGHTPATH TO MURDER
DEATH OF A PILOT OFFICER

STEVE DARLOW

Haynes Publishing

© Steve Darlow 2009

First published in 2009

A catalogue record for this book is available from the British Library

ISBN 978 1 84425 541 2

Library of Congress control no. 2009923201

Published by Haynes Publishing,
Sparkford, Yeovil, Somerset BA22 7JJ, UK
Tel: 01963 442030 Fax: 01963 440001
Int. tel: +44 1963 442030 Int. fax: +44 1963 440001
E-mail: sales@haynes.co.uk
Website: www.haynes.co.uk

Haynes North America Inc.
861 Lawrence Drive, Newbury Park,
California 91320, USA

Printed and bound in Great Britain
Typeset by Patricia J. Mills
Maps by TJ Design

CONTENTS

FLIGHTPATH TO MURDER

PREFACE

The published exploits of Second World War aircrew often highlight the glory and heroism, indeed the romanticism, of the air battles over Western Europe. Other books touch on the harsh realities of the air war. But this book details an untold and unique story from that period, dealing with the violence of the aerial conflict, the tragic consequences at a personal level and the post-war attempts to find justice amidst turmoil and chaos.

This book offers a fresh yet disturbing insight into another aspect of the air war over Europe and its repercussions. It can be viewed as part investigative story, part courtroom drama and part military and military law history. But at its core it is a human story, based on a considerable number of first-hand accounts and dealing with a widely overlooked aspect of the human tragedy of the Second World War.

I want to make it clear that, although I recognise the necessity to wage war against Nazi Germany and therefore support the bombing campaign, this is in many respects an anti-war book. It is an examination of how people are subjected to, and affected by, propaganda, and how they react in adverse situations. It tells of the levels of barbarity reached by both sides in the war. The book looks at the effect of applying military law to ordinary individuals swept along with the maelstrom of international conflict. It is a unique story of human beings who were subject to uncontrollable forces, which resulted in tragic consequences that have extended across the generations.

Looking at an individual case makes it possible to see in detail how such forces impact on individual lives. In the early stages of planning this book I did consider covering a number of war-crime cases concerning the lynching of Allied airmen. This particular case, however, allowed me to incorporate many aspects of the subject and to cover the issues, while humanising those involved. I feared that a general book on the subject would simply 'list' those involved. I wanted to highlight that they were people, humans, individuals, fathers, brothers, sons, friends, husbands, uncles.

The reader should note that throughout this book there are numerous quotations taken directly from investigation files and trial transcripts.

I have attempted to remain true to these documents. The reader will come across some inconsistencies in spellings, in particular the use of both American and British conventions, no doubt because the investigation was carried out by Canadians and the trial by the British. In addition, the punctuation, grammar and phrasing can be quite poor. Some of the statements and testimony at the trial were translated on the spot and recorded verbatim, and attention to punctuation and grammar was not a priority. Certainly the comma was used sparingly by whoever transcribed the trial proceedings. I hope the reader will understand that I have opted to reproduce these transcriptions exactly to maintain a feeling of authenticity in the narrative.

This has been a particularly difficult book to write. I have spent a considerable amount of time reading about, researching and looking at death. I have visited the graves of Allied airmen, the graves of German civilians killed in Allied bombing raids and the graves of war criminals. I have looked at autopsy photographs and read of exhumations. I have read of the means by which Allied airmen were executed and the means by which convicted war criminals, sentenced to death, met their fate. I have sat in the living room of an elderly German man, looking out across the Rhine, and heard how, sixty-four years previously, as a mere boy, he had identified the charred remains of two of his cousins. I have listened to a lady in her nineties as she told me how her mother was consumed by flames following an Allied bombing attack. Death has been ever present.

In some of my previous books I have highlighted the bravery and sacrifice of the Allied airmen and their contribution to the winning of the air struggle. My respect for these men remains intact, but the subject matter in this work has taken me into a new area, a new experience, and has given me a new perspective on the air war. The research for the book challenged my belief in the necessity of the bomber offensive to defeat Nazism – but necessary it was, because the war was necessary and victory was essential. But what it did to people and how it affected them . . . well read on.

LIST OF CHARACTERS

THE VICTIM
Pilot Officer William 'Spike' Maloney
    Royal Australian Air Force

THE INVESTIGATION
NO. 1 CANADIAN WAR CRIMES INVESTIGATION UNIT,
    NORTH-WEST EUROPE DETACHMENT
Major Neil C. Fraser, head of NWE Detachment, No. 1 CWCIU
Wing Commander Oliver 'Pat' Durdin, successor to Major Fraser as
    Head of NWE Detachments, No. 1 CWCIU
Captain Wady Lehmann, interpreter and investigator
Major L. S. Eckhardt, investigator
Major John Blain, investigator
Lieutenant George Drynan, investigator
Captain Harold Hunter, investigator
Corporal Klassen, investigator and driver
Lieutenant A. M. Fox, investigator and photographer

Major James Balfour, doctor of medicine and a pathologist
Flying Officer Duff, Royal Air Force

IN GERMANY
PEOPLE OF ELTEN
Paul Barton, head of the local police
Hans Renoth, local police officer
Hans Pelgrim, local police officer
Friedrich Grabowski, local customs official
Paul Nieke, local customs official
Hubert Franken, farmer
Johann Bosmann, farmer
Peter Peters, farm worker
Hendrikus van Boxen, farm worker
Franciscus Aalberts, farm worker

Albertus Konning, farm worker
Doctor jur Otto Weyer, Mayor of Elten
Elizabeth Heiting, ran the Hotelkur on Hoch Elten
Meta Rug, resident of Elten
Dominikus Arntz, sexton in Elten
Berhard Rutten, community labourer
Alex Kerkhoff, resident of Elten
Wilhelm Joseph van den Broek, farmer
Christine Franken, resident of Elten

Karl Doll, Superintendent North Cemetery, Düsseldorf
Wilhelm Peutz, attendant at the North Cemetery, Düsseldorf
Dietrich Hamann, District Superintendent of the constabulary at
 Wesel, district Rees

THE COURT
Lieutenant Colonel William Yaldwyn Kington-Blair-Oliphant OBE, MC,
 President of court, 2nd Kensingtons
Major John Leicester-Warren, legal member of court, Cheshire
 Yeomanry, Office of the Staff of the Judge Advocate General
Flight Lieutenant Atholl McLauchlan, member of court,
 Royal Australian Air Force
Major D. S. McNeill, member of court, 62nd Anti-Tank Regiment
 Royal Artillery
Major R. B. Sidgwick, member of court, 111th Heavy Anti Aircraft
 (HAA) Regiment
Captain H. Diamond, for the prosecution, Judge Advocate
 General Branch, HQ British Army of the Rhine
Doctor Walther Göbel,* for the defence, German barrister of Elten
Lieutenant R. E. Milman, for the defence, 1/5 Welch, solicitor

* In the trial transcripts he is referred to as Gobbels. For consistency, we
 have used this spelling through the book.

*What is absurd and monstrous about war is that
men who have no personal quarrel should be trained
to murder one another in cold blood.*

Aldous Huxley

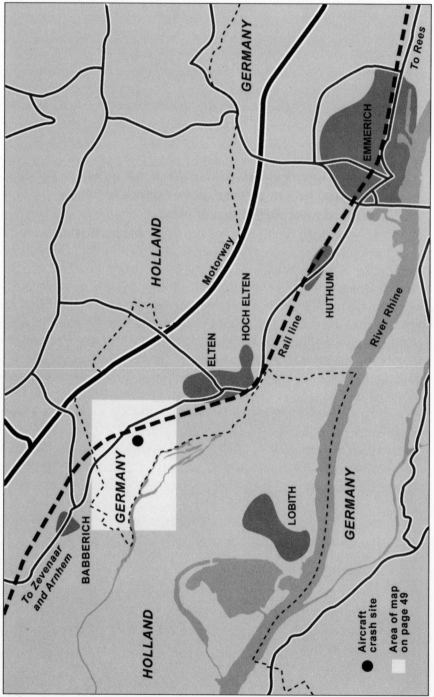

Modern Map of Elten and the Surrounding Area

PROLOGUE

Reichswald Forest Commonwealth War Graves Cemetery, Germany,
10 March 2008

I was looking the wrong way, then quickly realised my mistake; they drive on the right here. So I turned to my left to see if any cars were approaching down the long road flanked by the tall trees of the Reichswald. There was a hint of spring in the chill air, but the trees were still naked, creaking in the slight wind. I crossed the road, pushed open the wrought-iron gates and cast my eye over the architectural simplicity of the cemetery, bounded by a low stone wall. A plaque next to the gates informed me: 'The land on which this cemetery stands is a gift of the German people for the perpetual resting place of the sailors, soldiers and airmen who are honoured here.' I stepped onto a paved area. Directly in front was a slightly off-white plinth, the Stone of Remembrance, rising from the lush green, bearing the inscription 'Their Name Liveth for Evermore', and beyond that the off-white crucifix, the Cross of Sacrifice, with the embedded bronze sword at its centre of axis. To the right extended one 'wing' of the cemetery, countless rows of headstones; the same to the left. Turning right, I entered a small enclosed area to view the cemetery grave register.

I had been to many of the Commonwealth War Graves Cemeteries spread across Western Europe. I had paid my respects at individual graves in the grounds of village churches. I had been humbled by fields of memorialised remains, and overwhelmed by the sheer scale of death, in areas such as Normandy and the Somme. But the Reichswald Cemetery certainly had one of the thickest green register books. Identified in the well-thumbed pages were 7,495 casualties; 176 of those buried had no known identity, and 79 graves held men of other nationalities, the majority being Polish. When bodies were exhumed and brought in from all over western Germany in the aftermath of the Second World War, the Reichswald Forest Commonwealth War Graves Cemetery became the largest Commonwealth cemetery in Germany.

I found the name I was looking for and, noting the grave reference – Plot 7, Row F, Grave 18 – I set off to walk amidst the rows of white headstones that made up the left 'wing' of the cemetery. The first grave was an airman, as were the second, the third and so on. Some headstones had small Canadian flags at their base. As I neared my noted 'reference' I spotted a man crouched nearby, pulling up weeds. I had yet to visit a Commonwealth War Graves Commission cemetery that was not immaculately presented. I could hear the cars going past, the birds in the trees. The wind picked up slightly; agitated twigs crackled faintly and a weary bough creaked. A few leaves, remnants of seasons past, swirled between the headstones. And there in front of me was the grave of the man whose story I had been researching, whose family I had been corresponding with and whose photographs I had studied. The etched inscription on the headstone recorded his rank, 'Pilot Officer', his name, the air force he had served with, the date of death, 16 September 1944, and his age, 23. Then below a crucifix were three words: 'My Jesus. Mercy.' I looked around at some of the other headstones. A few nearby could record only that an airman of the war was buried there, his identity simply 'Known unto God'.

Directly behind grave number 18, in row F, plot 7, lay an Australian air gunner, Flight Sergeant Nicholas Robinson, killed during an accurate and successful Bomber Command operation to the synthetic oil plants at Sterkrade on 6 October 1944. Only one man survived from his 466 Squadron Halifax crew of eight, Sergeant P. Jack, who was set upon and brutally beaten around the head by three German civilians prior to internment in Stalag Luft VII.[1] All those who lost their lives now lay in the Reichswald cemetery.

In front was the body of Royal Air Force flight engineer Sergeant Halwood Jones. From his 115 Squadron Lancaster crew of eight, seven men lost their lives on a Bomber Command attack on Duisburg on the night of 21/2 May 1944. Areas of south Duisburg were blasted away that night by over 500 RAF aircraft, and a further 124 names could be added to the extensive list of Duisburg residents killed by the intensive bombing the previous year. Originally buried in the Nordfriedhof (North Cemetery) at Düsseldorf, all the 115 Squadron Lancaster crew were subsequently moved to the Reichswald cemetery.

To the right were the remains of air gunner Pilot Officer Thomas Hennessy of the Royal Canadian Air Force. His entire 635 Squadron Lancaster crew of seven lost their lives in a Bomber Command operation to the oil plants at Scholven-Buer on 12 September 1944. The crew were initially buried in the Nordfriedhof at Düsseldorf prior to transfer to the Reichswald cemetery, where their bodies now lie, side by side.

To the left lay air gunner Sergeant George Charlesworth of the Royal Air Force, killed on the night of 16/17 September 1942. Essen had been hit hard that night by 369 aircraft, although 39 of the bomber crews would not be returning to England. Some of the bombing had been scattered, and surrounding towns had also been hit. In addition to the material damage, notably at the Krupps factories, seventy-nine people had been killed.[2] Bomber Command had called in crews of their operational training units that night to strengthen the attacking force. No. 11 Operational Training Unit contributed three of their Wellingtons to the overall loss statistic. Sergeant Charlesworth had sat in the rear turret of one of these. Following a total loss of life, the crew of five were originally buried in the Nordfriedhof at Düsseldorf, then reinterred in the Reichswald cemetery.

I took one final look at the grave I had come to see and the name etched into perpetual commemoration. But I knew that for quite some time after he had lost his life this man's body had been recorded as unknown. When his body had first arrived at the Düsseldorf Nordfriedhof, in September 1944, the identity had been logged as 'unbekannt'.

PART ONE

A KILLING

Chapter 1

'UNBEKANNT'

Herr Karl Doll
Betriebsmeister
Nordfriedhof
Düsseldorf

23 July 1945

I, Captain Harold Alexander Hunter, an officer of No. 1 Cdn War Crimes Investigation Unit, acting on behalf of the said unit, have ordered the exhumation for post-mortem examination of the unknown body in grave number 544 in field 111c.

The pilot's skull showed evidence of terrible trauma. And it was clear to pathologist Major James Balfour of the Royal Canadian Medical Corps that death from such injuries would have been almost instantaneous.

Earlier that morning the simple wooden coffin had been lifted from grave No. 544, Field 111c, placed on a trolley and trundled to the Düsseldorf Nordfriedhof mortuary. In the meantime a Major Hazen, also from No. 1 Canadian General Hospital, and Balfour had met Captain Harold Hunter, a war-crimes investigator. Hunter, a pre-war Royal Canadian Mounted Policeman, who had volunteered for overseas duty, had been described by a supervisor as a 'keen investigator, aggressive', showing 'good judgment', skills well suited to the war-crimes investigation business.[1] On the outskirts of the shattered and crumbling city, Hunter met Hazen and Balfour, and they set off for the Nordfriedhof, detailed to examine the body of an unidentified airman. At the mortuary the three men, accompanied by a Royal Air Force representative, Flying Officer Duff, and another investigator armed with a camera, Lieutenant Fox, looked on at the coffin. The rectangular wooden casket was prised open, revealing a blackened decomposing corpse lying in a pool of sludgy liquid.

Before them lay what was clearly the thickset body of an adult male, the features of the young man unrecognisable owing to ten months of death's corruption. He was clothed, wearing a buttoned and collared RAF shirt. Balfour estimated a height of approximately 6 feet and weight in the

7

region of 200 pounds. The clothing was cut away to examine the body further. No identification discs were found around the corpse's neck. In fact, there was nothing on the body or the clothing to help identify the airman, no insignia or badges on the uniform. Specialist medical training was not necessary to identify the probable cause of death. The right side of the skull had been smashed, the inside of the cranium now a dark cavity. Balfour noted the injury was consistent with strikes from a blunt instrument, 'used with a great deal of force'. Was this the only fatal injury? That was difficult to discern, owing to the extent of decomposition and damage to the skull; in particular, Balfour recorded that he could not conclude whether there were any gunshot wounds to the head or body. Further examination of the skull area revealed that, although the upper jaw was intact, there were no upper teeth.

Four days previously Captain Hunter and Lieutenant Fox had come to the Düsseldorf Nordfriedhof to try and locate the body of a flyer whose death they were investigating but whose identity was unknown. That evening one of the cemetery attendants, Leichenwarter Wilhelm Peutz, had shown the two investigators an entry in the cemetery records – 'unbekannt' admitted 2400 hours, 16 September 1944. Peutz could not say for certain, but he believed it was an airman. Hunter and Fox sought out the Superintendent (Betriebsmeister) Karl Doll. Doll directed them to the morgue register to gain further information.

> Entry number – 59332
> Name of deceased – unbekannt
> Coffin number – No. 110
> Received by morgue attendant Peutz
> Date of burial – 17 September 1944 at 0900 hours.

Doll was able to assist the investigators further, providing information from the individual casualty report of the Fliegerhorst Kommandantur (air base headquarters).

> Particulars of death:
>
> Place – Elten Grondstein, meadowland
> Enemy aircraft type – Thunderbolt
> Date and time – 16 September 1944, 1145 hours

Unit – unbekannt
Rank and name – unbekannt.

With this limited but highly relevant information, Hunter had tangible evidence to support the reports, rumour and hearsay of an alleged war crime his team was investigating. Just over a week before, colleagues of Hunter had visited the scene of a killing with two German civilians, both witnesses of the incident, which Lieutenant Fox had recorded on film. Now there was further evidence that an Allied pilot had been killed and the circumstances were not consistent with an act of war. Hunter visited No. 1 Canadian General Hospital the next day, 20 July 1945, to arrange the post-mortem.

During the examination on 23 July Balfour asked Fox to record the grim sight on film, from a position to the side of the casket, which had to be propped up to improve the light and give a better angle. Balfour would later confirm his belief that the injury to the skull would have been sufficient to cause death without a gunshot wound. When questioned as to whether a shot had been fired into the skull, Balfour responded that that would be impossible to say, as 'the damage to the skull was so extensive'. The men departed, and the coffin was resealed and placed once more in German soil.

The Canadian team now set about building its case, to discover what exactly had happened to the airman, and who was responsible. Part of this would be the proper identification of the dead pilot. Flying Officer Duff was tasked with cross-referencing the information he had with RAF records, to try and prevent the body of someone's son being recognised in perpetuity as merely 'Known unto God'.

Chapter 2

BEGINNER'S LUCK

On 11 July 1945, twelve days before the exhumation in Düsseldorf, Lieutenant Fox stood in a field, near the German village of Elten, preparing to capture on film the scene of an alleged unlawful killing. Fox closed one eye, and with the other peered through the camera's eyepiece, ensuring everything relevant was in the frame. Two German farmers and two Canadians were facing the camera, standing erect amidst the mounds of straw that were scattered across a field of stubble. Each man held a numbered placard; a further separate placard was on the ground. The placards displayed the numbers 1 to 4 respectively, from right to left, with the farmer Johann Bosmann, supported by a walking stick, standing holding number 1 on the right, and forward of the man holding number 2.

To Bosmann's right, on the ground was placard 5. Fox was satisfied and opened the shutter to capture the scene, later making a note of what each placard represented.

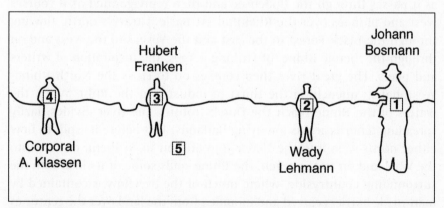

Franken's field, near Elten, Germany, 11 July 1945; the relative positioning of Johann Bosmann, Hubert Franken, the Canadian war-crimes investigators and their respective placards.

Placard number 1, held by Bosmann, was 'where physical violence against the airman commenced'. Standing with placard number 2, 'where the airman was located when he was shot', was Canadian war-crimes investigator Wady Lehmann. A second farmer, Hubert Franken, was displaying placard number 3, 'where Bosmann found the corpse', and

German-speaking Canadian war-crimes investigator Corporal A. Klassen displayed placard number 4, which represented the position of a man currently in custody 'when he fired at the airman'. A further note was added stating that, at the time of the original incident, 'Bosmann approached the scene from the background of the picture and finally stood about 10 metres behind . . . position No. 4'. Placard number 5 represented the location of the aircraft.

Behind, to the south and left, a few kilometres away and just out of shot, a tall spire stood proud amidst a tree-lined hill, the only high ground in the area, at Hoch Elten. To the left, a few hundred metres away, was the main rail line to Holland. Directly behind, in the direction Johann Bosmann was pointing, at a distance of just over one kilometre, was his home. To the right, and west, the land was dotted with the occasional farm building and fragmented with the ditches and dykes that had been maintained over the centuries to protect the area from any breach of the banks of the river Rhine.

From the Alps to the North Sea Western Europe is dissected by the Rhine – a natural waterway, a natural passageway, a natural resource, a natural barrier. It begins life as a churning stream in the Swiss mountains, settling as it passes through the Bodensee and then reinvigorated as it courses west and plunges over the Rheinfall. At Basle it travels north, flowing through the Black Forest to the east and the Vosges to the west and on through the 'heroic Rhine' of striking gorges, the inspiration of writers and poets. The great river then courses on to cross the North Rhine-Westphalia,[1] quenching the thirst of industry in the Ruhr. When the waters of the Rhine reach the Dutch frontier, the river divides, lazily spreading tendrils across low-lying flatlands. Just before its split to flow either north-west into the Neder Rijn and on to Arnhem, or east into the Waal and on to Nijmegen, the Rhine spills some of its load into the surrounding countryside, where much of the overflow is contained by man-made barriers carved and moulded from the land over the centuries by the local farmers to preserve their livelihoods.

The last major German town to flank the Rhine before the split and the Dutch border is the ancient Hanseatic League town of Emmerich, through which a major rail line runs almost parallel to the river. A few kilometres outside the town, to the north-west, the railway passes through the small border village of Elten, having just skirted the base of the only high ground in the area at Hoch Elten. Clear for all to see, dominating the skyline at the summit of the wooded contours, is the church of St Vitus.

Exact details of the martyrdom of St Vitus are sketchy. Believed to be the son of a Sicilian senator, he became Christian at a very early age, his apparent miracles bringing him to the attention of the administrator of Sicily, Valerian, whose attempts to quash his faith failed. Vitus, with his tutor and servant, fled to Lucania and then to Rome, where he is reported to have rid the Emperor Diocletian's son of an evil spirit. When he then declined to take part in a sacrifice to the gods, refusing to take part in the worship of idols, he fell from grace. He apparently managed to survive torture, and some sources report that he was then freed when a storm destroyed some temples, whereupon he went back to Luciana, dying at the start of the fourth century.[2] Through the centuries the saint and his relics became associated with healing, and in the tenth century, at the peak of the Hoch-Elten slopes, building work began on a church that would carry St Vitus's name. Over the next thousand years the Church grew in size, and, despite the ravages of numerous wars and the challenges of new religious and social ideologies, by the year 1944 the spire of St Vitus reminded all around that the Catholic faith had survived a whole millennium, and was continuing to survive.

At the north-western foot of Hoch Elten lies the village of Elten itself, and a few kilometres further on the railway and the main road cross the border. West of these tracks a few minor roads allow farmers access to their fields and farm buildings. It was by such a road that Lieutenant Fox, Wady Lehmann, Corporal Klassen and the two German farmers gained access to the scene of the alleged crime.

By the 1930s the Bosmann family had been working this rich farmland area for nigh on six generations, rearing cattle and growing crops. The Bosmann farm building, like all the others in the area, was raised above the general ground level as a precaution against flooding and was just a hundred metres or so to the west of the rail line and the main road. The current head of the Bosmann family, Johann, was, in fact, the local chair-man of an organisation set up to maintain the dykes that protected their livelihoods. In 1944 Johann had also taken on extra responsibilities, becoming a member of the Landwache, a sort of 'Home Guard', which met once a week to receive instruction.

Johann Bosmann was certainly no supporter of Nazism. It went against his strong Catholic convictions, and he had no reason to thank the regime for any support to farming. Farming, as in all facets of life in the Third Reich, had been subject to dictatorial regulation, but promises to farmers made when the Nazis had gained power had not been kept.[3] At one time some local party members had entered Johann Bosmann's home and asked where the pictures of Hitler were, to which they were told, 'only on the postage stamps'. Catholicism dominated spiritual thinking in Elten: a census of 1930 recorded 2,911 Catholics, 146 Protestants, 5 Jewish, and 1 without faith resident in the village. And the *National-sozialistische Deutsche Arbeiterpartei* (*NSDAP*) or Nazi party never attained a majority mandate from the people of the village before seizing power in 1933. In 1932 there were two elections for Germany's Reichstag. In the first election the *NSDAP* gained 21.6 per cent of the Elten vote, against 61.2 per cent for the *Zentrum*, the Catholic political party. In the second election the Nazi party polled only 19.6 per cent of the vote (and *Zentrum* 57.1 per cent). In the 1933 election the Nazis were still in the minority with only 31 per cent of the vote (with *Zentrum* on 48.9 per cent). At each election the remaining votes had been cast for the Social Democratic Party (*SPD*) and the Communist Party (*KPD*).

Throughout much of the war the Bosmanns had farmed the land around with very little disruption from the international conflict that was raging. Johann had seen the Allied bombers flying high and deep into Germany, and he had also seen the Allied fighter-bombers attacking the railways. Indeed, aircraft had occasionally come down in the area. But neither his farm nor his family had ever been in real danger. The devastating bombing of Emmerich in October 1944 had brought the realities of war closer, but, even when the Allied armies crossed the Rhine in 1945 and overran the area, the Bosmann farm was never in the line of fire. Yet there had been one particular day in which Johann had experienced directly the harshness of war; he had witnessed violence and brutality at first hand, and it was something he could never forget. And it was something he was willing to talk about. On the morning of 11 July 1945 Johann prepared to tell some Canadian investigators what had outraged him on this occasion and he had taken them to the spot where it had happened in a neighbour's meadow.

By July 1945 the years of hard toil had begun to take its toll on the 46-year-old farmer. Johann needed a stick to support himself, and, when Wady Lehmann and driver Corporal Klassen drove him to the scene of the aircraft crash, they then supported him by the arm as they led him to the exact location of what he had seen ten months earlier. Accompanying

Bosmann and the investigators was Johann's neighbour, another farmer, Hubert Franken. He also had been a witness to the incident Lehmann and his colleagues were investigating. Hubert's cousin Johann Franken farmed the field they were standing in. During the war Hubert had kept his dislike of the Nazis quiet for obvious reasons. He had previously lost a position of authority in a local union of farmers when he had refused to become a party member. Hubert had always told his seven children that Hitler's leadership would destroy Germany. It had.

Having parked the car close to the scene of the alleged incident, the Canadians accompanied the two German farmers across the field to where the aircraft was reported to have crash-landed. They had no trouble finding the spot. Although the main parts of the aircraft had been removed during the war, scarring of the ground with what were clearly skid marks, and small metallic airframe fragments, revealed where the aircraft had come to an abrupt halt. Bosmann began to describe what he had seen, ten months previously: where exactly the aircraft had been, where the pilot had initially been found, where everyone had stood, where he had come from and where he had been standing, and where the pilot had been so savagely attacked and beaten. Then, extraordinarily, Bosmann and Wady Lehmann spotted a piece of evidence pressed a few inches into the ground that would be crucial for the identification of the unknown pilot. Wady would later call this 'beginner's luck'. The war-crimes investigation business was new to Wady, as it was to most of the Allied investigators, and indeed to the Allied governments they were representing. Wady Lehmann, although not Canadian by birth, was there representing Canada.

Within weeks of his birth, Wady Lehmann, born near Tallinn, Estonia, on 22 October 1917, and his family, parents and one sister, fled the Communist revolution to Denmark. In 1927 the Lehmanns emigrated to Calgary, Canada, and a few years after that had moved to Vancouver, and then Burnaby in British Columbia.

Wady embarked upon his military career in 1941, taking basic training with the Westminster Regiment reserve, and then spending a year with 12 Canadian Field Ambulance. He then transferred to the 3 Armoured Brigade as an intelligence clerk/driver. Indeed, Wady's future lay in intelligence, helped, no doubt, by his sound understanding of the German language, gleaned from his family background and his time at school in Denmark. When Wady crossed the Atlantic to come to the United Kingdom, he received his commission, serving with the fledgling Canadian

Intelligence Corps, and then underwent specialised training in signals and battle intelligence with the British Army.

Wady's nomadic war continued in January 1944 when he travelled by sea to Italy with the Canadian Wireless Intelligence detachment serving with the 1 Canadian Corps. His linguistic skills were put to good use as a prisoner-of-war interrogator, then as an intelligence officer with the 1 Canadian Infantry Division and then on the intelligence staff of the 1 Canadian Corps, focusing on enemy documents, weapons and dispositions. When the Corps moved to Holland, Wady went with them, and was promoted to captain. There was one particularly notable encounter when he accompanied Lieutenant General Charles Foulkes in his meeting with General Johannes Blaskowitz, the German commander-in-chief in the Netherlands, as they discussed a ceasefire to allow food to reach the desperate population of western Holland. When hostilities in Europe ended, and a few days after assisting in the debriefing of General Blaskowitz's head of intelligence in Holland, Wady, as one of the better German speakers, and with a background in intelligence, was posted to a Canadian war-crimes investigation unit.

The novice investigator took on a number of roles within his unit while it was based in Germany: interpreter, translator, interrogator and investigator, operating in one of several teams of about five people each. Included in such teams were linguists, mainly German but one French, who acted both as official interpreters and as investigators. Wady describes the unit make-up and personnel.

Their army or air force operational experience helped them to understand the military aspects of the German organisation and customs. Our legal components, the lawyers and court reporters, had valuable experience in military law and procedures. Indispensable to each team was the driver, untiring, resourceful and patient. We usually managed to pack ourselves, rations and belongings into one vehicle, a Jeep, passenger car, or HUP (Heavy Utility Personnel). Our work routine consisted of tracking down witnesses who might be dispersed anywhere in Europe, including the Russian Zone, taking down depositions which would stand up in court, and examining public records, and, of course, ultimately apprehending and delivering the suspected war criminal.

The Elten case, as it came to be classified, would be the first Wady was involved in following his arrival early in the summer of 1945 at the headquarters of the North-West Europe (NWE) detachment of the No. 1 Canadian War Crimes Investigation Unit (No. 1 CWCIU). It was based in the spa town of Bad Salzuflen, which proved a somewhat idyllic location to carry out such unpleasant work, with its saltwater springs, baths, scenery and timber-framed houses.

Wady, inexperienced in the war-crimes business, decided on a somewhat novel way to learn the basics of the tasks he was about to perform, which would bear fruit when he visited Franken's field in July 1945.

To put myself in the mood for crime investigation I had brought an Ellery Queen thriller with me and reading through it I noted that his first move was to make a thorough search of the site. When I arrived at the spot in the meadow where the plane had gauged out its skid mark I had a good look around. What should I see but glinting through the sward was the outline of a dental plate! Beginner's luck.

Wady showed his compatriots and the farmers Bosmann and Franken what he had discovered, between three and four metres to the south of where the aircraft had been. Hubert Franken confirmed that they were the same teeth that he had seen lying beside the airman's corpse in September 1944. Wady pocketed the evidence. After the scene had been marked out and Lieutenant Fox had captured the layout on film, the five men returned to the car. Bosmann and Franken were taken back to their farms, Lehmann informing them that he would be returning with other colleagues at some point to take statements.

On the way back to Bad Salzuflen Wady pondered the next steps in the investigation. Over the next few weeks the 'Elten case' files grew as the investigation expanded, with the taking of statements from eyewitnesses and the exhumation of the body believed to be that of the pilot. In his possession Wady had the last piece of the jigsaw, the dental plate, which would finally confirm the name of the man who had died, ten months previously, in Franken's field, between the shadow of St Vitus church spire and the flowing waters of the river Rhine.

At the 23 July 1945 exhumation, a thorough examination of the corpse had revealed nothing on the body to aid identification directly – no papers or identity tag. A trawl through official records was required, using the basic information obtained so far from eyewitnesses, the cemetery records and the exhumation. But the evidence was scant, and there were a few red herrings. It was reported as a single-seater aircraft, believed to be a Republic P-47 Thunderbolt, but clearly this was very likely to have been a mistake; the Thunderbolts were predominantly used by the American air forces in Europe. The dead airman was wearing Royal Air Force clothing, although it was not clear exactly which country he came from. Airmen from all over the British Commonwealth had served with the RAF in Europe, including Canadians, Australians, New Zealanders, South Africans, Rhodesians and Indians. Then there were the men who had fled their countries to take up arms against the Nazis, such as the French, Belgians, Dutchmen, Norwegians, Poles and Czechs. The RAF was a truly multinational force, and the dead airman's nationality would require further investigation, but it was nevertheless unlikely that the aircraft was a Thunderbolt. It was certainly a single-engine aircraft, probably a Spitfire, Tempest, Typhoon or Mustang, and witnesses had stated that there was a red, white and blue rectangle on the rudder and a red, white and blue roundel on the fuselage. So it was clearly an aircraft from an operational RAF squadron. In addition, one witness had said that the number 662 was on the fuselage.

Time and date would certainly help narrow the search, and from witness statements it was believed that the crash probably occurred between 1045 and 1100 hours, the aircraft flying low before crash-landing in a cloud of dust. The aircraft had apparently been one of six attacking a train in the vicinity of Elten, Germany, between 1000 and 1200 hours on 16 September 1944.

The exhumation and investigation had, to date, uncovered some biographical information. The pilot was smallish in stature, with long black hair, and had an upper dental plate. He was believed to be Canadian, as recorded in the Düsseldorf Nordfriedhof records, although it had been mentioned by a witness that he might have been Australian. Witnesses had also informed the investigators that the pilot had had a rosary in his trouser pockets and some English, German and Dutch money, although none of this was found at the exhumation. His uniform was dark blue, apparently similar to German training uniform – dark blue coveralls. A witness indicated that the colour of the coveralls was similar to the Royal Canadian Air Force blue, the uniform being of rough material coverall style and not battledress style. He wore low, black shoes and a light blue shirt. A witness had said that there were badges of rank on the sleeve and lapel, some sort of silver bars and stars. There was no cloth name badge on top of the sleeve and no epaulettes. At the exhumation it had been noted that the shirt on the corpse was of an RAF pattern.

With such material the identification of the pilot was entrusted to a Captain T. W. Platt of the No. 1 CWCIU by the chief administrative officer Captain G. K. M. Johnston. Platt informed Johnston of his progress on 1 August 1945. His first line of enquiry involved contacting a Flight Lieutenant Daley of the Royal Canadian Air Force and Historical Officer for RAF Fighter Command. Daley supplied the following from the command war diary, concerning Canadian losses on 16 September 1944.

F/O McEachren, missing believed killed. McEachren's plane was seen to burst into flames at 300 ft and crash.
J28384 F/O Le Gear, F.S., missing in Typhoon of 263 Squadron after shipping recce over Beveland.

With these two men the only Canadians listed as missing that day – Le Gear's Typhoon missing near the coast and McEachren's plane crashing in the vicinity of Tilburg, Holland, both many miles from the Elten area – Platt broadened the enquiry and contacted the historical officer of the RAF Air Ministry. The diary of the Royal Air Force's 2nd Tactical Air Force, which had supported the Allied invasion in Normandy and the subsequent advances, and of its constituent 83, 84 and 85 Groups, were checked. The 84 Group diary revealed:

Missing from operations 16 Sep 44 W/O Lewczinsky 317 (Polish) Fighter Squadron, W/O Lewczinsky baled out at 1502 hours.

Platt informed Johnston:

One other officer was reported missing on that date but on checking with records he has since been reported as safe, while Lewczinsky is still listed as 'Missing presumed dead'. RAF and RCAF HQ could give us no help in identification of plane with numbers 662; as you know no doubt, all numbers are prefixed by a letter or letters of the alphabet, however 2nd TAF who are still in Europe may be able to help in this respect.

But this line of enquiry became redundant as further information came in from other sources. At the same time as the paper trail was being scrutinised, the dental plate found by Wady Lehmann was submitted for examination.

On 2 August a Major Johnson of No. 60 Field Dental Laboratory submitted a detailed report from an analysis of the denture, 'Origin – most likely made in the United Kingdom at private expense. If this denture was made by the Services it is a remake of a previous denture.'

On 9 August Platt wrote to Captain Johnston of No. 1 CWCIU, attaching a copy of a report that had been sent to the Air Ministry Casualty Branch on 1 November 1944 from the commanding officer of 80 Squadron, which had been operating with the RAF Air Defence of Great Britain. Although primarily concerned with defending the United Kingdom against aerial attack, the command's squadrons had flown many operations over Europe, supporting the Army and the 2nd Tactical Air Force.

> Tempest V, E.J.662 - Aus.414715 P/O W.E. Maloney.
> With reference to this unit's casualty signal A.35 dated 16 September 1944, herewith circumstantial report.
> At 1025 hours on 16 September 1944, the squadron were airborne on an armed recce on 'Big Ben' [V2 rocket] sites and M.T. [Military Transport] north of line Hague–Arnhem. During the operation P/O Maloney was seen to touch down with glycol streaming out of his aircraft, just west of Arnhem. ['West' is then corrected to 'East'.]

Platt added further information in his letter.

> Records RAAF have given me the following.
> Date of birth: 25-7-21
> Religion: R.C.
> Weight: 158 lbs
> Height: 5 foot 9½ inches
> He had an *upper denture* but full particulars are in Melbourne. These particulars could be obtained if necessary.

On 20 August Flying Officer Duff was able to add the following information to the Elten case files of the NWE detachment of the No. 1 CWCIU.

> Information has now been received from Air Ministry that it has been established that the victim was AUS.414715 Pilot Officer W. E. Maloney who was the pilot of aircraft Tempest EJ.662 operating on an armed reconnaissance north of line Hague–Arnhem on 16 September 1944. During this operation he was seen to touch down with glycol streaming out of his aircraft, just west [*sic*] of Arnhem.

With this information it appeared that Australian W. E. Maloney was indeed the airman who had been exhumed from grave No. 544 Field IIIc at the Düsseldorf Nordfriedhof in July 1945, and was the airman who had been killed in Franken's field in September 1944. However, absolute confirmation would not be forthcoming until some six months later. On 15 February 1946 the Air Ministry Casualty Branch wrote to the offices of the Judge Advocate General, War Crimes Branch, Headquarters, British Army of the Rhine.

> Pilot Officer W. E. Maloney, Aus. 414715 . . . we have received information from the Royal Australian Air Force Overseas Headquarters that from a comparison between the dental chart of the above-named officer and the description of the victim . . . it has been established that the murdered airman was Pilot Officer W. E. Maloney and steps are being taken to have the grave 544, Field IIIc, Nordfriedhof, Düsseldorf registered in his name.

Chapter 3

SPIKE – THE BOY FROM AUSTRALIA

On 3 September 1939 Australian Prime Minister Robert Gordon Menzies broadcast the grim news to his countrymen that they were at war with Germany.

> Fellow Australians, it is my melancholy duty to inform you officially, that in consequence of a persistence by Germany in her invasion of Poland, Great Britain has declared war upon her and that, as a result, Australia is also at war. No harder task can fall to the lot of a democratic leader than to make such an announcement.

On 4 September Menzies cabled British Prime Minister Neville Chamberlain: 'Your broadcast message moved Australia deeply. We ourselves have proclaimed a state of war and I have broadcast on behalf of the Commonwealth government that we stand with Great Britain. We firmly believe we have right on our side and in that strength victory is sure.' In the following months he set about turning political rhetoric into real action, ensuring his country stood by that commitment.

At the outbreak of war it was not just the members of Menzies's government who felt an affinity towards the 'home' land. In 1939 there still remained a general sense of British national identity; Australian nationalism was a post-war phenomenon.

In October 1939 Menzies had informed his nation that Australia would join the Empire Air Training Scheme, a programme that would prepare hundreds of thousands of British Commonwealth airmen for operational duties. Menzies called the scheme 'the most decisive joint effort to be made by the British nations in this war' and he went on to confirm his country's war allegiance with Britain: 'We are with you. Your danger is our danger; your effort is our effort; your success will be our success.' Menzies was clear in his statement that he believed he was acting as Australians 'would have wished'.

A recent study by Dr Peter Stanley, then Principal Historian at the Australian War Memorial,[1] supports this. 'In 1940 many Australians maintained a dual loyalty: to Australia and to Britain. They were proud both of their distinctive identity as Australians and of their membership

in an imperial partnership. Britain was "home": the great burst of enlistment in Australia occurred not when the war began, but when in 1940
Britain faced invasion and defeat.' News of the Battle of Britain, the home
land's heroic defensive struggle against the onslaught of the Luftwaffe,
was reported through Australia. Such news proved an excellent recruiting
tool for the Australian air forces. A young man could fight a more
'romantic' war than his forefathers, out of the trenches, defending his
'home land', experiencing the thrill of flying and perhaps enjoying the
social status and the perks of being a clean-cut and dashing warrior, a
fighter pilot. Many young men could not resist.

Approximately 25,000 Australians would fight as Royal Australian Air
Force servicemen with the Royal Air Force, the vast majority serving with
RAF's Bomber Command. Memories of the First World War, the sacrifice
made by the soldiers at Gallipoli and on the Western Front, were firmly
fixed in the Australian national conscious, and this directed many men
towards one particular form of waging war, a newer, exciting and cleaner
way to fight. Dr Stanley's research revealed some interesting insight into
the motivations of young Australian airmen, who were prepared to travel
halfway around the world to fight a war. Stanley claims that

> airmen's letters and diaries display little explicit interest in the Allied
> cause and even less in the morality of the bomber offensive . . . Nor did
> they expend much energy on abstract loyalty to the air force. Though
> many men volunteered for the air force because of its supposed glam-
> our (and their jovial contempt for 'brown jobs') and many were proud
> of being members of the RAF or RAAF, airmen seem to have attached
> relatively little importance to their status as airmen. They were arguably
> more proud of the wings denoting their musterings.

William Edmund Maloney, born on 25 July 1921 in the small town of
Clifton, south of Toowoomba, Queensland, Australia, was the eighth child
of Maurice and Gertrude Maloney. Maurice's parents, Edmund and
Catherine, were both Irish, as was Gertrude's mother, Mary, who had
married an Englishman, William Judd, from whom Bill drew his name.

Bill had been a most welcome addition to the family in that he was only
the second boy. Bill's early years were spent in an agricultural district called
Back Plains, his father, Maurice, being the schoolteacher in that area.
A month before Bill's third birthday the family moved to another farming
area, Glenvale, a few miles to the west of Toowoomba. Bill had one brother,

Patrick (Paddy), and six sisters Josephine (Jo), Kathleen (Kit), Gertrude
Veronica (Von), Clare, Sheila and Frances. Frances recalled:

> Paddy, being reared among 6 girls, had a very gentle nature, but Bill
> had a more forceful disposition, and was inclined to like his own way.
> He was more spoilt than the rest of us. Each child was looked upon as
> one of the 'team' and had little jobs to perform. Bill's jobs were to carry
> in the kindling wood for our wood stove, and to clean the lamp glass.
> We had kerosene lamps and the glass became very smoky. I couldn't
> bear to see him get into trouble so I would do his jobs, when he went
> off to Cricket or Rugby, every Saturday.

Bill certainly loved his sport, mainly rugby league. As Frances recalled:

> He was in his element when he finished Primary School and attended
> St Mary's Christian Brothers College in Toowoomba. Bill was a good
> scholar, and popular with his school mates. He was always mentioned
> in inter-school matches. He wasn't 'fast'. Dad used to say, 'Paddy is very
> speedy on the field, but Bill is as slow as an old duck!'

Frances remembered that Bill could be a little boisterous, 'but could be
kind also'.

> On few occasions we were allowed to go to a Matinée film in town
> [Toowoomba]. Stories like *Uncle Tom's Cabin* would find me bawling my
> eyes out. He would try and warn me by sending a message along our
> group of friends – 'Tell Frankie not to look.' Also, when our sister,
> Sheila, contracted 'Infantile Paralysis' (Polio) at the age of 9, she had
> to be kept from too much movement. My job was to read to her every
> afternoon from 3.30 to 4.30 pm. Bill would sit beside me for company
> and enjoy the stories as well.
>   When changing from 'boy' to 'youth', he became very conscious of
> his appearance. As a boy his hair stood up like a porcupine's, but in
> High School his hair turned into waves and he coaxed it along with
> 'Brilliantine'. He liked his new image and took his waistcoat to school
> in his school bag. After school, he walked downtown to meet our
> sister, Jo, who taught at the East School. She took him to and from
> school every day. He would wear the waistcoat in town and his school
> mates called him 'Waistcoat Bill'! He wasn't offended. He had a sense

of humour. When someone mentioned that he resembled his sister, Kit, he quipped, 'Oh! I thought I was good-looking!'

Bill seemed to enjoy the thrill of speed and machines. When he was old enough he purchased a motorbike. 'It was his pride and joy, and many friends enjoyed being pillion passengers.' And Bill certainly seemed to be a popular young man. 'He didn't have a special girl friend, but many girls enjoyed his friendship. He loved "dancing" and "socials".' Pictures of Bill at a dance show a clean-cut, healthy and good-looking young man, with his hair slicked back. There is a vibrancy about him – a distinct energy for life behind his eyes.

Bill's first job when he left school was to work for a Brisbane company called Steel Pipes. But his love of rugby league seemed to interfere with his work. When he broke his hand one weekend, he received a warning from the manager that if he played again he would lose his job. Bill played again and was sacked. On his return to Toowoomba Bill found a job at Cloakes Tannery, tanning hides and leather. Here he met and became friends with Vic Cloake. The two young men would join the air force together.

Frances recalled:

Why Bill joined the Air Force, I'm not sure. Maybe he wanted to do his 'bit' for his Country. Australian children learned early in life to be patriotic and to love their Country. From Grade 1 to Grade 7 it was customary for pupils to stand in the courtyard of their schools, watching the flag being raised. They saluted that flag, saying the words – 'I love my Country, I honour her Flag! I will do all in my power to obey her laws!'

Bill joined the Royal Australian Air Force in 1940, although it was not until April 1942 that he gained his first service flying experience. All through his training in Canada and the United Kingdom, and his operational service in Europe, Bill was a good correspondent. He wrote to his mother and father regularly, and to his siblings. Five of his sisters were teaching in schools scattered over the country, and his other sister, Sheila, had became a psychiatric nurse. Paddy, who had developed a real love of the land, had become a farmer. Ultimately the family received the news they were dreading.

The news of Bill's death was a sad blow for us. We received the news that he was missing a year before, and we hoped he was 'in hiding' somewhere. When the war was over the telegram, stating that Bill had been shot, shattered Dad. He was devastated. He said, 'If Bill had been killed in fair circumstances, it would have been easier to accept.' We thought all the pilots were lined up and shot. We didn't know the full story. After that, if Dad was introduced to any man bearing a German name, he would refuse to shake his hand. Dad died six months later, at the age of 71.

Mum was made of sterner stuff. She had reared a big family, lived through the Depression in the early '30s, and helped in Army Canteens during the war. She had a strong faith and often received letters from a Mrs Peggy McGuiness from the Officers' Club in London. In one of her letters she told Mum how she envied Bill his strong Catholic faith. Every time Bill returned to the Club after being at Sunday Mass, he would say he felt as though he was walking on air.

The news of Bill's death caused us, his siblings, to shed many tears, but we were young and knew life had to go on. To 'know' that he had given his life for his Country was comforting.

On 2 April 1942, at No. 2 Elementary Flying Training School (EFTS), Archerfield, Queensland, Bill Maloney made his first entry in his service flying logbook having flown as a passenger on a 30-minute flight in a De Havilland Tiger Moth. Over the next few days, flying dual, his instructor took him through 'effect of controls, taxying, familiarity of cockpit, straight and level flying, taking off into wind, powered approach and landing'.

The training at Archerfield was fairly intense, as it was at No. 5 EFTS Narromine, New South Wales, when he transferred there in mid-April. Bill amassed 60 hours 5 minutes of flying, of which just over 24 hours was solo, in the run-up to his 'Final Test' on 20 May 1942. Clearly it did not go too well, although he did pass, with the lowest assessment possible of 'Below Average'. He was described by the Chief Flying Instructor at Narromine as 'Under Confident'.

The next stage in Bill's journey to become an operational pilot took place overseas, as part of the Empire Air Training Scheme, and shortly after his arrival in Canada, he wrote home.

RAAF, Base Post Office
Ottawa, Canada
31–8–42

Dear Pop

By the time this reaches you, you most likely will have added another summer to your already strong line, but so long as it's a happy one – why worry. I spent my birthday dodging submarines in the Caribbean Sea. It was most pleasant. One of the boys, knowing of the event, smuggled on a bottle of 'Paul Jones' at Panama. We certainly needed it for we had a 'sub scare' that afternoon. It's too hard to describe the whole trip to you – I'll leave it till I get back again – then perhaps we will write a book together.

I have had no mail since the last lot, last week. We are expecting it any day now. So sorry to hear mum was not the best. That cold place would turn anyone off colour. Perhaps though, it would be better than 40° below.

By the way, mum is entitled to wear the Overseas badge. Any mother whose son is serving with the RAAF overseas must get them. I don't just know what she has to do or where she would obtain it, but be sure she gets one. They look very neat I believe and should she ever get to the city again she may wear it.

We had a big sports day here last week. They were short of a tug-of-war team and a few of the Aussies got together and we really walked in. We had about half a doz pulls and won every one. In the finish the Officers instructing us challenged us, but we were much too good for them.

We all got a silver identification wrist band for it. I also came first in a sack race by yds. So I haven't lost any of my school day form.

I have not flown in the last week but look like getting up today. The weather is much against us.

I intend going to Niagara Falls (that doesn't look like the spelling but bugger it) next leave. They are a couple of hundred miles from here. It will be getting too cold to go outside the door soon.

We had a big corn roast last week. We all sat round the open fire, sang, danced and ate corn, till we were sick of it.

Well Pop the mail closes within a few minutes, so I must close. Fondest love to you Both. See that Mum gets her badge. Best wishes to all at Rockmount [the family farm] and be sure and have a rest on the 10th or 11th of Oct.

Bill

Bill's father had never been sure which day was his actual birthday. In 1942 he would be celebrating his sixty-eighth birthday on either 10 or 11 October.

Bill's flying training continued at No. 1 Service Flying Training School (SFTS), Camp Borden, Canada, on 20 September 1942, in an Avro Anson, as a passenger on a cross-country flight to familiarise himself with the area. Over the next few months he would develop his skills, flying North American Harvards, racking up the hours, 'cross countries, formation flying, instrument flying and high and low level bombing'. By the end of November 1942 Bill had recorded 192 hours 40 minutes' flight time in his logbook, almost half of which was as pilot, and there had been an improvement in his assessment: he achieved an 'Average' as a single-engine pilot, although a 'Below Average' was written against his assessment as pilot-navigator/navigator.

Bill finished his training at No. 1 SFTS in December 1942. His next aerial experience was back in the UK at No. 26 EFTS Theale in March 1943, once more at the controls of Tiger Moths, and after just over 35 hours of flying he managed to get a 'Good Average' as a pilot, and an 'Average' as pilot-navigator, enscribed in his logbook. At this point Bill would have become aware that he was destined to be a fighter pilot. It would be most unusual to find any trainee aviators not aspiring to be at the controls of a modern fighter aircraft, such as a Supermarine Spitfire. Many, many trainees were disappointed when they found they were destined to fly bombers. The quotas had to be filled and in 1942 the bomber offensive was escalating. No doubt Bill was thrilled, however, to find himself destined for fighters, although there were further training hurdles to overcome.

Bill's flying education continued at No. 17 (Pilot) Advanced Flying Unit at Watton, in the month of May, flying Miles Masters as he prepared for duties in control of his own single-engine weapon. Bill finished the course with an 'Average' assessment to take to No. 57 Operational Training Unit at Eshott, where, no doubt with great anticipation, he first clambered into a Spitfire I, taking it for a 35-minute solo on 6 June 1943. Further familiarisation with the Spitfire followed – formations, camera gun (air to air), aerobatics, low flying, cloud flying, spinning, drogue attacks, air-to-air firing, low-level bombing, formation and section attack, and even a 'Dummy Rhubarb' (low-level offensive fighter operation) – at the end of July 1943.

On 4 July 1943 Bill wrote to one of his sisters.

Dear Franc

This letter was started last week, but as leave cropped up suddenly I'm afraid your letter was put aside, so when I returned I decided I had better start again. Very little has happened in the meantime, just the same old life, day in day out. I might mention I received two of your letters last week, one of them being written way back in January last. Of course the news was stale but still very welcome indeed. You know getting two letters from you on the one day is almost too much for any young fellow to expect.

Well Franc, you will notice from the address we are in the middle of summer & it is not much different from our own winter weather. At the moment it is very foggy & plenty cold also. I don't know how I will ever stand the sun, if & when I see it again. Had a parcel of socks from Mary Lucas & a bundle of papers from Mrs Cloake. They made good reading for a few days.

Von wrote me a long letter a couple of months ago & I can't think for the world of me whether or not I answered it. Tell her, if I haven't, that it is an awful oversight. Do you think that will meet with success? Had a weekend in Scotland last week. Jolly good place to spend a few days. They have great beer in that part of the world. Have not heard from Vic for a while now, although he is not so far away. We have both taken to pipe smoking & Vic is really funny. He can't keep the thing alight at all.

Franc, I will keep my eyes open for the Rosary Beads you were talking of although I doubt if they will be easy to get in these parts. However, you never know your luck. I suppose Sheila will have taken the big step ere this reaches you. Wish her all the best for me.

As I write, I can imagine you & Von counting the days till the August holidays – you lucky people. I guess you intend heading to Perth Street [the family home in Toowoomba]. The family should be well settled in there now. What is it like at Currumbin [a small village where Franc was teaching] now-a-days. To use an old English term you will probably be 'Browned off'.

Well Franco this is it for now. All the best of luck & love to you for the present. Will write to you again as time goes by.

Fondest Love

Bill.

After his time at OTU there is then quite a gap in Bill's logbook: his next flight was not recorded until 3 February 1944 at No. 2 Tactical Exercise

Unit, Balado Bridge, Scotland. It is not clear why there is this fallow period, although Bill, with some Australian air force colleagues, did have some extended leave in London, which he found somewhat frustrating – not the leave, which was enjoyed to the full, but the delay in a posting to an operational squadron.

At Balado Bridge, Bill, still flying Spitfires, carried out further shooting practice with a camera gun. On 17 February 1944 he inscribed in his log-book: 'Became a Caterpillar'. Membership of the Caterpillar Club was extended to all those who had used a parachute to save their life. Bill earned his having baled out of his aircraft owing to engine failure.

At the end of April 1944 Bill completed his course at No. 2 Tactical Exercise Unit, having also had the chance to fly Hurricanes, and at the beginning of May he arrived at an operational unit, No. 80 Squadron, to fly Spitfire IXs into combat.

Chapter 4

DEATH OF A PILOT OFFICER

No sirens had sounded. It could not have been a flying bomb. By September 1944 the sound of that particular menace was familiar to Londoners. As long as the engine drone could still be heard, those beneath could feel safe as the bomb flew onwards. But, if the engine cut out while it was overhead, they knew they were in mortal danger.

But on the morning of 8 September in Chiswick, London, there had been no warning. Following the sound of the explosion a double thunderclap had cracked the air and then a fierce whoosh as the sound waves of the rocket piercing the sky at supersonic speed caught up. Three people were killed, and seventeen seriously injured, and houses were blasted to rubble, around a massive crater. The V2 rocket had been fired only minutes before from the Hague area, in Holland. Shortly after the Chiswick explosion another rocket slammed into open ground at Epping, fortunately without claiming lives.

The fact that these were rockets was kept from the British public, and rumours that they were gas explosions spread, without correction from those in the know. But it was apparent to certain members of Allied intelligence that the German threat of a rocket attack had at last become a reality.

Unfortunately Duncan Sandys, the junior British Minister who had been charged with leading the investigations into the German secret weapon campaigns, had just made the claim, publicly, that the flying-bomb terror had been all but extinguished, that the 'Battle of London' was over. In fact there would be further V1 attacks, following the re-grouping of the retreating German launching organisation, against some British and continental cities, notably the crucial port of Antwerp. But the main assault against London was over. By the end of the war the V1 campaign had cost the lives of 6,184 civilians, with 17,981 seriously injured and 23,000 homes destroyed.

The development of the German secret weapon programmes had been under close scrutiny for a number of years, and there had been counter-measures, notably RAF Bomber Command's crucial intervention against V2 development in a devastating attack on the Baltic research station at Peenemünde in August 1943. However, the V1 campaign against London, which had opened in the middle of June 1944, had held the attention and drawn resources. The Allies had launched a bombing campaign against the launch sites in France to reduce the firing rate, fighters patrolled the approaches to London, anti-aircraft artillery was positioned beneath the flight paths and balloons were deployed to shield the city. Each flying bomb counter-measure met with varying degrees of success, but following the opening of the V2 attacks it was clear that none of these could be used to counter the rockets. They were launched from mobile transports and were too fast for any aircraft to pursue or for ground fire to hit. The respective transports had to be hunted down and the V2 supply lines to the firing areas cut.

Late in the afternoon of Friday, 15 September 1944, senior Allied air force commanders met at the headquarters of the Allied Expeditionary Air Force (AEAF) at Versailles for the ninety-seventh Allied Air Commanders (AAC) Conference.[1] The AEAF, under the control of Air Chief Marshal Sir Trafford Leigh-Mallory, held control of the tactical air forces supporting Operation 'Overlord', the invasion of north-west Europe. Leigh-Mallory could feel very satisfied with the contribution of his tactical forces in the previous three months. His fighter pilots and bomber crews had exploited the local air superiority over Normandy seriously to hinder the movement of the enemy on the ground. In particular, his fighter-bomber pilots, on low-level bombing or rocket projectile attacks, had often left carnage in their wake whenever sighting enemy concentrations on the ground, or when encountering German transport moving in daylight. The German soldier rarely saw a friendly aircraft. A notable example of the tactical air forces' destructive power fell upon the German army retreating from the closing jaws of the Falaise pocket. As the fighter-bombers returned from the skies above the battlefield, they left behind burning wreckage, smouldering animal carcasses and twisted human corpses. In Normandy German soldiers quickly learned to fear and hate the Allied fighter-bomber pilots.

Around the table at the 15 September AAC Conference were the most senior men in command of air operations in Western Europe. Sir Trafford Leigh-Mallory was joined by the Deputy Supreme Commander of the Allied Expeditionary Force, Sir Arthur Tedder, General Carl Spaatz of the United States Strategic Air Forces in Europe, Air Chief Marshal Sir Arthur Harris of Bomber Command, General 'Jimmy' Doolittle from the American Eighth Air Force, Air Marshal Sir Arthur Coningham in command of the 2nd Tactical Air Force, and General Hoyt Vandenberg of the American

Ninth Air Force. In addition, there were numerous intelligence officers, meteorological officers and a representative of the Air Defence of Great Britain.

The meeting opened with a summation of the weather conditions, which had been extremely poor that day in England, but for the following day the bases in the UK would be operational. A summation of the general military situation, as the Allies overran Belgium and further French territory, following the break-out from Normandy, reported 'satisfactory progress' but 'no spectacular advances'. Next to report was a Lieutenant Colonel Bennett from military intelligence, who explained to the assembled air chiefs what was known and what was expected from the opposing forces, notably: 'The German intention must be to fight a delaying action to the Siegfried Line and the river Waal.' The Siegfried Line, or Westwall, a defensive system stretching from the town of Kleve near the Dutch border to the frontier with Switzerland, incorporated bunkers, tunnels, tank traps and tons of concrete. Hitler had recently ordered a strengthening of the Westwall. Bennett went on to outline the thinking around German reinforcements.

> It was appreciated that two Infantry Divisions and three or four Panzer Brigades might be brought from Germany, and eight or nine inferior Divisions might be raised in Germany by 30 September. Two or three Divisions could be brought from Denmark and the Germans would probably have to withdraw their troops from the Balkans. Recent reconnaissance showed that main rail movement was in the area of Frankfurt, Mannheim and Coblenz. There was also heavy activity at Kaiserslautern, Halle, Homberg and Bingen.

A summation of the 'Big Ben' (V2 campaign) followed: sixteen rockets were believed to have been fired in all, fourteen against London and two against Paris, and, of those fired against the British capital, seven had fallen in the city and two in the sea. It had become clear that the rocket firing points were in the area north of The Hague and that some had been found and attacked by Royal Air Force Tempest squadrons.

Each of the Allied air forces then summarised their activity. The American and RAF tactical air forces were mainly employed on armed reconnaissance, searching for, and attacking, enemy road and rail transport, behind enemy lines. The RAF's fighters had also attacked shipping in the Scheldt estuary. RAF Bomber Command's Air Chief Marshal Harris's heavy bombers had maintained their onslaught, with major attacks in the previous few days and nights against Dortmund, Munster, Frankfurt, Stuttgart and a number of oil targets. Harris could be pleased with what his airmen had achieved. Information from initial post-raid reports, bombing photographs and reconnaissance indicated successful attacks. Subsequent information proved the case. On the night of 12/13 September a firestorm in Stuttgart had caused severe damage: the city would suffer its highest fatalities of the war, with 1,171 killed. On the same night, areas of Frankfurt were also obliterated, a troop train was hit and 172 people lost their lives in a public shelter. In total, 469 people lost their lives. The situation was hindered by the fact that an attack the night before on Darmstadt, a few miles to the south, targeted because of its rail communications, had drawn in firemen and rescue workers from Frankfurt. The emergency services based in Darmstadt had been overwhelmed, as fire had consumed much of the city with a terrible loss of life. Initially 8,433 people were reported to have lost their lives, 1,766 men, 2,742 women, 2,129 children, 936 servicemen, 492 foreign worker and 368 prisoners of war. After the war the United States Strategic Bombing Survey recorded that this preliminary figure was probably short by about 5,000.[2]

The AAC Conference concluded with a general discussion on operational commitments over the next few days. As military intelligence reported that German reinforcements were making their way by train to the battle fronts, the Allied tactical air forces were detailed to continue their strafing attacks on trains. With the imminent launch of Operation 'Market Garden' – an attempt to secure bridges over major waterways in a thrust through the Netherlands to Germany, outflanking the Siegfried Line – and with the knowledge that the V2s were being launched in the Hague area, the rail communications to Arnhem, Nijmegen and the Hook of Holland were to receive special attention from the RAF fighters.

Following the meeting, the commanders' wishes were turned into operational orders and passed to their operational units and men, including the Tempest pilots of 80 Squadron.

'A good tough bunch' is how 80 Squadron Commanding Officer Bob Spurdle described the group of men with whom he was to fly into battle. When he arrived at the squadron he found 'a mixture of Commonwealth pilots forming just the sort of squadron I'd always considered the best'. The New Zealander had sailed from his home country to England in

June 1940, earning the right to be named as one of Churchill's Few, and gaining valuable combat experience. Spurdle claimed some enemy aircraft late in the Battle of Britain, though on one occasion he would have to rely on a parachute to save his life. More of the enemy would fall to his guns over the next two years, and he was recognised by the award of a Distinguished Flying Cross in August 1942. A return to New Zealand to pass on his knowledge to air force trainees preceded a posting to operations, piloting Curtiss Kittyhawks against the Japanese in the Solomon Islands. In March 1944 Spurdle returned to England, spending a short time with 130 Squadron before a posting to 80 Squadron.[3] He found an air force whose character had altered since he was last in the UK, but it was one he still felt proud to serve in.

> I could see how the Air Force was changing – as war's attrition thinned out the original air crews, and as survivors were withdrawn from operations, or promoted to higher ranks, the RAF became for the much greater part an air force of duration-only personnel. It was the sheer numbers and fresh innovative outlook of these volunteers, leavened by tradition and the guidance of switched-on Regulars, that created the mightiest Air Force ever. Air crew or ground staff, men or women, machine for machine, the RAF was incomparable. Weeded-out wallies and wankers disappeared into the woodwork – relegated to jobs where they could potter about and do little harm.[4]

Spurdle joined the squadron prior to the D-Day assault of the Normandy beaches, taking up responsibility as a flight commander. Then in July 1944 he took over command of the 'Bell boys' (the squadron badge incorporated a bell). The pilots of 80 Squadron, including a certain Hugh Ross, certainly felt comfortable with their new leader.

> A really great CO. All the lads liked him, very down to earth and he didn't flash his rank. He had a long history of operations and led the squadron really well when attacking targets. He had a stabilising effect on us; at times it seemed quite dire, but it didn't affect morale too much.[5]

Another of Spurdle's 'boys' was Bill Maloney, who had joined 80 Squadron early in May 1944. Bill's first operational sortie took place on 25 May, flying a Spitfire IX, and over the next few weeks his operational hours accumulated. On 6 June he was involved in a convoy patrol, enscribing into his logbook 'D-Day, Ju88 attacked convoy', and the next day in a fighter sweep over the beachhead: 'Scads of everything to be seen.' From the opening of the invasion to the end of the month Bill would fly sixteen sorties, either over the beachhead or in protection of the convoys: 'Carried out patrol round Le Havre,' 'Caen still burning after heavy bombing,' 'Jerry pushed bags of flak up from Caen. Very close,' 'Jerry had a few fighters up, but we just missed out on them,' 'Few Huns about but nothing seen,' 'Very quiet afternoon,' 'Grim trip, bags of clouds, no joy.'

Early in July Bill flew in two escort sorties supporting bomber attacks on a V1 target and on German positions in Caen, and recorded the spectacle in his logbook: 'Wonderful bombing,' 'Greatest show ever seen.' For the remainder of the month it was mainly escorting the heavy bombers, with the odd shipping patrol and a fighter sweep. There are no entries in Bill's logbook indicating that he had any encounters with enemy aircraft. Bill, his squadron colleagues and the rest of the Allied air forces exploited the local air superiority over Normandy.

And so into August. The first half of Bill Maloney's month was taken up with target cover for bomber attacks, fighter sweeps and convoy patrols. During the second half of the month Bill flew on only three operational sorties. The Germans were in full retreat from Normandy, and the Allied land armies were pushing their enemy out of north-west France. As the month of August neared its end a significant change took place at 80 Squadron. Bob Spurdle certainly welcomed the appearance of new aircraft.

Our Tempests arrived. Brand new; shining in the sun! They seemed huge after our dainty Spitfires. But could they go! We found they cruised at almost 100 mph faster than the Spits, climbed like rockets and dived at incredible speeds. They were magnificent gun platforms and, apart from a slight tendency to swing on take-off, had no real vices. We were delighted.

Hauled along by the Napier Sabre engine, the new single-engine Hawker Tempest, a larger fighter aircraft than the Spitfire, certainly packed a considerable punch, armed with four 20mm Hispano cannon – a weapon created not just to fight in the skies, but also to strafe and destroy the enemy on the ground. Hugh Ross, like his CO, also came to appreciate the squadron's new weapon. 'It was a magnificent aircraft and climbing was great. When it came to ground attack it was as solid as a rock. There was no movement, just put your gun-sight on the target and go in on it.'

With the arrival of the Tempest came a move to RAF Manston, Kent, at the end of August, the squadron taking on the responsibility of intercepting the V1 flying bombs – and, as Hugh Ross recalled, 'hoping to clobber one'. Bill Maloney flew two 'doodle bug patrols' on 1 September, one the next day and one on 8 September. But there was no sport for Bill or the rest of the squadron. At this stage the V1 threat was diminishing rapidly, the German launch ramps had been abandoned in the path of the Allied land advances in northern France, and the launching troops were in full retreat. Not surprisingly the 80 Squadron diarist would regularly record 'uneventful' against the day's operational activity. Indeed on 7 September he would record: 'With the Diver [V1 codeword] menace quickly declining a relaxed state of readiness was brought into effect.' The lack of activity was not met with enthusiasm by the squadron, who were now armed with a new powerful air weapon and were seeking any opportunity to make contact with anything even vaguely German. Bob Spurdle knew that he had a group of men who had spent years honing their flying proficiency and their fighting skills. To maintain morale, if the enemy was not coming to them, he had to take his pilots out and find opposition. The squadron diarist recorded on 9 September:

The Squadron are getting rather browned off – the only sorties carried out in the last few days have been those to the 'bar'. The CO submitted a request for the first offensive operation to Planning last night in the form of a Ranger to Leeuwarden airfield. The Ranger was accepted and eight aircraft took off at 0805 hours . . .

However, Bob Spurdle's attempt to get his men into action and keep up morale was frustrated by the weather. Spurdle put in a request again the next day, it was accepted, the weather improved and a visit was made by 80 Squadron to Leeuwarden, with some success: the Tempests tore across the airfield, 'one unidentified enemy aircraft was damaged in the ground dispersal, blister hangars, gun emplacements and probable control tower were strafed'.

It is likely that Bill Maloney was enjoying a period of leave at this time. Following his uneventful V1 patrol on 8 September Bill would not be in the air again until 14 September. While Bill was away, the rest of the squadron went looking for the enemy.

In the few days following the Leeuwarden raid, 80 Squadron escorted bombers. Then on 13 September the diarist recorded: 'A new task was allotted to the Squadron in connection with the German V2 rocket, which mainly consisted of spotting and attacking sites and storage dumps.' 80 Squadron responded and on 13 September was detailed to attack a Big Ben storage dump to the north of The Hague. 3 Squadron would also be involved in the operation, led by its CO Squadron Leader Kenneth Wigglesworth, DFC. Bob Spurdle recorded his experience of the operation. The perils of ground attack, if not already known to Spurdle and his pilots, were about to be made quite clear.

We flew along about 400 yards apart in line-abreast at about five hundred feet ignoring the odd bursts of light flak. Suddenly I spotted a huge Meillerwagen V2 transporter under some trees and then the fifty foot needle-pointed rocket standing upright ready for launching, 'Target at 2 o'clock under trees! Break starboard!'
Wigglesworth was quite close to it and turning quickly he opened fire still banking. I saw his shells on the monster and then a colossal explosion as almost eight tons of liquid oxygen and ethyl alcohol blew. The warhead of over a ton exploded and my comrade flew directly into the huge ball of flame – and didn't come out.
Absolutely horrified, I flew around the scene of desolation – the huge crater and flattened trees. Odd nameless lumps smoked and fumed on the ground; brush burned, but there was nothing to indicate what had been a Tempest.

Ken Wigglesworth did not survive.
The next day 80 Squadron was detailed to continue its counter-offensive against the V2, with two Big Ben armed recces in the Hague area. Bill took part in the first, but the Tempests were recalled on reaching the enemy coast, owing to the fact that the targets had already been blasted by heavy bombers. Bill remained at Manston, while other pilots took part in the second recce of the day, the squadron diarist recording: 'Barges and transport were clobbered.' But it did not go all the squadron's way. Hugh Ross would not be returning that day. Following an attack on a 'big white barge', Hugh noticed his oil pressure dropping, so he called up his colleague Johnny Heap, who replied: 'You lead the way, and I'll keep an eye open.' Hugh, not wishing to fall into enemy hands, decided he would risk a flight across the sea, but the engine cut while over the water.

The huge prop just stopped dead. So I thought I'd better get out. I opted to fly straight and level and jump out over the side. I had all my straps undone, but when I jumped the cord on my R/T [radio telephone] caught on something and I was half in and half out for a while, being buffeted about by the wind. I managed to get back in, undo the helmet and then jump out and pull the parachute. I had my dinghy attached to the Mae West. I inflated it and got in. Johnny Heap stayed quite some time and I always wondered how he got back with any petrol left in his tank. He was a great bloke. Everybody looked out for everybody else, quite prepared to take pretty fair risks to see that the other chap was alright.

Hugh was eventually picked up by a Walrus, an air–sea rescue aircraft, and after a couple of days arrived back at 80 Squadron. Meanwhile, his fellow pilots continued to hunt the enemy. Further success would come their way on 15 September. Bill Maloney took part in yet another armed recce in the Hague area, the diarist recording: 'A 30 cwt truck was attacked and after a few attacks was left in flames. On the way out a vertical white vapour trail was seen topping to approx 25,000 feet. This was apparently caused by a rocket fired from the Hague area.'

There is no doubt that Bob Spurdle was enjoying leading his 'good tough bunch', and his pilots were seeing action.

It was a fantastic thrill to have my own squadron – to lead this bunch of fine pilots flying the best fighter in the Allies' stable. Looking first to one side and then the other at my boys flying in perfect formation; all of us so confident in each other and our powerful machines. With over two thousand four hundred horse power the 24 cylinder Napier Sabre motors let us outperform anything else to about 14,000 feet. Above that height the super-chargers of other aircraft gave them the edge but below this ceiling we were kings!

Spurdle's 'kings' were on the offensive; targets were being found, attacked and destroyed. While commanding, Bob Spurdle was yet to lose a pilot. Morale was certainly high. On 16 September 80 Squadron was detailed again for an armed recce in the Hague area. They would not be alone in the skies over Holland. Spitfires and Tempests from other squadrons roamed, providing cover to RAF heavy bombers, spraying lead into barges, motor vehicles and trains. The Luftwaffe did little to oppose their counterparts. The main threat to the Allied pilots came from the ground. Fighter Command lost eight aircraft on low-level operations that day, six as a result of enemy action; four of these pilots lost their lives. Two Spitfires were lost in a collision over Kent; one pilot was killed.

The 80 Squadron diarist recorded that day, 'Germany was entered for the first time. A loco together with 45 wagons were attacked . . . and strikes were seen on loco – black and white smoke soon appeared. The wagons were strafed well three times.' Bob Spurdle would never forget this attack. He was about to lose his first pilot.

> I attacked a train of flat cars and covered vans. Olaf [Captain Ullestad, Norwegian] flew across 'Spike' Maloney's slip stream and was hit by the streams of empty 20mm shell cases pouring out as 'Spike' fired and was wounded in the face.

80 Squadron's attack on the train did not go unopposed. The Tempests flew through a hail of flak, some of which punctured Bill Maloney's aircraft. Bill was unharmed, but it quickly became clear that there was critical damage to his aircraft. His fellow pilots looked on as glycol began to stream from his engine. Bill had to react quickly: it was too low to bale out and it would not be long before the fighter-bomber became a mere lump of metal, with gravity overcoming aerodynamics. He still had some control over his aircraft but had to get it down fast. While radioing to his colleagues, telling them of his intentions, Bill scanned the ground below. Easily visible was an area of high ground, with a church spire prominent on top. Bill could easily avoid that. Beside a rail line, there appeared to be a good-sized field. That would have to do – there was little choice.

Bob Spurdle would later recall seeing Bill, with the Tempest, on the ground.

> He waved to us from his cockpit. Returning to Manston we quickly refuelled and four of us flew back to try to locate Spike's machine and destroy it. We couldn't find the blasted thing, but a loco, which we dis-integrated plus a truck and trailer. That night we were advised to go to bed early as next day we'd be on a special op.

Bob phoned his wife Shirly: 'a selfish thing to do but it had been a bad day for me. Spike was my first loss and I felt it keenly and needed some loving words to cheer me. Besides I knew what the morrow entailed [Operation 'Market Garden'], and had the twitch. I couldn't speak of it but wanted to hear my wife's voice again.'

There is no doubt that Bill's loss was a shock to the squadron, but the reports from returning pilots were promising. Bill had definitely been seen alive on the ground. Evasion was a real possibility. Bill had crash-landed virtually on the Dutch–German border and, assuming that he had sustained no injury, he could have got away from the scene quickly and found cover. Then, in the days following, perhaps he would be able to make his way into Holland and find some friendly civilians. All speculation of course.

Any emotional response at 80 Squadron had to be quickly suppressed. There was still a job to do, and the following day Spurdle's Tempests were defending the paratroop drops as Operation 'Market Garden' was launched. Over the next few days operational activity was intense, and the squadron would suffer further losses. On the first operation of 17 September the squadron diarist recorded: 'Flak was plentiful.' Bob Spurdle recalled seeing his 'No. 2 Warrant Officer "Blondie" Godfrey, buy it with a direct air-burst'. Later that day Flight Lieutenant Irish's Tempest suffered engine failure, fortunately over England, and he was able to bale out. The next day brought further support to the Army's thrust into Holland. Flying Officer 'Lofty' Haw was hit by flak, the squadron diary recording: 'He attempted to ditch but eventually baled out at 1,200 feet and is missing believed killed. Flying Officer Haw and Tempest were seen to crash into sea, his parachute being only half opened.' Indeed Haw did not survive. The diarist also recorded: 'Flying Officer Bob Hanney disappeared mysteriously and no facts are available about him.' He too had lost his life. The diarist summed up: 'It was a day of suicide flying.'

Despite these losses, Bill Maloney would not be forgotten, particularly by his close flying colleagues. But he was becoming one of numerous losses, and there was firm belief that he had survived. Once Bill failed to return from the 16 September operation, the Air Force bureaucracy set about recording the known details of his fate. To those who did not know him, he was another casualty, another faceless name, another faceless service number. But, of course, the paper trail would ultimately lead to despair, yet through uncertainty there was cause for hope.

On 7 October 1944 Bill Maloney's parents received a telegram. The news any mother and father feared had arrived.

414715 P.O. W. E. Maloney missing. Regret to inform you that your son Pilot Officer William Edmund Maloney is missing as result air operations on 16th September 1944. Known details are he was pilot of Tempest aircraft detailed for operations against the enemy which failed to return to base. Regret delay notification due to breakdown in communication from your son's unit. This information is confidential and not for publication. The Minister for Air joins with Air Board in expressing sincere sympathy in your anxiety. When any further information is received it will be conveyed to you immediately.

There exist today letters that put into words the sense of loss to Bill's colleagues and to his parents. A colleague of Bill's, Frank Lang, wrote to Mr and Mrs Maloney on 13 October 1944. Hope remained.

Dear Mr and Mrs Maloney
    You will have already received our CO's letter stating that Bill's 'catterpilla' [*sic*] and squadron badge would be sent later. Enclosed you will find the catterpilla. The squadron badge unfortunately was locked in his kit which will be sent to you later.
    Bill was a very good pal of 'Bluey' Rankin and I and we are anxiously awaiting news of him. We have every reason to believe that he is alive and well. You will hear just as soon as any word is received. Please excuse the paper but I have just arrived in London for a short leave and have nothing.
    Please do not worry too much. 'Spike' will turn up
    Yours very truly
    Frank A Lang

Frank wrote another letter on 2 February 1945 to Bill's sister, at St Mary's Convent, Ipswich, Queensland.

Dear Clare
    Many thanks for your air letter of the 9th Jan. Am very glad to hear that you received the brooch and 'catterpilla' quite safely. I was wondering if they had arrived or not. You must ask your family to forgive me for writing such a make shift letter. I was in a great hurry and had no paper material. I am surprised to hear that you did not receive our CO's letter. I will try and give you what details I have. As I did not take part in the particular operation I have to repeat what I heard from those

who were. Bill was taking part in a strafing operation when his aircraft was hit by light flak. He called up on the radio telephone and said that he would have to crash land. He was seen to make a successful crash landing and it is all our opinion that he is still alive. The Hun is not very helpful in notifying us so all we can do is wait patiently. All his friends on the squadron are anxious for what news we can get.

Bluey and I are both looking forward to our return to Australia. With a bit of luck we should be there some time around the middle of the year. Our people will be glad to have us home I am sure. It is a great worry for mothers and fathers. Am afraid that Bluey and I are both from Victoria. There used to be some quite good arguments between Bill and us regarding the north and south.

You will have noticed that we are no longer in England. At the moment we are having lots of real bad weather which does not improve our opinion of Holland. Believe me this is not the romantic place that story books tell about. It is a very flat damp and uninteresting country.

Hope to hear better news in the near future

Yours very sincerely

Frank

But ultimately the hope that Bill was safe would be replaced with grief and heartache. Although the exact dating of the following telegram is not clear, it is likely to have been sent to Bill's parents after the war, probably at some point in the second half of 1945.

Deeply regret to inform you that your son 414715 Pilot Officer William Edmund Maloney previously missing lost his life on sixteenth September 1944. This reclassification has been made by Air Ministry London and is based on information from Canadian investigating unit which states that an aircraft crashed approximately five miles north-west [sic] of Arnhem on 16th September 1944. The pilot landed safely but was captured by the enemy and shot. It has been established that the pilot was your son and he is buried in grave 544 field IIIc Nord-friedhof Düsseldorf Germany. The Minister for Air joins with Air Board in expressing profound sympathy in your sad bereavement.

On 19 November 1943 Australian Flight Sergeant Frank Cummings, a close friend of Bill's, lost his life on active service, killed in an accident at South Tealing. There are numerous pictures of the two men together during training. On 4 November 1944 Frank's mother wrote to Bill's mother.

Dear Mrs Maloney

Now I have started I don't know what to say, what can one sorrowing Mother say to another sorrowing mother – there is just nothing to say that can in any way ease the heartache and desolation that comes when news such as yours comes. I wonder if you know who I am. I feel sure you do because I seem to have known your Bill so well through my dear son. He & Bill left Australia together and were staunch pals until my dear one was taken last November. They were together through their long leave in London last year, which was so irksome to them both, as they wanted action, poor darlings both of them. I received a letter today from Mrs McInnes in London, who knew and loved our two lads and she told me the tragic news and sent me your address.

There was evidently a very strong palship between our two lads. They were always together according to Sono's letters and photos and today when we read the news hubby and I could only say, well perhaps they are together again. I cannot express words of comfort, they mean nothing to the bereaved, all one can say is they were doing what to them was their duty and were happy in so doing. To me it is a waste of lovely young lives and all so useless and senseless. I only wish I could meet you as our boys were so much to each other,

I have a very lovely photo of them together taken in London last September, they look so happy. Let me know if you have one of them and if not I will have one taken off and send it to you. It is a lovely picture. Well dear friend there is nothing to say. We just know the heartache you are experiencing and yet we cannot help. Was Bill an only child too? When you are able to write I would appreciate a letter from you.

Yours sincerely L Cummings – Franks mum.

On 14 June 1944 Australian Flight Sergeant Donald Kairton of 19 Squadron, another good acquaintance of Bill's, lost his life on a dive-bombing operation supporting the battle in Normandy. It was believed that the blast from his own bombs may have resulted in the crash. Donald's mother wrote to Bill's mother on 3 January 1945, at a time when Bill's fate was still unclear. A most moving letter written by a mother who did not know the person she was writing to, yet they now had something in common.

Dear Mrs Maloney

I expect you will be wondering who I am, writing from Lithgow. Well I'd better tell you right away. My name is Mrs Kairton. My son Donald was a great pal of your son Bill, whom Mrs McInnes (of the club to which the boys used to go in London) tells me is missing. I do hope and pray Mrs Maloney that by this time you will have good news of him.

Mrs McInnes wrote to me so kindly when our son Donald was reported missing believed killed on 14 June 1944. For six months we've had high hopes that Donald may be a prisoner, but we got word on 14 December to say that the mayor of a small town in France had informed the RAAF that a fighter pilot belonging to an Australian unit had crashed and was killed instantly, they gave all the details as to what was found near his body, so that there can't be any mistake.

Mrs McInnes said your son and mine were very good friends and my brothers in England spoke of your son too when I asked if they had heard Don speak of any of his cobbers.

Mrs McInnes seems to think Billy will return, she didn't even think that Don would I'm sure. It nearly breaks a person's heart to think of such fine lads not coming back.

Your son Mrs Maloney was just 'missing' wasn't he? There is a good chance that he may be prisoner. God grant that he is. Donald was our only child, we unfortunately lost two other children previously, one 9 months, one 4 years, which made this blow to us trebly hard.

I do hope dear friend (may I call you that?) that you won't mind my writing. I just felt that I'd like to write to the mother of one of my son's pals. I'd be very glad to hear from you if you would care to write and I do hope that you have got some good news of Billy.

And finally another letter exists, sent to Bill's mother and written on 26 September 1945.

Dear Mrs Maloney

Since the end of the war I have thought of you very often, knowing that as the boys were getting home to Australia, how much more you would be missing Bill. It is wonderful to feel that there will be no more fighting, and one is so happy for all those who are going home, and for the families who will be there to receive them. But it does make one's loneliness greater.

I have met thousands of boys during the war, from all corners of the Empire, but there are some who will always remain in my memory and my thoughts, of whose friendships I will always be proud. Your Bill was one of those. He was so fine, so clean and honest and so friendly and happy. One cannot feel he has gone. May I quote from a passage in one of the London papers at the end of the Pacific war? The article was on the thanksgiving one felt and this paragraph I found very helpful.

'. . . and in Him we commend on this day all those whose hearts ache still, perhaps now more than ever. For those near and dear to them, who, so far as the sight of these eyes is able to discern, can never come back. But they are safe, safer perhaps than we. Their lives have not been lost nor their warm human comradeship withdrawn. They too are re-joicing with us here and now in a fellowship that remains unbroken. Such is our faith. It has upheld us. It shall continue to uphold us. Thanks be to God for his unspeakable gift.'

Two of Bill's pals came along to stay here occasionally. Frank Lang and 'Trev' Trevorrow. We always speak of Bill when they come – and of 'Bluey' Rankin another pal who is with Bill now [he had fallen victim to flak on 30 March 1945]. The friendships the boys have made in this war are very wonderful.

Please give my best regards to all your family. Someday, if I am fortu-nate enough to make a long-hoped-for trip to Australia I shall look forward to meeting you.

In the meantime please believe that though I don't have a great deal of spare time to write, I have not forgotten Bill's family, and think of you often, and of the families of many other young friends who have flown 'beyond the stars'.

Sincerely yours

Gina Murphy

(Victoria League Officers Club, London)

So what had happened to Bill Maloney on 16 September 1944? He had been seen on the ground by his squadron colleagues. He appeared unharmed. Yet he had died that day, 'captured by the enemy and shot'. And that was all that Bill's family ever knew about his fate. They were never made aware of the detailed investigation into Bill's killing and the resultant war-crime prosecution. For sixty years they were oblivious to the fact that those who had been involved in Bill's death had been held to account.

Chapter 5

WITNESSES TO MURDER

L ate on the evening of 19 July 1945 Elten farmer Hubert Franken told his Canadian interviewers that 'the whole population talked about this incident with disgust'.

Many who lived in the Elten area heard and saw the 80 Squadron Tempests in the skies above their village on the morning of 16 September 1944. It was actually nothing that unusual. Elten lay beneath the flight-path from England to the Reich, and American and RAF aircraft were regularly overhead. Yet there was something slightly out of the ordinary: one of the aircraft appeared to be in trouble. But other Allied aircraft had come down in the area before, so it was still not something that caused great concern.

What happened next, however, would shock the local community. And not just in the immediate aftermath of the incident, but for generations

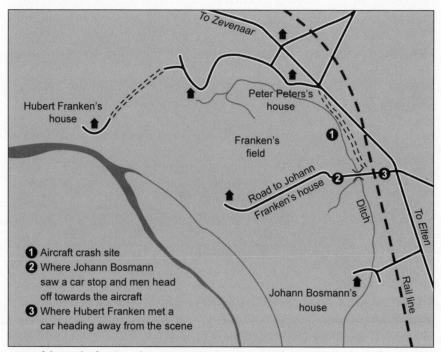

Scene of the crash of 80 Squadron Tempest EJ662, 16 September 1944.

to come. The incident fuelled rumour, which combined with hearsay to spread around the district in the days following. The local people would be divided into those who believed the stories of the witnesses who had watched the events unfold and those who believed the accounts of the men who had been directly involved in what actually happened. Feelings that had been kept suppressed would surface, and a different side of people's character would emerge.

Using statements from the key witnesses, taken shortly after the war, one side of the story can be pieced together. On 19 July 1945 a small team of Canadian investigators arrived in Elten to start taking statements. The 'Examiner' was Major Neil Fraser, then head of the NWE Detachment of the No. 1 CWCIU, and the 'Cross-Examiner' was Major L. S. Eckardt, with the translation carried out by Lieutenant Wady Lehmann, who had visited the scene of the alleged war crime just over a week before. Included in the statements are accounts from Hubert Franken and Johann Bosmann respectively, the two men who had accompanied Lehmann when he visited the scene of the incident and found Bill Maloney's dental plate. Franken's and Bosmann's evidence lay at the core of the investigation.

Frau Meta Rug, 41 years old, whose husband was serving away, lived in Elten at the time. Something had happened on the evening of 15 September that would firmly place the events of the next day in her memory.

> A woman who lived in the colony near my home, and who was responsible for the distribution of ration cards, came around to my house and found the door locked. I was out shopping, and seeing my doctor. My son, who was outside, told her, 'Mother is not at home', to which she replied, 'If you want cards you can come yourselves'. When I arrived home I saw her bicycle standing two houses away and I went to her and asked for my ration cards. As an answer I was told, 'You must say, Heil Hitler'. I repeated my request and she insisted I give the greeting. I said, 'Away with your Heil Hitler' and I assured her I would come and pick up my cards personally in the future rather than have her deliver them. I proceeded to the town office. The woman called after me, 'We always greet the Führer'. I thought it was over, but when I returned home I was hit in the face by the same woman.

On the morning of 16 September Frau Rug was in Elten, and she noticed the presence of the Allied aircraft, but it was something she was getting used to: 'There were attacks almost daily along the railway . . . We had just arrived back from Emmerich about eleven o'clock with a friend . . . when we were surprised by fighter-bombers and sounds of intensive gun fire.' Frau Rug took cover behind a building near the town hall: 'I saw one come very low over us, travelling in the direction of Babberich, in the direction of my home, which is not very far from the meadows of Johann Franken . . . I had sent one of my children ahead as I had to do some shopping and was very worried about the child.' The aircraft passed over some trees and out of Frau Rug's sight.

Hubert Franken recalled it was 'a fine morning' that day, as he stood in his backyard, looking to the south-east, where he 'saw a number of English aircraft flying around the way they had been doing the last few days and shooting up the trains'. The farmer watched as one of the pilots, clearly in considerable trouble, fought to control his fighter plane, flying low over Johann Bosmann's house and into one of the fields belonging to his neighbour Johann Franken. As a member of the *Landwacht* (similar to the Home Guard), Hubert Franken 'was responsible for taking prisoner any pilots who had landed and preventing their escape across the border'. Franken would later recall that he 'stayed back intentionally', although he would never say why, perhaps fearful of a confrontation.

A half mile or so along the road eastward from Hubert Franken's, farm worker Peter Peters recalled spending a quiet morning in his house, unable to work outside, owing to a problem with his leg. His wife had also seen the fighter planes approaching from the south-east, and it soon became apparent to her that one was in trouble, losing height and heading in the direction of their house. She shouted to her husband to take cover quickly. They both retreated to their basement.

In the cockpit of the aircraft that Frau Rug saw flying low in the direction of Babberich, that Hubert Franken saw in considerable trouble and that Peter Peters saw losing height was Australian pilot Bill Maloney. Bill's crippled Tempest angled downwards directly over the house of 48-year-old Johann Bosmann, who had come outside to watch the aircraft shooting up a passing train. Bosmann stood transfixed as 'Spike' struggled to get the spluttering aircraft to ground safely and watched as the Tempest hit the ground a kilometre to the north in Johann Franken's meadow: it 'turned over and I thought that no person could have survived . . . it did a complete loop and landed in a cloud of dust'. Bosmann retrieved his identification papers from the house (he was also a member of the

Landwacht) and then set off for the crash site. After a few minutes' walking Bosmann looked up to see a car travelling westwards on the road to Johann Franken's; it pulled up between him and the wrecked Tempest, and he watched as a group of men 'got out of it and went toward the aircraft'. Bosmann would recall that three were in field grey and two in SA uniform: 'They took their service rifles and carried them in a ready position.' He continued on his way, watching the men ahead, who occasionally took cover from the RAF fighters, piloted by Bill Maloney's colleagues, which were still flying low overhead. When Bosmann was a few hundred metres from the scene, 'the men came with an airman, who had hidden in the bushes, and they brought him to the aircraft . . . a struggle ensued . . . they began to fight with their fists'.

Bosmann was not the only person watching. Peter Peters spent only a short while in the basement of his house. He soon returned to ground level again and went to his door, where he 'saw an aircraft lying in the distance', he estimated 1,200 metres to the south-east. He went back inside again, then half-an-hour later came out once more. Looking in the direction of the aircraft, he saw 'three or four men who were fighting', but was unable to recognise any of them. He then watched as three men, 'in field grey', 'as if to attack', approached a man who was standing but drawing back, 'in darker attire'. 'I suddenly saw an object being raised, which was being used to strike something, exactly what it was I couldn't see, it may have been a rifle'. The men then went out of Peters's sight into a depression in the field. Hubert Franken had by this time joined Peters.

Twenty minutes after seeing the aircraft crash Hubert Franken had set out to where his sisters lived on the Zevenaarer Strasse, between Elten and Babberich, stopping at Peter Peters's house on the way. Peters told him what he had seen from his house: that 'someone was being beaten in Johann Franken's meadow'. Hubert Franken recalled seeing 'four men proceeding across the meadow towards the road, which comes from Johann Franken's meadow towards Elten. On each side I saw a SA man; in between were two men in dark uniform, i.e. *Wehrmacht* uniform.'

Meanwhile, Johann Bosmann continued to make his way to the scene of the crash and, when he was about 100 metres away, he recognised one of the men, local police officer Hans Pelgrim. A 'struggle' then escalated. 'I saw the airman beaten with rifle butts.' He then watched as the pilot 'tried to ward off the blows, but it was to no avail'. Bosmann recalled that Pelgrim 'had the rifle in a raised position and jumped in amongst the others'. All this had been taking place on the far side of the aircraft. 'Then they came around the aircraft where I could see everything very clearly. The airman was bleeding and his skull was smashed in. He was bleeding terribly. While he was bent over, and four men were beating him, one man came and kicked him in the face with his boot. I shall never forget the scene.' Bosmann recognised another one of the men, police officer Hans Renoth, who had been separate from the beating. Bosmann listened as Renoth 'told the men to go away. He took aim with his carbine and at that moment I turned away. When I had gone a few steps the first shot was fired. The airman uttered a cry. When I had gone a few more steps, the second shot was fired. Thereupon I went home.'

Christine Franken, 58, had lived on the road from Elten to Babberich ever since childhood. She had heard the shooting but did not see Bill Maloney's aircraft crash-land. 'My sisters and the farmhands were out working and a few soldiers came in when the shooting began.' The soldiers had gone into the basement, and a labourer by the name of Schepper and the farm-hand Hendrikus van Boxen also returned to the farm. 'He said he was scared, he had stayed under a haystack, there was a ditch in front of him and across that in the meadow was the aircraft.' At this point Christine Franken recalled two of the soldiers, strangers who were probably infantry, going over to have a look: 'As far as I can remember they were two elderly men who came past with their packs on their backs on the way to Holland.' The soldiers returned between 10 and 15 minutes later. 'They said a man came out of the reeds with his hands up and they began to beat him and they couldn't stand to look . . . My sisters asked who they were and they said they were from the Schupe [police] and members of the Party.' Christine recalled that the soldiers had returned because 'they couldn't stand the sight of the beating'.

Hendrikus van Boxen, a 37-year-old farmhand for the Franken sisters, was working, spreading manure, when he heard aircraft overhead and shooting. 'I took cover under a haystack. I heard something fall. I thought it was a bomb, so I crept around to the far side of the haystack. I didn't see anything as I was under the haystack, until the shooting ceased and things quietened down. It could have been about 10 minutes.'

When Hendrikus came out from beneath the hay, he saw an aircraft less than 100 metres away, in Johann Franken's meadow, with the engine broken off. 'It was grey, single-engined; I saw circular markings on the fuselage and wings.' He did not hang around, having to run back to the Franken sisters' house in pursuit of some horses that had bolted, about one kilometre. On arrival at the house, he discovered that some soldiers had taken cover in the cellar. 'Four or five – I think there were only four. They were *Wehrmacht* but I don't know the unit. I told them that an aircraft had come down and one or two of them went down to have a look. They didn't remain long . . . at the most a quarter of an hour.'

Hendrikus recalled that one of the soldiers told him that someone had brought out a pilot from the ditch with his hands up. 'He said that the *Landjägers* [Gendarmerie] had come across the meadow and taken the pilot off him and began to beat him . . . they beat the pilot with rifles. He said he couldn't stand the sight and came back to the house.' Hendrikus also recalled that later in the day some more German soldiers came to the Franken sisters' house.

> Two groups of soldiers came past the house, one of them about fifteen strong; some of them had also been down to see the aircraft but not all of them came in. The second group of soldiers who came along stopped by the first soldier who told the story and one of them said that the pilot had been killed.

Hubert Franken left Peter Peters at his house and cycled on, to the road leading to Johann Franken's farm, 'in order to see what airmen they were'. Here he came across a car. 'In it were sitting two men in SA uniform, one of whom I recognised as [customs official Friedrich] Grabowski. The other two were in *Wehrmacht* uniform.' Hubert continued on his cycle and then saw the car of the local head of police, Paul Barton, by Johann Franken's meadow.

> I saw Barton walking across the meadow towards the aircraft. I proceeded along the field track and both Barton and I arrived at the aircraft at about the same time from different sides. Renoth stood beside the aircraft, he was very excited. Then close to the aircraft I saw the pilot's corpse lying on the ground, his face was horribly disfigured from beating and his teeth lay alongside. The engine of the aircraft had broken off, the clockwork in the aircraft was still running, the safety belt in the cockpit was unbuckled. As I could see no trace of blood on the seat or on the panel in front I concluded that the pilot had been murdered. Barton then went through the pilot's pockets, in them he found bundles of English, Dutch and German money, then he brought a rosary out of his trouser pocket, then Barton made a remark about the

Catholics over the fact that they had been allowed at large among the people. As I am a Catholic myself, I departed at once. I went over to my sisters. About 200 metres from the aircraft on the road to my sisters I saw two soldiers running in *Wehrmacht* uniform and without weapons. When I arrived at my sisters I heard that their horse had bolted. My sister's hired man had been spreading manure very near the aircraft and the hired man, van Boxen, arrived at my sisters soon after. Then my sisters told me that two soldiers had taken cover in their cellar, they were supposed to have been at the aircraft and had returned almost immediately. They had not been able to stand the sight of the beating and had therefore returned immediately. I then went home. At about four in the afternoon Customs Official Vierchow came to me at my farm and said that in Elten it is generally talked about that the pilot was murdered by the officials. At about five o'clock I started to Emmerich with my wife and I heard already at the bicycle shop of Wittenhorst, here in Elten, that the pilot had been beaten to death.

I heard the same rumour the next morning, i.e. Sunday morning in the church in Babberich where I always went to church. When I returned on Saturday evening I heard from my children, who had been down to see the aircraft, that the chemist shop proprietor of Moers by name of Frehe and a daughter of my cousin who works at the shop, that is the chemist shop, had also been at the aircraft. An assistant customs official had come there also who had said, 'He came out alive and how he met his death I refuse to say.' Chemist Frehe told me the same thing at noon the following day during a visit at my home. I know the name of the customs official but I cannot remember it at the moment although I know he was originally from Stettin. On Sunday morning I was detailed to stand guard over the aircraft, on the occasion the assistant custom official Vierchow came again. I told him that it wasn't the people of Elten who had spread the rumour but that his own Colleague had said yesterday evening that the pilot came out alive and that he would not say how he had met his death. He then admitted that the pilot had been beaten to death.

After watching the beating and hearing the shooting, Johann Bosmann 'continued home without looking back. It was lunch time but I proceeded straight to bed.' Early in the afternoon he rose, returned to the scene and looked on at the dead pilot.

I went back to the aircraft with the intention of seeing what had actually taken place. I found the body near the aircraft and Renoth was standing guard. The other people had gone away . . . the body had the Rosary lying on him and his head was completely bashed in . . . Renoth started to tell me what had occurred. I told him, however, that I myself had been present. He replied, 'In my excitement I didn't see anyone.' Then I went home and did not see any more of the affair. I recognised the victim as a pilot because he was wearing blue uniform and shoes and I could not understand his language.

Bosmann would also tell Allied investigators that 'when Barton saw the corpse and the rosary he said, "This is how we can recognise the sign" . . . Catholics were despised by Barton because he was an atheist himself.' Bosmann would add that on a later occasion he heard Barton say: 'This is going to cause a lot of trouble, it would have been better if they had shot him in the forest in an attempt to escape.' Bosmann also recalled other incriminating evidence when he met Barton: 'In the Landwache a rifle was missing and a broken rifle stood in a corner, Barton said, "Too bad the rifle's broken. It happened that time in the Pelgrim affair . . . when Pelgrim was in on the beating. You know the story don't you?"'

It is interesting to note that during his interview Bosmann was also asked by the Allied investigators if Pelgrim was 'ordinarily a man who would participate in such barbarity?' Bosmann replied: 'Yes, no previous case like that had been reported but he had stepped out of the church.' Asked if it was 'generally a practice of the Nazi Party to step out of the church', he replied: 'No, it was only the custom of the extremely bad ones!'

In the above account, the events of 16 September 1944 are described using the main points from some of the witness interviews. But there were other witnesses, and quotations from the notes made following their interviews provide important additions to the account.

Doctor jur Otto Weyer, the Mayor of Elten, described how Gendarmeriemeister Barton had told him that, while he had been away,

a pilot made a crash landing here in Elten and wounded so severely by a private soldier that the Gendarmeriewachtmeister Renoth of the reserve gave the pilot the *coup de grâce* by firing a rifle on the orders of a Hauptmann Kuehne. On another occasion Renoth came to me and showed me the written order from Hauptmann Kuehne, which proved that he [Kuehne] had given Renoth the order to fire the *coup de grâce*. Renoth added that the pilot was lying on the ground in convulsions and was already dying before he shot him and that he only shot him to put him out of his pain.

Frau Elizabeth Heiting, who ran the Kurhotel on Hoch Elten hill, told examiner Neil Fraser and his fellow investigators that she knew a Captain Kuehne, whose Christian name was either Karl or Otto, and whose unit was Festungs-Nachrichtenstab P.I. 21 (Fortress Signals Headquarters Engineers) and that he was billeted in the hotel in September of 1944. She added that she believed Kuehne was a barrister in Hamburg in civil life. She stated that an Oberstleutnant Heye, the senior officer, was also billeted in the hotel, as was an Obershalmeister Werner Von Den Eichen. Frau Heiting stated that she 'overheard a certain conversation between Kuehne and another about a crash landing and that a soldier came out of the plane alive, and also some talk of a rifle butt'.

Albertus Konning, from Babberich, worked for Johann Franken and recalled seeing Maloney's Tempest crash.

Soon after [I] went over to the aircraft and arrived there about the same time as Pelgrim and someone else, whom I could not recognise in uniform. Also I saw Grabowski and Nicke [*sic*], who were there in party uniforms. Pelgrim asked me if I had seen the pilot and I replied 'No' and went back home. Half an hour or three-quarters of an hour later I again visited the plane and the pilot was then lying beside it and Renoth appeared to be in charge.

Dutchman Franciscus Aalberts, who worked as a farmhand for the Franken sisters, remembered the aircraft crashing and that later in the afternoon he went to Johann Franken's meadow, 'I saw the aircraft and lying nearby was the pilot. At the time Renoth was standing guard and preventing people from approaching closer.'

Bill Maloney's body now had to be disposed of, which would bring in more witnesses to the course of events. Each would tell Allied investigators their recollections of the day.

Wilhelm van den Broek, a 43-year-old farmer, had lived in Elten since 1916: 'I worked for myself and also looked after the cartage business of my neighbour who was in the army.'

In the morning I was at the railway station working on the goods for the cartage business. We were standing by the tracks when the aircraft were flying. One came from the north-west, another one from the south, gliding in and we thought it would land – that was about ten or half past ten. At about twelve o'clock I was instructed by the town office to pick up a corpse.

Van den Broek went to the morgue to pick up a coffin and then made his way to Franken's field on a cart, followed by two men on bikes, who had been detailed to help: Bernhard Rutten and a man called Wienhof.

Bernhard Rutten was 63 years old and had lived in the Elten area for thirty-nine years; at the time of the incident he was working as a community labourer. He recalled that he had been told to go and pick up the corpse: 'I was in the process of digging potatoes, about three o'clock.' Rutten cycled to Franken's field with Wienhof. Van den Broek, in the pony-driven wagon, with boarded sides, arrived first, followed shortly after by Rutten and Wienhof. Rutten recalled: 'The aircraft was completely destroyed and I saw a man lying on the ground with his head opened from the back of the right side to the forehead by a gash about 2 inches wide.' He also noticed a rosary lying on the body.

Van den Broek continues with his recollection.

I saw the aircraft, the engine lying on one spot and the main body about 20 metres further on. The fuselage was in an undamaged condition and between the two lay the corpse . . . As far as I could see the corpse wasn't injured from the landing, the back and side of his head on the left showed a gap. He couldn't possibly have received that injury from the landing of the aeroplane . . . The corpse was dressed in a blue overall, black low shoes, and socks, the pilot's helmet was still in the cockpit. And there was a rosary on his breast. He was lying on his back.

When van den Broek arrived, before Rutten and Wienhof, he recalled only seeing a Gestapo man there with Pelgrim and Barton. Van den Broek watched as

they searched the aircraft and looked for the tank. They found it and opened the protecting cover and tried to siphon the petrol out of the tank with a rubber tube . . . I didn't speak to the Gestapo man although he said to Barton, pointing at the pilot with the rosary on his chest,

'Those are the fruits of Catholicism, one should burn all priests and churches,' whereupon he stepped upon the chest of the corpse. Barton replied, 'Here you can see, with the rosary in their pocket they let these people loose to shoot women and children.'

Bernhard Rutten recalled finding Pelgrim, Renoth and Barton at the scene with a soldier he did not recognise: 'They were waiting for a higher officer and they helped themselves to the petrol.' Rutten recalled the party member, whom he could not identify, saying: 'All Christian churches and ministers should be burned,' and he stamped his foot on the pilot's chest. Rutten looked at the corpse. 'I asked Barton, as I didn't have a good pair of shoes, whether I could have the shoes, as I would be able to make better use of them when the corpse was buried.' Barton agreed. After taking the shoes, Rutten suggested: 'Since we have to wait so long here let us go ahead and load the corpse into the wagon.' He recalled seeing a dental upper plate, which 'lay on the meadow', but he also claimed that he picked it up and put it in the coffin beside the corpse. The expected officer did not arrive, and at about 5.45 p.m. Maloney's body was taken away to the morgue. Rutten went home with his new shoes. 'An hour after I returned home Pelgrim came and took them,' saying, 'You are no longer the owner of those shoes because I have to take them along.'

Dominikus Arntz, 71, had lived in Elten since the turn of the century. Originally a cooper, he became sexton in 1917, his duties including digging graves and recording the arrival and burial of the dead at the local cemetery. As evening drew in on 16 September 1944, Dominikus went to the morgue, 'and there I saw the pilot's corpse, badly mutilated about the head, particularly in the back . . . the corpse had neither shoes or socks, he had no jacket on, only a sort of blouse'. Dominikus left the morgue, recalling that he locked the door behind him.

Important testimony on the movement of Maloney's body would also come from 15-year-old Alex Kerkhoff. He recalled Barton asking him for the key to the morgue that day, and replying: 'I'll get the key from the sexton' (Kerkhoff was related to Dominikus Arntz). Alex completed his task, met Barton at the morgue, gave him the key and was told to wait a few minutes.

Alex, somewhat inquisitive, followed Barton into the morgue. There is an unexplained contradiction in the testimony here concerning the coffin, as van den Broek and Rutten had mentioned putting Maloney's body in a coffin at the scene. Alex Kerkhoff recalled that a lorry pulled up.

About four soldiers stepped out. They went into the morgue with a coffin and they placed it beside the pilot's corpse . . . It was said he was a Canadian . . . He wore blue trousers and light blue shirt and a blue tunic. A darkish blue. I could see that he had an opening in the skull from the back to the forehead. He had bare feet . . . Just before that Barton and Pelgrim, who was also there, had searched the corpse for an identity disc. The soldiers picked up the corpse and placed it in the coffin. They took the coffin out, put it on the lorry and drove away. Barton returned the key to me and I took it back to the sexton.

Alex believed the 'soldiers' were from the air force and that Barton and Pelgrim did not find any identity discs or papers.

Why did Arntz let Barton have the key? His response to the Allied investigators was 'because Barton had gone to my cousin's house to get his son Alex to get the key from me . . . occasionally people come in to see their corpse or prepare them, or the coffin maker might drop in'. Allied interrogators would later press him on this matter, asking him if he had had any other cases in the previous six years where a body had come into the morgue to be taken out again without any record. Dominikus replied that he had; 'many people came from Emmerich badly burned', and 'there was one pilot who was killed in an accident. He was badly burned, and he lies buried in this graveyard.'[1] As sexton, Dominikus was merely 'responsible to see that the grave was properly dug with the proper burial'; he also claimed that he acted on instructions from the town office. Allied investigators would also press him on whether he was afraid of the police. He answered with a definitive 'No'. And whether he feared the Gestapo. Again his response was 'No'.

When the witnesses mentioned above gave their statements to the investigators, some of those alleged to have been involved in the beating and killing were in captivity. Notably, the head of local police Paul Barton was not. Barton's reported activities clearly fuelled suspicion. Why was he trying to move the body on so quickly? Why was he searching for identity discs? When Maloney's body was exhumed, no identity discs were found. Barton would not be at large for long, however, and he was to face a grilling from a man of considerable legal, investigative and military experience in more than just a clash of interrogator and prisoner. It was a clash of democratic law and free thinking with dictatorial law and blind obedience.

PART TWO

A REASON

Chapter 6

RISE OF THE *TERRORFLIEGER*

W hen Bill Maloney was killed on 16 September 1944, the war had raged in Europe for just over five years. Nine months of battle, death, brutality and killing remained before the Allies would take control of a shattered Germany and before the victors would set about imposing their understanding of justice upon the people of the nation they blamed for causing such humanitarian catastrophe. To understand fully the development of the Elten case, it is important to outline the context within which the investigation was set, in particular the experiences and influences of the men involved, and the progress of aspects of the air battle over Europe.

The Luftwaffe pulverisation of Warsaw in September 1939 and of Rotterdam in May 1940; the Blitz on London in 1940–1 and the devastation of Coventry in November 1940; the RAF 'Thousand Bomber' attack on Cologne in May 1942, the firestorming of Hamburg in July 1943 and the arduous Bomber Command winter campaign of 1943–4 against Berlin – these are all notable 'highlights' on the timeline of escalating aerial bombardment.

Early in the war Churchill had exclaimed his faith in the bomber offensive: 'The fighters are our salvation, but the bombers alone provide the means of victory.' Soon, however, it became clear that bombing by night was by no means a precision exercise. In August 1941 an investigation of night raids in the previous June and July, published as the Butt Report, exposed Bomber Command's operational ability. One finding from the analysis of the bombing photographs showed that just one in four bomber crews who claimed to have bombed a target was within 5 kilometres of the aiming point. A major rethink of the bombing policy followed, and dramatic changes were made.

In February 1942 Sir Arthur Harris took over the command of the RAF's heavy bomber force. He had witnessed at first hand the Blitz on London, when, as he described it, the Luftwaffe had 'sowed the wind'. He was forthright in stating that his force would ensure that, in return, the Germans would 'reap the whirlwind'. The senior British politicians and the Air Ministry created the framework for the escalation of the bomber offensive, adopting the controversial area bombing policy, targeting the 'morale of the enemy civil population'. German cities were now in the front line. The RAF was to attack the entire German war machine, and the definition of a 'civilian' became blurred. Was, for example, the sheet metal worker whose end product made artillery shells a legitimate and worthwhile military target? The British War Cabinet thought so, as did the Air Chiefs.

With every bombing attack on Germany, as had happened earlier in the war at Coventry, Liverpool and London, the civilian casualty numbers rose. Despair, grief and fear spread, and, under the absolute control of the Nazi party, German newspapers and radio protested vehemently against the terror attacks. With millions prepared to listen and to accept the propaganda and published casualty statistics, slowly but surely every word uttered by the Reich Minister of Public Enlightenment and Propaganda Joseph Goebbels gave weight to the cause of revenge. New weapons were developed to answer terror with terror, and incitements for reprisal were published and broadcast.

The forces that drove the growth of Nazism in Germany have been well documented – the sense of injustice over Versailles, the fear of communism, economic crisis. Even though the National Socialist party had never previously polled a majority in the elections for the Reichstag, President Hindenburg was persuaded to offer Adolf Hitler the Chancellorship on 30 January 1933, at which point he headed up a cabinet in which his colleagues of the NSDAP were in the minority. The next step towards Hitler's domination followed the Reichstag fire on 27 February 1933. Blame was allocated to the communist factions, and they were quickly eradicated from the political scene. With one major opponent eliminated, Hitler manipulated the other parties in the Reichstag, culminating in the adoption of the 'Enabling Act', which effectively allowed Hitler to impose his will further, and to suspend civil liberties. The government no longer needed parliamentary approval in passing laws. Germany was a one-party state. Hitler's dictatorship became total.

Hitler believed in the power of 'struggle' – that, through conflict, the healthiest and the strongest would win through. Struggle and conflict characterised Nazi governmental style. Containment and control of the will of the German people were essential, by whatever means necessary. All opposition had been suppressed, by assassination if necessary, and laws were created to bring the nation in line with National Socialist doctrine. When power was secured, Hitler set about rearming Germany. The armed forces had to be kept in line, and the implementation of the soldier's oath of allegiance to Hitler proved an extremely powerful contract. After the war, at the Nuremberg International Military Tribunal, Albert Speer, the German Minister of Armaments and War Production, had included in his final statement:

> Through technical devices such as radio and loudspeaker 80 million people were deprived of independent thought. It was thereby possible to subject them to the will of one man. The telephone, teletype, and radio made it possible, for instance, for orders from the highest sources to be transmitted directly to the lowest-ranking units, where, because of the high authority, they were carried out without criticism.

It is now known that behind the film, radio and printed propaganda image of order and efficiency lay administrative confusion. In *The Nazis: A Warning from History*, written by Laurence Rees, documentary-maker and author,[1] Rees comments that the political structure, a 'working towards the Führer', was 'one in which those at the lower end of the hierarchy initiate policies themselves within what they take to be the spirit of the regime and carry on implementing them until corrected'. It is necessary to follow the development of this 'spirit of the regime' in respect of the Allied bomber offensive, as such thinking may well have been what determined Bill Maloney's fate when he came into contact with the lower echelons of the Nazi hierarchy.

A few months after the RAF bombing of Cologne of 30–31 May 1942, a pamphlet written by a Nazi party elite speaker, Toni Winkelnkemper, who was also involved in radio broadcasting in Cologne, received widespread distribution. 'Der Großangriff auf Köln' (The Attack on Cologne) criticised the growth of British 'senseless terror attacks', which were 'aimed only and exclusively at the civilian population'. Winkelnkemper described the bombing, the aftermath and the cost in lives.

> Cologne buried its dead eight days after the attack. They were buried together, just as they had died together. The whole city took leave of them in a powerful and moving ceremony. Formations of the party and its divisions, units of the military, the police, and other public services, accompanied them to the grave, along with thousands of citizens. In silent sorrow, family members, many of whom still bore the wounds of the British attack, stood before the long line of graves. A mother

rested between two of her children. A third child who survived wept at the graves. Here two sisters were buried next to each other, there a whole family of four. Here, several siblings, their grandparents and a grandchild. And so it went – a long line of coffins.[2]

In Joseph Goebbels's weekly newspaper *Das Reich* of 14 June 1942 he wrote of 'Der Luft- und Nervenkrieg' (The Air War and the War of Nerves). Goebbels attacked the bombing policy, the 'blind and destructive terror', calling it 'random bombing warfare against the civilian population for reasons of revenge or dark hatred'. Throughout the article Goebbels blamed Churchill, who 'chose random bombing, and he will be paid back in the same coin. That is an unfortunate and painful method of warfare for both sides, but he who began it bears the responsibility.' Goebbels was obviously able to put to the back of his mind the September 1939 bombing of Warsaw and the May 1940 bombing of Rotterdam. 'Terror can be broken only by terror,' Goebbels informed readers, and then gave a warning on the Allied view on the bombing: 'It would do the Jewish press in New York and London too much honour to give any attention to their bloodthirsty commentaries on the air war and the war of nerves. They will have to pay for it with the extermination of their race in Europe, and perhaps far beyond.'[3] Three months later Goebbels ran an article in *Das Reich* attacking the English, stating that 'we Germans must still learn to hate' and that, while there was a war on, 'we hate them from the bottom of our souls because they threaten our very life, because they oppose our national existence out of envy, jealousy, and ill-concealed national pride'.[4]

On 10 August 1943, with the ruins of Hamburg still smouldering, with burial grounds full of thousands of dead civilians and with hundreds of thousands now homeless, Heinrich Himmler, head of the Schutzstaffel (SS), the police and security forces, issued an order to senior executives, SS and police officers, which was to be passed down the hierarchy by word of mouth. Included was: 'It is not the task of the police to interfere in clashes between Germans and the English and American terror flyers who have baled out.' Just over two weeks later, some guidance was sent to magazine editors in the Third Reich, concerning 'Themes on the 5th year of war', stating: 'These points should be made by German magazines on the anniversary of the beginning of the war on 3 September in compelling and effective ways.' Included in the suggestion to editors were statements such as: 'The German people is fighting in this war for its national ethnic existence, as so often in the past. The enemy this time wants actually to rob the German people of its existence and wipe it out as a people . . . Their last hope is the moral collapse of the German people, since they have seen that the German people cannot be defeated with weapons. They have again turned to terror and lies. They hope bombs and lies will wear down the German people, hoping to terrorize it . . .'.[5]

Through the winter of 1943–4 RAF Bomber Command focused its destruction on wearing down the people of Berlin. In *Das Reich* on 13 February 1944 Goebbels attacked the British bombings in 'Die Schlacht um Berlin' (The Battle of Berlin), calling them 'brutal and horrible attacks' on the Reich capital:

> he drops unimaginable quantities of explosive and incendiary bombs on densely populated residential sections of our large cities, he also rains down thick stacks of hypocritical leaflets. He apparently believes that our men and women who have lost everything through this cowardly and wholly unmilitary method of warfare will sit down in the glow of their burning homes and perhaps by the corpses of their innocent children to read these worthless leaflets.[6]

On 29 May 1944 Goebbels, in *Völkischer Beobachter,* the newspaper of the NSDAP, stated:

> It is only by the use of firearms that we can protect the lives of enemy pilots shot down during bombing attacks. Otherwise these men would be killed by the sorely tried population.
>
> Who is right here? The murderers who, after their cowardly misdeed, expect humane treatment from their victims, or the victims who wish to defend themselves on the principle of 'an eye for an eye and a tooth for a tooth'. This question is not difficult to answer. It appears to us intolerable to use our soldiers and police against the German people who are only treating child murderers as they deserve.

Hitler's private secretary and Head of the Party Chancellery Martin Bormann added to the growing clamour building against Allied airmen in a circular to Nazi party *Reichsleiters* (national leaders), *Gauleiters* (regional leaders) and *Kreisleiters* (district leaders) in May 1944.

> Several instances have occurred where members of such aircraft [which he stated had fired on women and children] who have baled out or

have made forced landings were lynched on the spot immediately after capture by the populace, which was incensed to the highest degree. No police measures were invoked against German civilians who had taken part in these incidents.[7]

Albert Hoffmann, the *Gauleiter* of South Westphalia, reported on to his subordinates, including police officers.

Fighter-bomber pilots who have been shot down are in principle not to be protected against the fury of the people. I expect all police officers to refuse to lend their protection to such gangsters. Authorities acting in contradiction to the popular sentiment will have to answer to me. All police and gendarmerie officials are to be informed immediately of my views.[8]

At the post-war Nuremberg International Military Tribunal, the German Foreign Minister Joachim von Ribbentrop was confronted with numerous documents implicating his complicity in promoting the slaying of Allied airmen – lynch law.[9] At a meeting at Hitler's headquarters on 6 June 1944 to establish a policy in respect of downed Allied airmen, 'to deter Anglo-American fliers from further raids on Reich cities', Ribbentrop's viewpoint was made clear. He was prepared to leave the airmen to the will of the mob – namely, lynching. Evidence for Ribbentrop's Nuremberg trial included:

Obergruppenführer Kaltenbrunner informed the Deputy Chief of WFST in Klessheim, on the afternoon of the 6th of June, that a conference on this question had been held shortly before between the Reich Marshal [Goering], the Reich Foreign Minister [Ribbentrop], and the Reichsführer SS [Himmler]. Contrary to the original suggestion made by the Reich Foreign Minister, who wished to include every type of terror attack on the German civilian population, that is, also bombing attacks on cities, it was agreed in the above conference that merely those attacks carried out with aircraft armament, aimed directly at the civilian population and their property, should be taken as the standard for the evidence of a criminal action in this sense. Lynch law would have to be the rule. On the contrary, there has been no question of court martial sentence or handing over to the police.

In addition there was the suggestion of a policy for those who managed to escape the mob.

> Deputy Chief of the WFST mentioned that, apart from lynch law, a procedure must be worked out for segregating those enemy aviators who are suspected of criminal action of this kind until they are received into the [POW] reception camp for aviators at Oberursel; if the suspicion was confirmed, they would be handed over to the *SD* [*Sicherheitsdienst*] for special treatment.

'Special treatment' from the *SD*, of course, meant execution. At the 6 June meeting Ribbentrop failed to achieve consensus on the lynching of airmen who had been involved in the bombing of a city, but there were situations outlined in which lynch law could be justified: 'Low-level attacks with aircraft armament on the civilian population, single persons as well as crowds'; 'Shooting our own men in the air who had baled out'; 'Attacks with aircraft armament on passenger trains in the public service'; 'Attacks with aircraft armament on military hospitals, hospitals, and hospital trains, which are clearly marked with the Red Cross.' Chief of Staff of the OKW Generaloberst Alfred Jodl held certain reservations on reviewing the findings of the conference, asking 'What do we consider as murder?' and 'How can we guarantee that the procedure be not also carried out against other enemy aviators?' Ribbentrop's Foreign Ministry concerned itself with avoiding international law on the matter, as evidenced in a Foreign Office document of 30 June 1944. 'In spite of the obvious objections, founded on international law and foreign politics, the Foreign Office is basically in agreement with the proposed measures.' With respect to provisions protecting prisoners of war in the 1929 Geneva Convention, it was decided that it would be 'futile to try to cover up any violation of them by clever wording of the publication of an individual incident'.

> An emergency solution would be to prevent suspected fliers from ever attaining a legal Prisoner of War status, that is, that immediately upon seizure they be told that they are not considered Prisoners of War but criminals; that they would not be turned over to the agencies having jurisdiction over Prisoners of War; hence not go to a Prisoner of War Camp, but that they would be delivered to the authorities in charge of the prosecution of criminal acts and that they would be tried in a

summary proceeding. If the evidence at the trial should reveal that the special procedure is not applicable to a particular case, the fliers concerned may subsequently be given the status of Prisoner of War by transfer to the Air Forces (P.W.) Reception Camp Oberursel.

Naturally, not even this expedient will prevent the possibility that Germany will be accused of the violation of existing treaties, and maybe not even the adoption of reprisals upon German prisoners of war. At any rate this solution would enable us clearly to define our attitude, thus relieving us of the necessity of openly having to renounce the present agreements or of the need of having to use excuses, which no one would believe, upon the publication of each individual case.

It follows from the above that the main weight of the action will have to be placed on lynchings. Should the campaign be carried out to such an extent that the purpose, to wit the deterrence of enemy aviators, is actually achieved, which goal is favoured by the Foreign Office, then the strafing attacks by enemy fliers upon the civilian populations must be stressed in a completely different propagandist manner than heretofore.

When Bomber Command historian Oliver Clutton-Brock summed up the June 1944 policy discussions concerning downed airmen, he could have gone further. 'Eventually instructions were formulated and everyone in power and authority in Germany knew of the "open season" on captured Allied airmen, such vitriol inevitable dripping its way down to the Luftwaffe rank and file.'[10] Nazi party officials, soldiers, seamen, policemen and civilians were also given leave to focus their malice against the *Terrorfliegers*.

Hitler's henchmen had eroded the rights of captured airmen. Individual prisoners would no longer be protected by international law. Allied aviators had been grouped as *Terrorfliegers*, no matter what their individual circumstances. But that was central to Nazi doctrine: the Jew, the handicapped, the gypsy and the homosexual had not received judgement as individuals. The 'will of the Führer' was placed in the hands and minds of the people who first confronted the airmen.

No doubt Goebbels's propaganda brought news of the *Terrorflieger* raids on Germany to the people of the village of Elten, and for some the impact of the bombing was emphasised – for example, when the body of Gerhard Kroes, who had been working with the *Reichs-Arbeitsdienst* (labour service) in Wuppertal, was returned, following a devastating attack in May 1943, for burial in his home town. The Ruhr had been a focus for Bomber Command in 1943 and the population suffered accordingly, with many people escaping to the country. With the evacuations came first-hand accounts, such as that of one young girl who had roots in the Elten and Emmerich area, Agnes Pelgrim.

Agnes witnessed directly the attacks on Essen, and she would often make contact with her family, living in Elten, to tell them of her experiences. Hans, her father, had been an electrician before the war, but had since taken up duties as a police officer. In addition to Agnes, Hans and his wife had one other daughter and a son who was in military service in the East.

One particular bombing attack remains fixed in Agnes's mind. She was working an apprenticeship at one of the bakeries in Essen, which was on the ground floor of some apartments housing four other families. 'It was a Saturday night. It was already dark and we decided to take shelter in the basement rather than go to the bomb shelter. The house above was totally destroyed. Two adults and a child, who were tenants, and who I knew, as they were regularly in the bakery, were killed.' Unsurprisingly, Agnes found it difficult to remain indifferent towards the *Terrorfliegers*. 'How can you, when you see the body of a child carried out of a bombed building.'

Having been bombed out, Agnes travelled to Elten to see her parents and tell them she was all right. When she arrived, her mother was absent; she had set out for Essen to check on her daughter. Agnes remained at her home until her mother returned. But soon Agnes returned to Essen. She still had to finish her apprenticeship; it was her job and she felt a loyalty towards the people who ran the bakery and who had found new premises. Agnes continued to keep in touch with her parents in Elten, occasionally returning home for the weekend by train.

Despite the failure to take the bridge at Arnhem, in the second half of September 1944 Field Marshal Bernard Montgomery still managed a significant thrust, the Allied spear making a deep penetration, but falling short of the overall objective of Market Garden – to secure a crossing over the rivers Maas and Rhine from which to penetrate into Germany and threaten the all-important Ruhr industry. Montgomery wanted to split Holland in two, outflank the Siegfried Line and push the Second Army on to the Zuider Zee. But frustration at Arnhem took the edge from the spear.

Nevertheless the salient placed German forces south of the Maas in great peril, and removed the threat of any German inclination to recapture the vital port facilities at Antwerp. Although the approaches to the port were far from secure, the north of the Scheldt estuary was still in German hands.

The overall failure of Market Garden placed the Allied forces at Nijmegen, south of Arnhem, out on a proverbial limb. Deputy Supreme Commander Sir Arthur Tedder in his post-war memoir summarised his and Eisenhower's view on the situation:

> It became clear that the enemy's real policy was to defend the western frontier of the Reich for as long as possible. The line chosen in the first place was that running from the water obstacles in Holland to the Moselle, the Vosges and then the Rhine. The Supreme Commander thought that the Germans might well attempt counter-attacks to restore the situation at those points where this line had been breached.[11]

To the right and left of the breach forced by Market Garden, the Allied forces therefore sought to gain ground to flatten the front line, and to the south the Americans were meeting stiff resistance in their attempts to seize Germany's most westerly city, Aachen.

This overall strategic situation now impacted directly on the locale of the area in which the main events concerning this book are set. To protect the Allied forces at Nijmegen, German communication lines to the exposed eastern flank came under attack. Two towns that were seen as important enemy communications centres were Kleve and Emmerich. The latter had previously been a target for the American Eighth Air Force. On 14 June 1944 sixty-one Liberator bombers blasted the oil facilities at Emmerich. A few days later, when the town buried the dead, local officials and organisations, in all their regalia, paid their respects at the side of the excavated collective grave. Little did they know that a much larger area was going to be excavated, for a similar purpose, in a few months' time.

On 6 October 1944 the situation at Nijmegen was summed up in a *Times* newspaper report from its 'special correspondent'.

> [The Germans] are racing against time in an effort to mass sufficient forces to mount a decisive attack . . . Enemy artillery concentrations on the north bank of the lower Rhine and in the Reichswald forest south-east of Nijmegen are the largest we have met since the invasion began.

They are able to reach out into many areas of the salient, including Nijmegen itself, which is under shell fire each day. Moreover, the German retreat towards the frontiers of the Reich has tended to eliminate the problem of ammunition, which bothered the enemy in Normandy . . . here they are within handy distance of the main dumps . . . It is clear that the German High Command has decided to try to use the line of the River Waal as one of the main obstacles in barring the allied entry into Germany. This is the reason: the West Wall, popularly mis-called the Siegfried line, ends at Emmerich, due east of Nijmegen, and the fact that the allies hold ground north of the Waal means that the West Wall is in imminent danger of being outflanked.

Emmerich, mentioned in the above report, now became a tactical target, as did the town of Kleve a few kilometres across the Rhine to the south. With rail communications to the front line passing through the two towns, a decision was made to block these rail lines. The heavy bombers were called in.

Chapter 7

BLOWING THE HELL OUT

At The National Archives in Kew, London, in file AIR 37/1237, '2nd Tactical Air Force: Air Marshall Sir Arthur Coningham: demi-official correspondence', there is a note to Captain The Rt Hon. H. H. Balfour, MC, MP, at the Air Ministry.

9 October 1944

I am glad that your journey to Normandy went off smoothly. Many thanks for your letter and for the note about your impressions.

When the P.M. does raise the ban please come over as we shall be delighted to see you.

After your view of the damage in Normandy you will understand my strong aversion to bombing Allied villages and towns merely because the army think that as road centres their destruction will hinder the enemy. I have been going through periods of considerable unpopularity in high places since June because I preferred to cut two or three roads outside the residential area rather than blot the population. The army now agree with my view and all is well. With German territory the position is different and there, without any doubt, we start bombing the centre of the villages and work outwards.

During the Normandy campaign, and the advance into Belgium, the Allied heavy bombers had been called in a number of times to break enemy positions. It had been a hotly contested issue at Allied commanders' conferences. The bomber chiefs were not in favour of this tactical role. They were fearful of friendly casualties, because of the precise nature of the raids and the close proximity of civilians and Allied troops. Their fears were often realised. Despite the protestations, the bombers had been called in. There was some success, but there was also tragedy. Army personnel lost their lives and French civilians were killed, in their hundreds. The bombing of places such as Caen and Le Havre, while militarily successful, caused severe destruction and wide-scale death.

With the war about to enter its sixth year, the RAF, now accompanied by the American Eighth Air Force, had taken the bludgeoning art of bombing to unprecedented levels. Years behind were the days of solitary bombing sorties by twin-engine bombers, rudimentary navigation and 1,000lb bomb loads. RAF Bomber Command could now attack targets *en masse*, using four-engine 'heavies', Lancasters and Halifaxes, with the capability of carrying bomb loads in excess of 10,000lb, manned by highly trained crews that had been taught by men who had learned their craft in the fast-track classroom that was war. These men had electronic navigational aids to find their way, and great advances had been made in bombsight technology to aid their precision. Raids were controlled by specifically trained crews that, with the use of various pyrotechnics, could find and mark targets for their colleagues. RAF Bomber Command had become a lethal weapon with which to realise both the strategic and tactical objectives of the Allies.

A few days before Coningham's memo was written, two towns near the German border became tactical objectives of the bomber forces. On 7 October 1944 the names of Kleve and Emmerich were being transmitted to RAF bomber stations. The numbers of aircraft required followed, along with H-hour, the plan of attack, the routes to and from the target, and the bomb loads to be used. There were eventually 351 aircraft that took off to attack Kleve, with the raid scheduled to open at 1353 hours and to last 25 minutes, ending at 1418 hours. Another 350 aircraft took off to attack Emmerich, with the raid scheduled to start at 1414 hours and to last 22 minutes.

At the RAF Bomber Command airfields of 1, 3, 4 and 8 Groups stretched along the eastern flank of England, aircrew inspected the serviceability of their aircraft and tested them in the air. Ground crews made adjustments. Specialist equipment was checked, bombs were hoisted into place, pumps filled fuel tanks and armourers loaded guns. The station cooks prepared the pre-operational meal of bacon and eggs. Eventually the crews assembled at the briefing room to learn of the operational requirements for that day; approximately 2,400 airmen would be going to Kleve, approximately 2,400 airmen would be going to Emmerich. Included in the latter were 217 men of 460 Squadron Royal Australian Air Force.

The aircrews of Bomber Command were drawn from all over the British Commonwealth. British nationals made up the highest percentage of airmen, followed by Canadians (including some Americans serving with the RCAF), then Australians, New Zealanders, some South Africans and a few from other dominions. Other Allied air forces also made their men available, including Poles, French and Belgians. By 1944 RAF Bomber Command was certainly a multinational force. While 460 Squadron was designated as a Royal Australian Air Force unit, it was not exclusively manned by Australians. Of the squadron's 271 airmen who would fly on the operation to Emmerich on 7 October 1944, 135 were Australian, 74 were British and 8 Canadian.

Conditions at 460 Squadron on 7 October were described by the squadron diarist as 'Fine but a trifle cloudy'. At 1145 hours the first of the squadron's laden bombers was airborne, and at 1232 hours the last of the thirty-one aircraft took to the air. The bombers climbed into a loose assembly, and the navigators set course for enemy territory, crossing the coast near The Hague, then on to Arnhem and to the target. After bombing they would fly south-east to Belgium and cross the coast near Ostend, to avoid the continuous flak that had previously been reported behind the German front lines in Holland. The force attacking Kleve preceded the Emmerich force on the same route in and out. Both forces' aircraft would experience some flak damage, with the intensity greatest at Emmerich. Two aircraft were shot down by flak during the accurate bombing of Kleve, and three aircraft would fall to the German gunners at Emmerich, including one Lancaster in the vanguard of the raid, which blew up following a direct hit.

One man piloting a 625 Squadron Lancaster on the Emmerich raid was Jack Ball. Having grown up in Kingsbury, on the northern outskirts of London, Jack had witnessed the Luftwaffe attacks in 1940. Jack had been on holiday in Warwickshire at the start of the bombing of London, and had returned on the back of his brother's motorcycle, recalling: 'You could see the flames from miles away, the glow in the sky . . . In the suburbs there was considerable damage. I used to cycle [as the tubes weren't running] in to work and I could see quite a lot of damage, houses and buildings down. We had quite a few bombs in Kingsbury and there were fatalities.'

Jack joined the RAF in 1940, largely because of his interest in aviation; it was something he was going to do whether there was a war or not. After a lengthy training period in Canada and the UK, he joined 625 Squadron and became operational in September 1944. His operations included a raid against a German secret weapon depot at Eikenhorst in Holland, and attacks on Calais to try and break the German garrison. On 7 October 1944 Jack flew his Lancaster and crew to Emmerich. In 2006

Jack Ball made a recording of his recollection of the raid, in which he believed that Emmerich was in Holland, not Germany.

It was a beautiful day, a Saturday I remember. Clear sky. The flak was very accurate but there was a tremendous column of smoke and dust from Kleve, which the Halifaxes were attacking, and we were all Lancasters going in on Emmerich. I remember thinking it was such a beautiful day everybody at home would be going on to football matches, or out shopping, and here we were preparing to blow the hell out of some Dutch town that was holding up the [Allied] advance.

When asked in his interview about concerns over civilian casualties, Jack replied: 'I was grateful for being up above quite frankly.'

I didn't feel too badly because my village had been bombed at home, although the raids had finished then. We had been through it. I regretted it, the civilian particularly, but it had to be done to get the blood and strife finished in Europe. The Germans had been so horrible. I never liked bombing French or Dutch targets quite frankly in that respect. And even on German targets, if you look at the casualty figures quite a number of foreign workers were killed who were friendly, fellow Allies. They always seemed to be placed in the way of danger.[1]

As Jack recalled, weather conditions were perfect that day and the bomber crews attacking early in the raid could clearly see the target. There was a slight haze at ground level, but no cloud, and visibility extended about 6 miles. The first red Target Indicators (TIs – coloured pyrotechnics used to mark targets) would later be assessed as accurate, although the green TIs did undershoot. Those at the front of the bomber stream had a clear view of the target; those following up found the town obscured, as thick smoke billowed to 12,000 feet. The crew designated to act as co-ordinators of the raid over the target, the Master Bombers, directed the other crews to bomb different areas of this smoke. 460 Squadron would later record that '4,000lb bombs were accurately placed, but there was a tendency for the incendiaries to fall short'. Later on the squadron diarist would summarise the expected results of that attack.

In view of the large force employed it is doubtful whether much can remain of this small town whose rail and road communications were so vital to enemy supplies to the Arnhem sector of the Front. It is considered to be a very successful attack . . . 30 × 4,000 bombs (one hung up [failed to release]), 12 No. 14 Cluster, 12 No. 15 Clusters and 69,960 × 4lbs incendiaries were carried.

In total, 644.6 tons of high explosive and 1,353.7 tons of incendiaries were dropped on Emmerich.

Reconnaissance photographs taken a few weeks later led to the following 'Interpretation Report'.

Emmerich, situated on the right bank of the river about 20 miles from Arnhem is on the main supply route between that town, the Ruhr and Central Germany. The town has been completely destroyed and all railway facilities severely damaged.

The town centre, occupying an area of nearly 160 acres, is a scene of almost total devastation and hardly a building in the whole area is visible which has not been gutted by fire or completely demolished by high explosive; moreover, the majority of buildings in scattered residential property within a radius of a mile of the town have suffered a similar fate.

The main Passenger Station, the Goods Depots, the Locomotive Depots and Customs Sheds have all been destroyed. At least nine tracks within the railway yard were severed, and some twenty damaged and burned out wagons were visible. Three weeks after the attack damage to the through running line was seen to have been repaired and through traffic was possible, but no other repairs and no substantial movement of damaged rolling stock was observed. The main line to Arnhem was out. A number of warehouses, customs sheds and covered wharves were destroyed or wrecked in the Rhine harbour. Four barges are seen to be damaged and others are possibly sunk.

At least 25 small unidentified industrial premises have been destroyed or severely damaged in the general destruction of the town and some additional damage is seen to the two more important factories in the area, the oil refinery of the Deutsche Gasoline A.G. and the Vegetable and Marine Oil Works of Oelwerke Germania G.m.b.H.

Militarily the devastating attack on Emmerich had been a success; this particular supply line to the Arnhem and Nijmegen area and to the V2 launching sites in Holland had been cut.

But with regard to the humanity of those beneath the bombs, a heavy price was paid that day. At a personal level, the suffering was horrific. In 1943 the bombing of Duisburg resulted in the closure of Theo Meenen's school. To the young boy, 'it seemed like every night there were bombs crashing'. Most of the other children in the area were being evacuated to the east of Germany, but Theo's mother decided it would be best if she brought her boys back to their family home in Emmerich. Theo's father had been sent to fight with a *Wehrmacht* unit against Russian partisans. He went missing in March 1944, and nothing was ever discovered concerning his fate.

During the summer of 1944 Theo, then a 14-year-old, worked on a local farm, between Emmerich and Elten, and he often saw fighter planes from both sides roaring overhead. In the build-up to the Allied Operation 'Market Garden' there had been a noticeable increase in activity. At one time Theo's horse had bolted when Allied fighters had attacked a nearby column of German tanks. The fighters had flown directly over Theo, but, he suspects, on noticing that he was a mere boy they had merely waved. Then, a few weeks after the Allied paratrooper landings at Arnhem, Theo witnessed a further devastating and awesome demonstration of Allied bombing power.

For Theo Meenen there appeared to be nothing that unusual about the morning of 7 October 1944. Theo had a busy day planned, harvesting potatoes. As he set about his work he became aware that Allied fighters seemed particularly busy that morning, and, when German fighters arrived, he saw two Allied planes shot down towards Holland. But this was merely a precursor to a much more awesome and terrifying spectacle. News started filtering through that Kleve was under bombardment on the other side of the Rhine. And it soon became clear that a large bomber force was heading in the direction of Emmerich. At the farm the young children and the women were quickly placed under cover, and Theo, along with a Dutch and German helper, went to look for the horses. Meanwhile, the RAF bombers approached Emmerich, and the markers fell to open the bombing.

Theo stood beside a wood, controlling two horses, and watched as the raid took its course. Nearby he noticed numerous empty boxes falling – the cases of the incendiaries that had fallen short. 'There was a terrible noise, terrible, and a very very dark cloud rose high above Emmerich.' There was little Theo could do, of course, except watch. Beneath the obscured sun, amidst the crashing turmoil of Emmerich, Theo could only wonder about the safety of some of his relatives.

When the raid closed Theo fetched his brother Hubert from the farm, and they went to a local school, where his father had been a teacher. People began to drift out of the bombed town, clearly extremely upset and somewhat at a loss as to what to do. On finding Theo, one of his cousins took him back to her house in Emmerich to see what they could save. The house was still standing, and they managed to retrieve some items from the cellar and put them in a pram. Shortly after they had come out of the house it collapsed. Theo also tried to locate his grandfather Johann, who lived with his aunt, Alvine Balmes, and two other cousins, Rudi and Norbert Meenen, but he could not enter their house. The stock of glass owned by his grandfather, a window maker, had melted and spread in the heat of the bombing. It was impossible to look inside until the glass cooled. A few days passed before Theo discovered their fate, when he once again returned to the house and was asked to identify some bodies that had been removed. He recognised the bodies of his cousins, 14 and 8 years old, who had clambered into a small bath in a futile attempt to protect themselves from the bombing, and also the body of his aunt. When he did eventually manage to get into the house almost a week later, he discovered a watch on some human remains that belonged to his grandfather.

On the afternoon of 7 October Herbert Schüürman and his father Theodor, standing in the street outside their house, noticed the bombers approaching. News of the attack on Kleve had already reached Herbert, and it appeared that Emmerich was next. Along with his sister, his mother, Agnes, his father and a neighbour, he quickly took shelter in the cellar of their house. And they waited. And hoped.

Herbert had failed to meet the criteria to become a German soldier. In fact he did not really fit into Nazi policy at all. The tuberculosis that developed in his leg when he was 16 resulted in him leaving his family in Emmerich to spend time in a special clinic near Düsseldorf. But as a result of the bombing in the area around the hospital he returned to his home town. Although Herbert's father did not agree with Nazi doctrine, he had had little choice but to allow his son, in previous years, to be part of the Nazi youth organisations that attracted young men with exciting boyish opportunities such as motor cycling or shooting. But now Herbert's disability did not really fit into the ideals of health and vigour.

Herbert was certainly aware of the air battle going on over Germany; they often watched the bombers flying east, but initially there was no expectation of any raids on the scale of those taking place in the Ruhr or against Berlin. But then the war got closer. A Dutchman living in the house next door used to risk his life listening to the BBC, and heard the news of the Allied advance from Normandy through Belgium and into Holland. Herbert began to fear that Emmerich might soon be subject to a heavy attack. On 7 October his fears were realised.

From within the cellar Herbert listened. The drone of the bombers preceded the incredible shattering sound of bomb blasts. The cellar ceiling vibrated, and the supporting struts shook, threatening a collapse. Fortunately the supports held, and, when the bombing ended, the family stealthily made their way to the staircase. As they clambered up, the strapping supporting Herbert's leg broke open. Upon reaching ground level, they met flames and heat: the whole house was burning. In fact, all the houses around were ablaze. In a house opposite two people had been cut down by flying glass. Quickly Herbert's father took his family away from the devastation to an open field, and then on to a farm, pushing Herbert along on a bicycle. As the day wore on further homeless people joined them at the farm, and by night there were twenty people sharing one room.

Herta Schieck first heard of the bombing of her home town of Emmerich on the radio. Two days after the raid, she received a telegram from her father, Carl von Gimborn, telling her that her mother had been killed; she was not to come to Emmerich, and he would come to see her. Herta had moved to Dresden some years previous to be closer to her husband's family.

It had been more than four years since the sound of bombers had been 'the music' for the wedding of Herta von Gimborn and Wolfgang Schieck on 11 May 1940, the day after the German forces had opened the Blitzkrieg, thrusting into Belgium and Holland. A telegram from Wolfgang's father, who lived in Dresden, had recently informed Wolfgang of his call-up for military service. Herta and Wolfgang wasted no time in speeding up the preparations for their marriage. Wolfgang's father had been the last *Ministerpräsident* of the *Freistaat Sachsen* (Free State of Saxony). Having intervened on behalf of the operatic conductor Fritz Busch, who was arrested during a concert for his opposition to the new Nazis, he had been dismissed by Hitler in 1933.

Shortly after the marriage, the newlyweds went to Dresden, where Herta's father-in-law managed to find them an apartment, in which she lived until early 1944. Wolfgang regularly wrote home from the war in the east, and occasionally they were able to meet up, one such encounter leading to the birth of their daughter Alexa. But their personal fears grew over the bombings of German cities and the approach of the Russians, and in the summer of 1944 Herta returned with her daughter to her family home in Emmerich. Although unaware why at the time, Herta noticed the build-up of soldiers in the area following the Allied landings at Arnhem; the children were forbidden to play in the garden because of the number of fighter aircraft that were flying low all over the area. The war was clearly getting closer. Perhaps Wolfgang was more aware of the situation than she was when he wrote telling her that it was no longer safe in Emmerich and it would be best if she returned to Dresden. On 22 September her father Carl von Gimborn took her north along the Dutch border and on to Rheine, where she boarded a train to Leipzig, changing in the night for Dresden. On arrival, she quickly came across hordes of people who were fleeing west as the Russians advanced. Here in Dresden, on 9 October, she received the telegram informing her that her mother Emma had been killed. When Carl arrived in Dresden he merely told his daughter brief details about the terrible loss of his wife and Herta's mother. Only in later years would he describe more fully what happened.

When the bombing started her mother and father had taken shelter in the cellar along with a 79-year-old aunt, a gardener and a young girl. The house was hit and a fire started. There was only a small window to the cellar, but the first bomb to fall had smashed a small hole into the underground chamber. It became the only way out, and Herta's father managed to clamber through. Desperately Carl sought help, pleading with some soldiers to help force open a larger hole. In the cellar next to where his wife was trapped, coal was stored; it was alight and the flames were spreading. They managed to create enough of a gap to extricate the young girl and the aunt, but the gardener was trapped beneath rubble. Herta's mother's leg was similarly trapped, and the only way they could have got her out was to have cut the leg off. Her father stayed in front of the hole listening to the cries of his wife as she and the gardener burnt to death.

Chapter 8

DEATH OF NAZISM

The British Soldiers' Pocketbook – 1944
You are going into Germany.

You are going there as part of the Forces of the United Nations which have already dealt shattering blows on many fronts to the German war-machine, the most ruthless the world has ever known.

You will find yourselves, perhaps for some time, among the people of an enemy country; a country that has done its utmost to destroy us – by bombing, by U-boat attacks, by military action whenever its armies could get to grips with ours, and by propaganda.

But most of the people you will see when you get to Germany will not be airmen or soldiers or U-boat crews, but ordinary civilians – men, women and children. Many of them will have suffered from overwork, underfeeding and the effects of air raids, and you may be tempted to feel sorry for them.

You have heard how the German armies behaved in the countries they occupied, most of them neutral countries, attacked without excuse or warning. You have heard how they carried off men and women to forced labour, how they looted, imprisoned, tortured and killed. THERE WILL BE NO BRUTALITY ABOUT A BRITISH OCCUPATION, BUT NEITHER WILL THERE BE SOFTNESS OR SENTIMENTALITY.

You may see many pitiful sights. Hard luck stories may somehow reach you. Some of them may be true, at least in part, but most will be hypocritical attempts to win sympathy. For, taken as a whole, the German is brutal when he is winning, and is sorry for himself and whines for sympathy when he is beaten.

SO BE ON YOUR GUARD AGAINST 'PROPAGANDA' IN THE FORM OF HARD-LUCK STORIES. Be fair and just, but don't be soft.

The failure of the German counter-offensive through the Ardennes at the end of 1944 and into January 1945, the Battle of the Bulge, essentially ended the *Wehrmacht* ability to counter the Allied advance into the Third Reich. Late in January and into February the overwhelming strength of the Allies punched holes through the German defensive lines, forcing the *Wehrmacht* back to the Rhine. When the Allies opened up

Operation 'Plunder', crossing the Rhine on 23 and 24 March 1945, reporters broadcast directly into the living rooms of those at home. The BBC's Wynford Vaughan Thomas recorded his experiences aboard a Buffalo amphibious vehicle, almost shouting above the roar of the engines as it plunged into the Rhine.

> Now he is opening up full power. We are racing across and side-by-side with us go racing the other Buffaloes, racing for that hell of the other side. The searchlights cast a white beam now right across the river on one side of us but ahead of us is only red water. The current's carrying us down and we are putting up our noses against it, going clean across it all the time. And the tracer is making a pass on either side of us beating down the opposition. Now we are utterly alone it seems right out in the midst of this swirling stream. You get a complete feeling of detachment. Waiting all the time for the enemy to open up. Waiting all the time for them to spot us as we lie helpless as it seems out here in this wide stream. The Buffalo swings, points its nose upstream now. We are drifting, fighting the current to get over. And now looking behind us the other wave of Buffaloes is dipping down and coming out behind and you get the feeling of irresistible power flooding now across the Rhine.

In addition to the waterborne troops, airborne infantry landed on the far side of the great river, and, by the end of 24 March, bridgeheads had been established and deepened. Over the course of the next two days bridges were constructed and the bridgeheads linked and enlarged. On 28 March 1945 *The Times* reported:

> German resistance seems to be cracked and disorganized generally all round the 21st Army Group's bridgehead. Today Canadian infantry of the 3rd Division are in the outskirts of Emmerich advancing along the causeway road running close to the railway into the town, and they find the German troops who are supposed to be resisting them, to say nothing of the civilians, showing signs of having had enough of the war. Demolitions and mines are by far the greatest obstacle to their progress.

Three days later *The Times* was reporting that the Canadians had taken Emmerich, and over the course of the next week they closed in on

Arnhem. On 2 April *The Times* displayed a photograph within its section 'Incidents in the Great Advance' of 'A general view of the ruined frontier town of Emmerich', and on the same day reported that the Canadians had cleared 'the Hoch Elten wood from which German guns for so long dominated our positions near Emmerich'.

Some British eyewitnesses of the advance through Emmerich recorded what they saw.

John Hayes was an aircraftman serving with an RAF repair and salvage unit. Since his arrival on the Normandy beachhead he had scoured the liberated countryside, acting upon reports of downed Allied aircraft, salvaging what he could for future use. His unit had followed in the wake of the advancing armies, and he had come close to losing his life, managing narrowly to survive a V2 attack. John crossed the Rhine at Emmerich, trying to locate a Typhoon that had crash-landed, to see if it could be repaired and flown back to its base. John witnessed, first-hand, the appalling conditions in Emmerich.

> We went across this pontoon and came up the other side and the town was completely destroyed. As we drove up we drove across bricks and rubble. Tanks had been before us, we were following their tracks. It reminded me of Lisieux in Normandy, which also had been just obliterated. The only thing that stood in Lisieux was the green-spire church. And here we were in Emmerich with a repetition of all this destruction. The British Royal Military Police had got across the Rhine and put a big notice up, obviously well prepared. It said 'You are now about to enter the uncivilised world. Be on your guard.' This was a warning to all of us. We weren't quite sure how the Germans would react to us.

John, who at the time had three younger sisters at home, then came across a young German girl.

> Our old Crossley [truck] had had the front blown off by shell fire but the motor was alright. We never had any windscreen, but we still had the turret where the sergeant used to sit and watch for any trouble. I saw a German girl walking towards us on the pavement and I could see that the girl was absolutely shaking with fear at the sight of British soldiers. I thought, 'What on earth is wrong with her. I couldn't believe it.' It was only later that I learned that some of these Germans were

petrified of what was going to happen to them. They must have been told that we were probably uncivilised.[1]

This was one of many scenes John witnessed as he went through Germany that had a life-changing effect. On another occasion John was driving the truck when it hit a donkey being chased by some German women. He pulled over and went back to where the donkey lay dead in the road. The women then set about cutting up the animal and putting the pieces in bowls, to take away and eat. Within minutes there was nothing left. John Hayes made the decision that he was never going to hate anyone ever again.

Denis Whybro served with the 1st Fife and Forfar Yeomanry, in Churchill Crocodiles (flame-throwing tanks), and crossed the Rhine at Rees. Tasked with taking the high ground overlooking their positions, they had to pass through Emmerich.

Took us three days to get through Emmerich . . . You had to bulldoze your way through it . . . [The civilians] were mostly in the ground and cellars. Most we saw were prisoners and they were bad specimens.

Once you got into Germany, anything that was standing you put a shell through. It's just frustration. The customs posts all had big swastikas on them and right bang through the middle of them would be a shell hole. Put that through them just to bust them up. Never took any notice of property once they got into Germany. I used to feel sorry for the Belgians and Dutch, but they didn't worry about the Germans, I think they had caused enough trouble.

While in the area Denis witnessed the treatment of captured Germans by some of his Allies.

French Canadians there were a right lot. I've never seen anybody treat prisoners like they did. But mind you they had had a hell of a hard time. They would run them out of action on a motorbike. If they didn't run fast enough they'd soon lift them up the back of the ear hole with the butt of a rifle. When you had seen things what they'd seen, I suppose that makes you do that. I thought that was a bit – after all the blokes, some of them, were on stretchers, carrying stretchers. That was a bit naughty really I suppose, but what can you do, they had probably seen their mates killed. That was in Emmerich.[2]

The crossing of the Rhine really signalled the end of any faint German military hopes. Hitler and his entourage were not going to accept defeat, and the Allies had, in any case, insisted on unconditional surrender. But it was now only a matter of weeks. The Ruhr was encircled, and the German army disintegrated as the Allied armies swept through the Reich. The Red Army lay siege to Berlin, and US and Russian troops exchanged hand shakes at the river Elbe. On 30 April a Russian soldier hoisted the hammer and sickle aloft the Reichstag, and Hitler took his life.

On 4 May, at Luneburg Heath, all German forces in north-west Germany, the Netherlands and Denmark surrendered. On 8 May crowds gathered and danced in London. The war in Europe was over. But a new struggle was about to begin. Germany was in ruin and the social order had disintegrated. Displaced persons roamed the countryside. The Allies now had to fight the peace.

In *The Devil's Tinderbox* Alexander McKee, who served with the 1st Canadian Army and then with the British 2nd Army through to the war's conclusion, and then worked in the British Zone for the next seven years, gave a summary of the conditions in the immediate post-war period. 'Apart from a few favoured cities, Europe had been reduced to a continent of cave-dwellers.'

> The British Zone . . . had an area approximately the size of Ireland and a population far greater – some 18 million people. In 1939 the population had been housed in 5½ million buildings. By May 1945, 1½ million had been totally destroyed and a further 1½ million severely damaged. The German population were starving and many millions of Hitler's former slave workers, ill-treated and armed, were on the loose. The bureaucrats, prim to the last, called them 'displaced persons', but truly, most of them were Russians, Ukrainians and Poles, forcibly uprooted from their homes in the East. War material of all kinds, from Tiger tanks in drivable condition to guns and ammunition, littered the countryside. The sounds of shooting began at nightfall and continued until dawn. Martial law was in force and enforced. The apocalyptic pre-war visions of H. G. Wells and other pacifist prophets had come true . . . [3]

Alexander McKee recalled that much of what he saw was 'burnt with fire from heaven or tornadoed into rubble by the passage of armies'.

In some towns, such as Emmerich and Arnhem, I was present while their final destruction took place. In Emmerich I saw no building whatever intact, although here and there the gutted shell of a house, one wall of a church tower, still stood. And it was German artillery fire now which vied with the British and Canadian guns in ploughing over the ruins. This process, when the town was an Allied one, we referred to with bitter mockery as 'Liberation'. When you said that such-and-such a place had been 'liberated', you meant that hardly one stone still stood upon another.[4]

Into such 'liberated' towns former inhabitants now returned. Theo Meenen had remained in Emmerich for another week following the devastating air raid of 7 October 1944, and then left with his mother and two brothers to stay with some relatives in Iserlohn, east of the Ruhr. But a return to Emmerich was forced in January 1945 because of the growing numbers of evacuees from Dortmund coming into the town. The Meenens took up residence in a cellar in Emmerich because of the continual shelling by the Allies from across the Rhine, but at least they had plenty of food, eggs and milk, brought in regularly by the local farmers. However, it was clearly not a healthy environment to be in, and just before the Allied crossing of the river the Meenens had once more returned to Iserlohn. Following the American advance through the town, Theo, accompanied by some female cousins, set out on bicycles to return once more to Emmerich. 'It was very difficult, all the bridges had been destroyed, we were not allowed on the main roads as they were reserved for the military. There were a lot of very drunk Poles about and it was certainly dangerous.'

On return to Emmerich, any fears the Meenens had concerning their new rulers were soon dispelled. 'The English officers were very clever and very polite.' Theo helped the British translate leaflets for general distribution, although he found little reward in the occasional 'good fellow' or 'wonderful boy' when some of the other boys were getting chocolate. In and around Emmerich food was scarce. Many people came from the Ruhr areas looking for food, bringing goods to exchange. In 1947 Theo had to spend three months in hospital because he was undernourished.

The Schüürmans remained at a local farm for only a couple of days after the 7 October 1944 bombing of Emmerich, at which point they were told to leave the town and head east. They were eventually entrained, with many others from the recently bombed town, finally disembarking and finding a farm in which to stay in Brandenburg between Magdeburg and Berlin, the whole family sharing a single room. Every farm in the area seemed to be accommodating an evacuated family.

As the war ground on to its climax, rumours reached the Schüürmans that the Russians were nearing and that it would be best to flee west. They left their farm and headed for the river Elbe, Herbert pulled along on a carriage, but on arrival at the water's edge they were told that only soldiers could cross, not civilians. After spending the night in the open, they returned to their farm; they knew there was food there. Eventually the Russians did arrive in the village; the first soldier Herbert met, who had come to take eggs, seized him by the arm and took his watch. At one time some Russian soldiers chased a woman through the village, clearly hoping to rape her. She found a place to hide but the soldiers prowled, looking. They entered the farm the Schüürmans were in and confronted them, asking where the woman was. A shot was fired into the ground to further assert their authority. Herbert's mother went and found a Russian officer, who came to the house, and the soldiers left. From then on the women were kept hidden.

The Schüürmans, like numerous other families, were eventually rounded up and put in a camp, still on the Russian side of the Elbe. They did finally manage to get across the river to the American side, and the discovery of a large store of cigarettes hidden in a village enabled them to persuade the current 'captors' to take them to a rail station, and they spent the next week on a goods train making their way back to Emmerich, arriving as 1945 was drawing to a close. Herbert had to go back to hospital. His father set about rebuilding their house.

Herta Schieck lived on the outskirts of Dresden, and along with her father managed to survive the horrific bombing of the city in February 1945, during which she saw the 'Christmas trees' (Target Indicators) coming down. On the day after the 'terrible bombings on Dresden', and as the Russians were getting nearer, they fled the area; it took Herta and her 4-year-old daughter ten days to cycle back to Emmerich. Her memories of Allied rule are split: 'Some were better than others; some Americans gave us chocolate; others put bread on the ground and drove over it.'

Agnes Pelgrim was most grieved when she found out some more of the detail concerning the bombing of Emmerich in October 1944. Some of her former school class mates had been killed in the raid. Her parents told her that they were going to head east, taking their other, sickly, daughter with them, moving away from the approaching battle front. At the end of the war Frau Pelgrim and her daughter were the first to return to Elten. Hans, Agnes's father, would follow later.

The German families in Emmerich, Elten and the surrounding farms did not really know what to expect when the Allies arrived. Willi Bosmann, the 9-year-old son of Johann, had been called into his house when Allied soldiers were seen approaching the farm, and he cowered with his family in their kitchen. But they had nothing to fear. The farm was merely checked over, and the soldiers moved on, though they took a few geese with them.

With the war over, and a seemingly friendly atmosphere pertaining with their new occupiers, Johann, still outraged by the incident he had seen, had not found it difficult to inform the local Allied military of what he had witnessed. Word spread around the community that those who had been involved had returned to Elten, which created some unease and tension in the village. Those under suspicion took it upon themselves to approach the military authorities.

Policeman Hans Renoth was the first to give himself in, arrested at 2200 hours on 30 May 1945 by 24 Coy CMP (TC), who noted that he 'admits having given the *coup de grâce* to a British pilot but claimed he was carrying out orders of a Captain, and that the victim was already dying from the blows he received'. He had returned from Leipzig at 1800 hours that evening and, because of the local gossip, had decided that it was best to report to the British authorities. Further details concerning Renoth recorded that his main profession was as a 'Gamekeeper. Born 30 Jun 1896 at Bischofswesen, Bavaria. Catholic. Married. Lives at Ammoddeichll [Am Moddeich] (date of this entry 7 Jul 28). Former place of residence: Elten. Police Reserve – Elten.'

Next to turn himself in was Elten customs official Friedrich Grabowski, at 1900 hours on the evening of 19 June 1945. The 42-year-old's arrest report recorded his details:

Address of last residence: 9 von Lochnerstrasse, Elten. Unit Making Arrest: 24 Coy CMP. Reason for Arrest: Alleged War Criminal. Statement after Arrest: States he was present at the time of the killing of a Canadian airman in Sept 44 [changed later in the report to Australian pilot]. Military or Civil Authority taking Custody of the Prisoner: 807 Military Government Prison Bedburg.

The arrest report then went on to record, at length, Grabowski's affiliations with the Nazi party and various associated organisations, since he had joined the *NSDAP* in May 1933. Just before the war Grabowski had been an *Ortsgruppenorganisationsleiter* (local group leader) in Elten. He had also been in the SA and had been a member of *Nationalsozialistische Volkswohlfahrt* (*NSV* – the Nazi People's Welfare Organisation) *ortswalter* Elten, the *Reichsbund der Deutschen Beamten* (*RDB* – German Civil Service), a paramilitary group, often performing anti-aircraft duties, the *Reichsluftschutzbund* (*RLB* – Reich Air Protection Association) and the *Volksbund für das Deutschtum im Ausland* (*VDA* – People's Association, for Germans residing in foreign countries), and since November 1944 *Zollgrenzschutz under Grepo* (border police).

While he was in custody further details were forthcoming.

Born 20 August 1902 at Thomareinen in district Osterode, *Gottglaubig* (believes in God but not in an established Church), Wife: Grabowski, Elisabeth, née Hellwig, born 14 Nov 1920 at Hasslinghaisen, in District Schwelm. *Gottglaubig*. Children (by first marriage): Hilmar, born 6 Apr 1934 in Elten, Ingeborg, born 27 Sep 1935 in Elten, Manfred, born 17 Jan 1938 in Elten. Profession: Oberzollsekretär (Customs Secretary). First Lieutenant in Frontier Control Service.

A further note was made to 'Check this man's connections with *VGAD* [*Verstärkter Grenzaufsichtsdienst* – Reinforced Border Control Service], *GREPO* [*Grepo Grenzpolizei* – Frontier Police], both of which are under control of Gestapo. Automatic arrest categories.'

Next to hand himself in was the colleague of Hans Renoth, who was already in custody. On his return to Elten, Agnes Pelgrim's father Hans quickly became aware of the rumours spreading concerning the death of the pilot eight months earlier. Hans was arrested on 2 July 1945 in Elten. A note on his arrest report stated: 'He was arrested on the instruction of Major Moody. OC "B" Coy 3 Mons for alleged conspiracy in the murder of a Canadian airman forced to bale out near Elten in Sept 44. Two others Renoth and Grabowski have already been arrested.'

The report recorded that he had joined the *NSDAP* in May 1933, had held the position of *Blockleiter* in Elten from 1935 to 1940 and had been a member of the *NSV* and *NSKOV* (Nazi War Veterans' organisation). He was in the Gendarmerie at Elten, holding the rank of *Bezirks* (area) *Oberwachtmeister*, his last promotion taking place on 1 November 1944.

The report noted that he 'admits having been present at the killing of Australian airman (not Canadian)'.

Further details recorded his civilian occupation as a plumber (although he was actually an electrician). 'Born 21 December 1896 at Elten. Left Catholic Church 19 May 42, now G.L. [*Gottglaubig*] Resides, Bahnhof Str 3. Wife, Elise P, née Kaultjes, born 4 Dec 1901 at Sterkrade, Catholic.' Listed were his three children, Frieda born 11 September 1922, Hans born 14 September 1923, and Agnes born 30 April 1926.

> He seems to have had his permanent address at Bahnhof Str 3, Elten but during the war he personally seems to have made the following moves; 18 Sep 1939 to Herchen, District Siegburg, 2 Aug 1940 to Koln – Lindenthal, 20 Jan 1941 to SS Nadritan Ers AbtNuruberg [*sic*][5] (Sigs Rft Unit), 31 Oct 1942 to Essen, 3 Linden 64, 10 Nov 1943 to RAD U.F. (Westphalia?) Check this man's SS connection. Automatic arrest category. On Elten Police Force.

To this report a note was added in pencil: 'He states that has never been in the SS, that it is his son Hans Pelgrim who entered the SS. Pelgrim Senior was a *Blockleiter* of the *NSDAP* in Elten 36–40.' There is also a hand-written note in the file (the signature is ineligible) stating: 'I ordered the arrest of this man because the *Burgomeister* [mayor] of Elten had stated that he was causing discontent in the village, and also that he had been a member of the party that murdered the Canadian airman.'

With three of the alleged perpetrators in custody, and prima facie cases established, a war-crimes investigation team, including Wady Lehmann, set about gathering the evidence required to hold these men accountable. But there were other men who had allegedly been involved who still remained at large. From statements provided by Renoth, Pelgrim and Grabowski, cutoms official Paul Nieke had been implicated, and on 14 August 1945 Captain Harold Hunter had received a note saying that Grabowski's colleague had returned to Elten. Nieke was subsequently arrested by Wady Lehmann on 29 August 1945 in Elten, his address given as 15 von Loch-nerstrasse, a few doors away from Friedrich Grabowski's home.

Four men were now in custody, three had given statements, and witnesses had opened up to the investigators. Slowly the story, or rather stories, concerning the killing of Bill Maloney developed. Evidence was gathered and preparations were made to put the perpetrators of the alleged crime on trial. But what exactly was the crime they had committed?

PART THREE

A CRIME

Chapter 9

CONDEMNATION

M ilitary training not only equips soldiers, airmen or seamen with the necessary skills to carry out their jobs; it teaches them to obey orders and to kill. Combatants must have the mental training to ensure that they can dismiss the humanity of the living being that moves in their sights, or is within the machine that is bearing down on them, or blocks their path, and that they must eliminate it from the battle. The vast majority of fighter pilots claim that in combat they are shooting at a machine. Whether on the ground, at sea, or in the air, warriors are motivated by the objective set out by their commander, by self-preservation and the collective unity, even by the collective unconscious of their peer group. But modern thinking requires that the ability to kill is moderated; it has to be controlled. Through the centuries such restraint was more often than not absent. On the ancient and medieval battlefields, the defeated, unless they were worth holding for ransom, were usually shown little compassion and either put to death or taken into slavery.

Enlightened thinking introduced the concept of restraint into the conduct of warfare. In 1863, during the American Civil War, President Abraham Lincoln put his signature to the Lieber Code, providing guidance to the Union Army on what was considered acceptable conduct. It was deemed outside the law to give 'no quarter' to captured enemy soldiers. The humanity of prisoners of war was recognised and required protection. In 1859 a Swiss national, Henry Dunant, had been horrified at the suffering of tens of thousands of wounded soldiers, many of whom were shot or dispatched with a bayonet when an Austrian army clashed with a French and Piedmontese–Sardinian force at the Battle of Solferino. So appalled had Dunant been that he wrote a book, *A Memory of Solferino*, bringing to the public conscious the horrific reality of battle, the woeful treatment of abandoned wounded men and the need to create some kind of organisation that could intervene on behalf of the wounded. In 1863 the Geneva Society for Public Welfare responded to Dunant's plea, subsequently establishing the International Committee of the Red Cross, and in August 1864 the First Geneva Convention or the 'Convention for the Amelioration of the Condition of the Wounded in Armies in the Field' was signed by sixteen states, and the emblem of the red cross on a white background adopted as the international symbol of those who aided the wounded.

The Hague Conventions of 1899 and 1907 took the international consensus on accepted conduct during conflict a stage further, codifying the 'laws and customs of war'. Included in the latter Convention was a series of articles listing the expectations of the signatories when dealing with prisoners of war, including: 'Prisoners of war are in the power of the hostile Government, but not of the individuals or corps who capture them', and that 'they must be humanely treated'. The Hague Conventions certainly provided a 'framework' for conduct during the First World War, although there were reported incidents of excesses and atrocities, and the Treaty of Versailles required that the defeated German nation surrender suspected war criminals. In response, the Germans decided to try the suspected criminals themselves, in Leipzig, but the original list of 896 was cut to 45, and only 6 were convicted, with their sentences measured in months – an early indication of a nation's reluctance to punish its own nationals.

With the harsh and horrific realities of the First World War still fresh in the minds of the warring nations, the 1929 Geneva Convention expanded on the provisions of the Hague Conventions, notably enhancing the protection and treatment of prisoners: 'In the extreme event of a war, it will be the duty of every Power, to mitigate as far as possible, the inevitable rigours thereof and to alleviate the condition of prisoners of war.' In the detail of the Convention certain articles outlined the treatment prisoners were entitled to. There was reaffirmation that captives were the responsibility of the hostile government and not of the individuals or formations tht apprehended them. Then the provision for humane treatment included protection against 'acts of violence, from insults and from public curiosity'. Moreover, 'measures of reprisal against them' were forbidden. In terms of disciplinary measures against captives: 'Imprisonment is the most severe disciplinary punishment which may be inflicted on a prisoner of war'; 'No prisoner of war shall be sentenced without being given the opportunity to defend himself.' Both Germany and Britain were signatories to the Geneva Convention. Russia was not. For individual combatants, the Convention provided some protection. Once they had downed arms, their status changed from a military target to a defenceless human being requiring humane treatment. It was a noble ideal in principle and one that generally provided protection to prisoners. But, as with other ideals, such as the early Second World War commitment to avoid bombing civilian areas, noble and humane tendencies in conflict can be subject to the corrosion of revenge, retaliation and retribution.

On Friday, 23 June 1944, incensed members of the British Parliament listened intently as Anthony Eden stood and told them of the reports he had received concerning the fate of a number of Allied airmen who had three months earlier broken out of Stalag Luft III, Sagan, Germany, in what came to be remembered as 'The Great Escape'.

> In my previous statement I told the House that 47 British and Allied Air Force officers had been shot as a result of an escape from this camp. This information was based on the figures given to the Protecting Power by the German authorities on a routine visit to the camp. We have now received an official communication on the matter from the German Government. This communication states that 50 officers have been shot [which included 6 Canadians and 5 Australians], and not 47, as previously stated. The next-of-kin of the three additional victims have been informed. The German note gives the same explanation and attempted justification of these shootings as was given to the Swiss inspector on April 17, namely, that these officers were shot while offering resistance when found after their escape, or while attempting a renewed escape after capture. The note adds that during the month of March there were a number of mass escapes of prisoners of war from camps throughout Germany involving several thousand persons: that these escapes were systematically prepared, partly by the General Staffs of the Allies; and that they had both political and military objectives. This situation is stated to have endangered public security in Germany. In order to repress these undertakings, specially severe orders were given to pursue at all costs all prisoners who failed to halt upon challenge, or offered resistance or made renewed attempts to escape after capture, and to make use of weapons until the prisoners had been deprived of all possibility of resistance or further escape.

Eden went on to explain that German authorities had informed them that 'weapons had to be used' against escaped prisoners in Germany, 'including 50 from Stalag Luft III'.

Repatriated officers had provided more details of the Stalag Luft III escape and subsequent shootings, including a Group Captain H. M. Massey, DSO, MC, who had been the senior British officer of the North Compound of Stalag Luft III, from which the break-out was made.

Massey, suffering with an injury to his leg, had been repatriated in exchange for a German airman. This was a grave mistake by the Germans, as he returned with a first-hand account of the planning and execution of the escape attempt and the terrible consequences as reported at the camp. Eden was able to pass on some of Massey's testimony to Parliament.

On April 6 Group Captain Massey was informed by the Commandant that he had been ordered by the German High Command to give him some information about the escape. He then read out a statement to the following effect – this is the German Commandant: 'With reference to the recent escape from the North Compound at Stalag Luft III, Sagan, I am commanded by the German High Command to state that 41 of the escapees were shot while resisting rearrest or in their endeavours to escape again after having been rearrested.' On being pressed for further information regarding the circumstances, and whether all the men were shot dead or some only wounded, the Commandant merely repeated the statement and said that he could not amplify it, except that all were killed, and there were no wounded. A similar statement, with the substitution of the figure 47 for the figure 41, was subsequently posted up on May 8 at the camp at Annaburg, to which Group Captain Massey and the other repatriates from Stalag Luft III were removed on April 11 on their journey home. With the exception of one shot fired at the last of the 76 as he got out of the tunnel, no shooting was heard by anyone in the camp at the time of the escape.

Eden provided information concerning the fate of those escapees who had been captured and survived. The Gestapo had taken over, and the men imprisoned in a Gestapo prison at Görlitz. Interrogations followed, and it was reported that they were threatened: 'We have got you here. Nobody knows you are here. To all intents and purposes you are civilians. You are wearing civilian clothes, and we can do what we like with you. You can disappear.' They were told that they were outside the protection of the Geneva Convention as they were in civilian clothes. It was reported that some prisoners were selected and 'driven away handcuffed and in the charge of the Gestapo officials, who were armed with tommy-guns, while the remainder were handed over to the Luftwaffe and brought back to the camp'.

When Eden stated that the explanation put forward by the German government was 'in fact the confession of an odious crime', he was greeted with a wall of cheers.

First, no orders have at any time been given to British prisoners of war to take part, in the event of their escape, in any subversive action as is alleged in the German note. Secondly, all these officers knew the futility of attempting any resistance if they were re-captured. Thirdly, as to the possibility of a renewed attempt to escape, we now know that owing to physical exhaustion and ill-treatment at Görlitz they were incapable of any such attempt. Fourthly, whether these officers escaped in small or large numbers there can be no justification for the German authorities executing them . . . Fifthly, and most significant, there were no wounded, as would have been inevitable if the shootings had taken place during an attempt to resist capture . . . Sixthly, the German statement omits all reference to Görlitz, and contains no account of the circumstances which led to the death of any single officer. Finally, the ashes of 28 of the escaped prisoners have now been returned to Stalag Luft III, although the Germans had previously refused to send back the bodies for burial. This is the only occasion known to his Majesty's Government or the Protecting Power upon which any British prisoner of war who has died during captivity has been cremated.

Eden was clear that he considered none of the men had lost his life in the escape attempt or while resisting recapture. And it was entirely unjustified to state that the wearing of civilian clothes by an escapee 'deprives him of the protection of the Prisoners of War Convention'.

From these facts there is, in his Majesty's Government's view, only one possible conclusion. These prisoners of war were murdered at some undefined place or places after their removal from the Gestapo prison at Görlitz, at some date or dates unknown. His Majesty's Government must, therefore, record their solemn protest against these cold-blooded acts of butchery (spontaneous cheers erupted). They will never cease in their efforts to collect the evidence to identify all those responsible (more cheering). They are firmly resolved that these foul criminals shall be tracked down to the last man, wherever they may take refuge (more cheers). When the war is over they will be brought to exemplary Justice (more cheers).[1]

Those responsible for the murder of the fifty officers who had broken out of Stalag Luft III were not the only German criminals that the Allies promised to pursue. Reports had been steadily filtering through from the early days of the war, from the German-occupied territories, of other alleged atrocities. At the time Eden was gathering his evidence and making his statements, reports were coming in from the Normandy battle front of further alleged war crimes. As the Allied troops advanced inland, following the 6 June D-Day landings, reports accumulated of atrocities against Allied servicemen, notably the shooting of prisoners. In response, the Supreme Headquarters Allied Expeditionary Force set up a court of inquiry to investigate the allegations.

The political momentum had been gathering for a number of years, to establish a means by which German war criminals could be held to account at the end of hostilities. Reports of alleged war crimes had been made during the invasion and occupation of Poland and Czechoslovakia, and in October 1941 President Roosevelt went public with his condemnation of the 'German practice of executing scores of innocent hostages'. In London, in January 1942 the representatives of nine countries then under occupation put their names to an Inter-Allied Declaration, which opened by claiming that Germany had 'since the beginning of the present conflict, which arose out of her policy of aggression . . . instituted in occupied countries a regime of terror characterized in particular by imprisonments, mass expulsions, execution of hostages and massacres'. The nine signatories committed themselves to 'place amongst their principal war aims punishment through the channel of organized justice of those guilty and responsible for these crimes, whether they have ordered them, perpetrated them or in any way participated in them'.

In October 1943, at a meeting of seventeen representatives of Allied nations, the United Nations War Crimes Commission (UNWCC) was formed and tasked with collating and recording the evidence pertaining to war crimes and then with informing respective governments of any prima facie case. Subsequently, if suspects had been detained with a view to putting them on trial, the UNWCC could advise respective governments on the necessary legal procedures. To assist the UNWCC, a Central Registry of War Criminals and Security Suspects (CROWCASS), set up towards the end of the war, provided a published list of those already held and those wanted in connection with alleged war crimes.

In addition to creating the bureaucracy necessary to control and manage the post-war war-crimes business, the Allies further expanded on the policy behind their executive machine. At the Moscow Conference, in October 1943 the three premiers of Russia, the USA and Britain issued a joint statement, the 'Moscow Declaration', warning their enemies, 'the Hitlerite Forces', that one day they would have to answer for any atrocities perpetrated in any of the occupied territories. The three main powers committed themselves, 'speaking in the interest of the thirty-two United Nations', that:

> At the time of granting of any armistice to any government which may be set up in Germany, those German officers and men and members of the Nazi party who have been responsible for or have taken a consenting part in the above atrocities, massacres and executions will be sent back to the countries in which their abominable deeds were done in order that they may be judged and punished according to the laws of these liberated countries and of free governments which will be erected therein.

They concluded the declaration by making it quite clear the lengths they were prepared to go to, as a warning to those who had, as yet, remained guiltless. 'Let those who have hitherto not imbued their hands with innocent blood beware lest they join the ranks of the guilty, for most assuredly the three Allied powers will pursue them to the uttermost ends of the earth and will deliver them to their accusors in order that justice may be done.'

Some in power wanted quick retribution against certain high-profile war criminals. Winston Churchill was quite prepared to have the German leaders declared as outlaws; their culpability was so obvious that a formal judicial procedure to prove their guilt was not necessary. Once their identity had been confirmed, Churchill believed they should be 'shot to death . . . without reference to higher authority'. He sought to avoid the 'tangles of legal procedure'.[2] Anthony Eden, then British Foreign Secretary, had stated at a Cabinet meeting in June 1942 that 'the guilt of such individuals is so black that they fall outside and go beyond the scope of any judicial process'.[3] Across the Atlantic similar thoughts pervaded. The Secretary of the Treasury Henry Morgenthau, on 5 September 1944, presented a memorandum to President Roosevelt, the Morgenthau plan. The United Nations was to produce a list of 'arch-criminals of this war whose obvious guilt has generally been recognised'. Morgenthau proposed: 'They shall be apprehended as soon as possible and identified as soon as possible after apprehension, the identification to be approved by an officer of the General rank. When this identification has been made the person identified shall be put to death forthwith by firing squads made up of soldiers of the United Nations.'[4] The American Secretary of War, Henry Stimson, challenged Morgenthau's plan, submitting his memorandum four days later: 'the very punishment of these men in a dignified manner consistent with the advance of civilisation will have the greater effect upon posterity. Further, it will afford the most effective way of making a record of the Nazi system of terrorism and of the effort of the Allies to terminate the system and prevent its recurrence.'[5] Ultimately Stimson's view won through, and, with the Russians also calling for some kind of a special international tribunal, the British would, eventually, give way, leading to the establishment of the International Military Tribunal at Nuremberg.

But it was not just the German leadership that was going to have to account for its actions. Provisions were also being made for the apprehension, prosecution and punishment of individuals who had gone against the accepted conduct of war, or who had, through their actions, carried out crimes against the basic principles of humanity itself. The political debate over war crimes had always afforded the 'ordinary' criminals some kind of process. There were concerns that revenge might taint the application of justice. The British Lord Chancellor, Lord Simon, stated in 1943: 'Do not let us depart from the principle that war criminals shall be dealt with because they are proved to be criminals, and not because they belong to a race led by a maniac and a murderer who has brought this frightful evil upon the world.' Indeed Henry Morgenthau in his 5 September memorandum was suggesting the establishment of military commissions to try 'certain other war criminals'.

At the top of the Allied political and military hierarchy the conviction to bring to justice the criminals was firm and focused. But it was the men on the ground who would have to hunt down, capture, incarcerate and punish the perpetrators. They would have to try and set aside any personal feelings in ensuring due process. But these men, the investigators, the gaolers and even the judges, were men who had been part of the drive into Germany. If they had not actually been to the scenes of the crimes, they had certainly heard about them, or read about them. If any doubt had existed, they could now be sure that the war against Nazism had full justification. And these men had been primed not to allow any sentimentality to cloud their ability to carry out their job.

For example, on 7 May 1945 reporter Matthew Halton of the Canadian Broadcasting Corporation broadcast from Holland, providing a graphic account of the aftermath of an atrocity.

The Nazis are now calling themselves werewolves. They are worse than that. The Nazis and the Gestapo are passing from the stage of Europe. But even as they go they leave a trail of slime and abominable crime. I saw one of these crimes today. A few miles north-east of the old Dutch town of Zutphen, which Sir Philip Sidney made immortal, there is a Gestapo concentration camp which the Nazis have made infamous. It was captured last night by a western Canadian regiment as they fought their hard way north. I visited the regiment today and when I went inside the concentration camp I saw 20 or 30 captured German paratroops digging graves. 'What's all this?' I asked . . . the man to tell it is the RSM, Regimental Sergeant Major James Austin of Halifax [who] unearthed it literally. Sergeant Major Austin was standing there making the Germans dig the graves. On the ground laid ten dead things who had been heroes of the Dutch resistance party. Austin led me a few yards away and showed me a brick wall which was spattered with blood and brains. He said, 'As soon as we saw that, we knew there had been atrocities here. Then we saw the fresh pile of earth at the foot of the wall and we found the ten Dutchmen newly buried under a few inches of earth. They have been beaten and tortured to death. Come and look.' As the frightened paratroops looked on, Sergeant Major Austin, cold with hate, bent over the dead men and showed me things much too horrible to describe. Some of these men had been tortured and then shot. Their hands were still tied behind them. But some hadn't even been shot. They had been tortured to death in unspeakable ways. The worst things you have ever read about in an account of Nazi atrocity were there. I saw and was sick. I don't know the names of these victims of the master race. There were no Dutchmen around because there was a battle going on ahead and to left and right and it's hard to get details during a battle. These men of a great Canadian division are having sticky fighting for Zutphen and Deventer but I knew the victims were Dutch Resistance and that the murderers were the Gestapo. Some of the paratroops dug graves, while others lay utterly exhausted on the grass after a gruelling battle. I looked them over and then spoke to one of them. I pointed at the ten Dutchmen and said, 'What do you think of this?' The young unshaven red-eyed paratrooper rose to his feet and stood shaking at attention. 'Das ist eine Schweinerei' (It's a swinish thing), he said in a trembling voice. 'Who did it?' I went on. 'Not us. Not us.' He said. 'We are soldiers. The Gestapo did it.' 'Do you understand why the world hates your country?' I asked. And for the first time in a reply to that question I heard a German say, 'Yes. Yes. I understand.' I put the same question to others. One of them almost cried and said, 'At home in Innsbruck I never dreamed of things like this.' No, these men hadn't done it, but as they looked at the stern-faced Canadian soldiers and at the murdered Dutchmen, they feared for their lives. And indeed, as Sergeant Major Austin said, 'It was hard not to go berserk and kill.' There were two German officers who thought they were going to be shot when they were captured. A Canadian officer said to them, 'Don't be such fools. You are officers. You should have more brains than to believe we shoot our prisoners.' Yet hours later he said the two Germans were still afraid. As we stood there we watched another Canadian regiment go through us to attack. We saw the smoke and fire of battle, heard the exploding mortars. Saw Typhoons rocketing enemy machine gun positions. Purging the Germans out, and none too soon.

Chapter 10

THE DRIVE FOR JUSTICE

O n 15 June 1945 the British Parliament published a statement making clear its plans with regard to war criminals.

It is the strong wish of the British Government to bring all classes of war criminals to trial and punishment as quickly as possible, and substantial progress has been made with the preparations. A start is to be made in about three weeks' time with the trial in Germany and Italy of ordinary war criminals whose victims have been our prisoners of war or other British nationals. A special Royal Warrant is to be issued at once to establish military courts for this purpose. Each of these courts will consist of from five to seven military officers and the prosecutions will be conducted under the direction of the Judge Advocate General. These courts will be exclusively British, and it is expected that it will be possible to set up immediately three or four of them in the British zone of occupation in Germany and one in Italy. When they are brought before the military courts, the criminals of this class will be charged with offences contrary to the laws and usages of war. The plea of having acted under the orders of a superior will not be in itself a defence, although regard will be had to the rank of the person charged. Cases of our prisoners having been shot while attempting to escape will be investigated with the utmost rigour. Those other ordinary war criminals in British hands whose offences have been against other nationals will be sent back for trial to the countries where their crimes were committed. If any small allied country should prefer to be relieved of that responsibility, the British Government will accept it.[1]

The day before, the jurisdiction of British Military Courts had been defined, stating that His Majesty 'deems it expedient to make provision for the trial and punishment of violations of the laws and usages of war'. By the end of the war the strong political will was clear, and a legal structure had been established to prosecute the perpetrators of war crimes. Now the criminals had to be found, and evidence had to be gathered, and, in the defeated German homeland, it was all the Allies could do to ensure that the social structure, or what was left of it, retained just a semblance of a civilised veneer.

When Canadian Prime Minister Mackenzie King informed his Parliament that six of the fifty officers shot following the Stalag Luft III breakout were Canadian, there was not only outrage in the chamber; newspapers fuelled a sense of public despair and anger. Promises were made along the lines of those expressed by the British government. In the days, weeks and months following the D-Day landings the Canadian government had further cause for alarm at how its nationals were being treated. Many Canadian prisoners had simply not been afforded the supposed protection of international conventions. In the aftermath of the fierce fighting, as the battlefront extended away from the Normandy beaches, reports of atrocities against captured soldiers filtered through. There were many incidents involving Canadians, notably the apparent execution of some captured Canadian soldiers at the Château d'Audrieu on 8 June 1944. When the British overran the area on 9 June, the bodies of thirteen Canadians, with head wounds inconsistent with battle, were brought to the attention of the British, and the Canadian Military Headquarters were informed. The Canadians instigated their own special investigation, concluding that an atrocity had clearly taken place. Early in August Mackenzie King broke the news of the Château d'Audrieu massacre to the Canadian parliament, and, as was reported in the press, 'instantly the atmosphere of the House congealed into a cold hatred'.[2] General Crerar of the First Canadian Army made it clear that he wanted to see the Château d'Audrieu investigation taken through to a damning conclusion against the perpetrators. SHAEF would retain control of investigations through the Court of Inquiry, including direct Canadian involvement, notably with the appointment of a certain Lieutenant Colonel Bruce Macdonald, who had studied and practised law pre-war and had seen action in the front line in Normandy. In the following months Canadian interests would centre on allegations against one particular German unit, the 12th SS Division, and the man, Kurt Meyer, who, having commanded the 25th SS Panzer Grenadier Regiment in the early days of the invasion, went on to command the division when his predecessor was killed.

In the context of this book it is of interest to note that one survivor of the fighting in Normandy, who had been captured but survived to escape later, was able to describe what he had seen as he had been marched off to captivity: how one prisoner injured by shellfire had been shot, and how, when they had passed through the town of Authie, he had seen 'seven of our men from our company lined up in the street. Every one of them was shot through the head.' He also told how a German truck driver had deliberately driven into, and killed, two prisoners. He also reported on why some of the enemy men behaved in such a manner: 'There was one fellow who said it in English. He said that we were bombing their wives and mothers back home.'[3]

As the Allied war machine rumbled on and the occupied countries were liberated, the CROWCASS list lengthened. By the end of the war the responsibility for investigating war crimes lay with numerous units attached to the Headquarters of the Allied Forces in Europe. In Germany investigations were conducted under the auspices of the 21st Army Group, which would later become the British Army of the Rhine, although, with the evidence concerning the Kurt Meyer and 12th SS Division case still being accumulated, the Canadians received a formal submission to continue with this particular investigation.

On 8 May 1945 Bruce Macdonald had suggested that a separate war-crimes investigation unit be established within the Judge Advocate General's Department at the Canadian Military Headquarters, which would share information pertaining to Canadian investigations with SHAEF, 21st Army Group and the UNWCC. The Canadian High Commissioner of London, Vincent Massey, gave it his backing, and the No. 1 Canadian War Crimes Investigation Unit (CWCIU) came into being, headed by Macdonald, on 4 June 1945, tasked with investigating cases 'reported against Canadian nationals and members of Canadian Armed Forces and to prepare cases for trial in which sufficient evidence is available'. With offices in London, this 'UK Detachment' would be focused on the Meyer case. On 2 July 1945 another unit was established, the North-West Europe Detachment (NWE) operating out of Bad Salzuflen in Germany, formed by Major Neil Fraser and Major L. S. Eckhardt.

Initially Fraser and Eckhardt had to find the men with the necessary aptitude for such investigative work. Servicemen of legal training who had taken part in the European conflict would fill many of the vacancies, including a certain Wady Lehmann. In due course, Neil Fraser would be succeeded by the then Squadron Leader Oliver 'Pat' Durdin, and, in the light of the fact that many of the cases concerned crimes committed against airmen, he would bolster his team by recruiting RCAF investigators. Wady Lehmann recalled Durdin as 'stocky, energetic and outgoing, easy to get along with and strict in the application of the emerging rules of law governing war crimes'.

At detachment headquarters in Bad Salzuflen, a peace-time spa, we were attached to a British Mess presided over by a moustachioed major of horse-drawn artillery, who invariably dressed for dinner in formal blues complete with spurs and mail. Tennis and soccer matches were laid on, and the spa provided evening relaxation to the music of a string ensemble. We shared these amenities with ladies of UNRRA (United Nations Refugee Relief Agency, paraphrased as 'You Never Really Relieved Anybody), and other organisations. On one occasion, ENSA, the British services entertainment corps, even featured a troupe of the Rambert ballet. These diversions, however, did not deter us from diligently pursuing our assignments.

We regularly exchanged information with the British War Crimes unit at nearby Bad Oyenhausen at the headquarters of the British Army on the Rhine (BAOR – nicknamed 'Beyond All Ordinary Reason'). Many of our cases were filtered to us through them. Much of the investigation consisted of routinely checking out these leads. This could be very frustrating. After explaining the procedure to the witness and the swearing-in, there would follow the invariable opening remark, 'That I can no longer remember today'. As interpreter I was then caught between a perplexed witness and an infuriated legal interrogator. Often we barely got a corroboration of the original testimony, which would bring the case to a dead end. However routine, the excursions were never dull.

I can't say we were frustrated over the number of cases we could not follow through to a conclusion because we soon realized the fact that our sources and witnesses were going to be hard to trace due to the displacements in the post-war populations. Any flagging in morale was offset by the fact that we were slated for repatriation as soon as our turn came without giving us time to brief a successor.

The Germans I met appeared mostly still in a state of shock, although generally cooperative. One witness in a walk-up in East Berlin could express nothing relevant beyond his craving for cigarettes while all the time trying to light a miserable wad of dried tobacco stalks. Outside the streets had been dug out in channels around gutted ruins and end-less piles of rubble. The Brandenburg Gate was still there but it looked somewhat battered . . . People who had managed to leave the city were bedding down with their bundles of belongings in ditches by the fields. A German lady doctor told me how she and a female friend had evaded the Russians by hiding in hay stacks until caught and then only saved

themselves by finding work in an army kitchen where they were also fed
... A young English Military Government officer complained to me that
the only competent civil service staff he could find had been members
of the Nazi party. He also mentioned that Germans had told him that the
English occupation was more highly regarded than the American,
because they realized that the English were making sacrifices from their
own stocks to help the Germans through the first hard winter.

A case in East Berlin involved a plane which had crashed into one of
the lakes. After futilely interviewing the two witnesses referred to us,
we were only too eager to exit from the east zone, as the Russian
patrols were beginning to take too great an interest in our activities.
Even the Allied Control Commission pass was not enough to prevent a
lengthy detainment. East Berlin was an eerie city by day as well as by
night. In the daytime refugees and German soldiers in tattered
uniforms and feet wrapped in rags were drifting in from the eastern
battlefields. At night rubble in the darkened streets lay in huge mounds
etched against the starry sky. Yet in the shell-pocked opera house I sat
in a capacity audience of survived Berliners and Allied service people
alike taking in a performance of *Fidelio*.

In the industrial Ruhr a British security detachment showed us an
arsenal of improvised weapons – sawed-off Mauser rifles, vicious skull-
cracking lengths of steel cable welded at the ends, etc. These had been
taken off liberated Russian forced labourers who roamed the ruins
nightly to extort food and avenge themselves of their former German
masters. Everywhere were rusting remains of huge foundries and
rolling mills with massive armour plate still in place. On a street
corner civilians crowded around a spouting end of a water pipe
protruding through the pavement to fill their pots and pails. Overhead
droned a four-engined Lancaster taking sightseers over the ruins of
armaments factories it had taken part in bombing a short time before.[4]

When it became clear to the Canadian investigators that the airman killed
in Franken's field in September 1944 was not a fellow countryman, a deci-
sion was made to transfer further investigation and trial preparation to the
British, although there was little more to be done. A note was sent to the
NWE detachment of the No. 1 CWCIU on 9 August 1945 naming
'Aus 414715 P/O W.E. Maloney', who was 'NOT a Cdn as originally thought'.
The handing-over of the case to the British caused some consternation,
particularly when the validity of the evidence that had already been

gathered was questioned. The war-crimes investigators were still inexperienced in such matters, although many of them had legal training, and when it came to a multinational investigation and trial they were not helped by inconsistencies between respective countries' war-crime regulations. The law as applicable was still in its infancy, and there was little previous case law to provide maturing precedent.

If there was going to be a problem with the admissibility of the evidence, it was compounded by the fact that the war was over and many of the Canadians, who had been serving in Europe for a number of years, were looking forward to returning home. They felt that their procedures for recording evidence were sufficient for presentation at trial, without them being there. However, Major G. Johnston, the administration officer at the No. 1 CWCIU, wrote to Durdin at the NWE Detachment on 19 October, following a response he had received from the British Judge Advocate General, informing him that statements given by witnesses and also officers of the Detachment, including details of the exhumation and Wady Lehmann's discovery of the dental plate, were 'not satisfactory in their present form'. The British Judge Advocate General was considering sending a British team to obtain a new set of affidavits from the accused and witnesses. Durdin replied on 25 October, saying that the letter had 'caused considerable concern among the personnel at this detachment'.

> The concern felt by the personnel is that after repatriation or leaving the detachment if evidence formally recorded as in the Elten case is unsatisfactory for trial without the attendance of a legal officer, the interpreter or court reported, they may be called back to the theatre at any time the trial takes place, possibly long after their repatriation. It has however occurred to the writer that the unsatisfactory state of the evidence may arise as the result of the difference in the regulations governing the admission of evidence at trials by the British War Crimes Commission and those respecting Canadian cases; it would appear that under the Canadian Regulations . . . the evidence recorded in this case would be admissible without the attendance of any witnesses in person . . . Lieutenant Drynan . . . states that he will be extremely reluctant to sign certificates on any evidence recorded in future, unless some assurance can be given that by so doing he will not incur the risk of delayed repatriation or recall for the trial.

Durdin's concerns clearly met with sympathetic British ears, as early in

November Durdin was informed that one member of the 'Court of Inquiry' (the investigative team from the previous July) would be sufficient at the trial to prove the evidence of the witnesses then provided. As it was, Major John Blain, a member of the original team, who had not actually been present at the main examinations of witnesses, but had been when minor witnesses had been questioned, was notified that his presence would be needed at the trial to authenticate some of the evidence.

As 1945 drew to a close, the Elten case was virtually ready for trial. The accused were in custody, witnesses were available and investigation statements had been declared admissible. Final preparations were made, including the appointment of the judges to try the case, some of whom had been in the thick of the fighting in Germany, the overrunning of the Reich and the imposition of post-war order.

Chapter 11

VIOLATING THE LAWS AND THE USAGES OF WAR

On 15 April 1945 British troops entered the Bergen-Belsen concentration camp, coming face to face with unimaginable horrors: thousands upon thousands of emaciated and diseased prisoners drained of life energy, amidst piles of skeletal corpses. The BBC's Richard Dimbleby reported that 'this day at Belsen was the most horrible of my life'.

> Here over an acre of ground lay dead and dying people. You could not see which was which except perhaps by a convulsive movement or the last quiver of a sigh from a living skeleton too weak to move. The living lay with their heads against the corpses . . .

Dimbleby's graphic description of his revulsion was initially met with incredulity and some disbelief at the BBC. But it was all, of course, so terribly true, and as German territory fell into Allied hands, other abominations were exposed. The name 'Bergen-Belsen' would become synonymous with the horror of Nazi doctrine, as did those of places such as Dachau, Mathausen, Buchenwald and Auschwitz. If any members of the British, American, Canadian or Australian public, any politicians, or any of the military, still needed a reason to be given for the war against Germany, Dimbleby, Matthew Halton of the CBC and their media colleagues, with their explicit reports and shocking photographs, provided the justification.

On 23 April 1945 the *Sydney Morning Herald* used a full page of its broadsheet to show 'German Camp Horror which has Shocked the World'. The 'Murderer of Belsen', Josef Kramer, was pictured under armed escort, his ankles manacled: 'Commandant of the horror camp in which 60,000 dead, dying and starved people were found.' Next, Eisenhower, with Generals Patton and Bradley, stood looking at the 'charred bodies of prisoners on a camp near Gotha'. Then two men were shown carrying a women's body suspended by her scrawny limbs, her hair brushing the ground and her dress having ridden up. Behind, two more men were in the process of picking up another emaciated body from the end of a long line of death. British soldiers looked on as the 'brutal SS guards captured at the Belsen camp [were] forced at bayonet-point to remove and bury the bodies of the victims of their Nazi frightfulness'. In another picture two women attempted to do some washing, 'with a tin of water taken from the only supply for the camp, a filthy pond'. Some open ground was littered with skeletal bodies, some naked, some in rags: 'Starved and tortured bodies of victims lying unburied on the open ground.' Finally a young girl, her dark hair, apart from a few exposed curls, contained by a woollen hat. She wears an oversized great coat with the collar upturned, and manages to force a smile for the camera. Despite everything she still smiles. Two bloodied dressings cross on her forehead, with another across her nose. 'Beaten by Nazis. One of the girl victims in Belsen concentration camp shows evidence of having been brutally beaten by the Nazi guards'.

On the evening of 10 June 1945 Field-Marshal Sir Bernard Montgomery broadcast a message to the German population of the British Zone concerning fraternization:

> This time the Allies were determined that you should learn your lesson; not only that you have been defeated, which you must know by now, but that you, your nation, were again guilty of beginning a war. For if that is not made clear to you and your children you may again allow yourselves to be deceived by your rulers and led into another war. You have often wondered why our soldiers do not pay any attention to you when you wave to them or bid them 'Good morning' in the street, and why they do not play with your children. Our soldiers are acting in accordance with orders. You do not like this attitude: neither do our soldiers. We are by nature a friendly and kindly people. But the order was necessary, and I will explain to you why. During the war your rulers would not let you know what the world was thinking of you. Many of you seemed to think that when our soldiers arrived you could be friends with them at once, as if nothing had happened. But too much has happened for that. Our soldiers have seen their comrades shot down, their homes in ruins, their wives and children hungry. They have seen terrible things in many countries where your rulers took the war.

Montgomery, never one to hold back with his opinion, told the German people that, following the First World War, 'your leaders spread the fairy tale that your armed forces had never been defeated, and later on they repudiated the war guilt paragraph of the treaty of Versailles. They assured you that Germany was neither responsible nor defeated.'

Montgomery accused the German nation of applauding when their leaders 'once more wantonly unleashed' war.

> Once again, after years of devastation, carnage, and misery, your armies have been beaten . . . You think that, not you, but your leaders are responsible for all these things. But these leaders have risen from the German people, and this nation is responsible for its leaders, and so long as they were successful you were jubilant, you celebrated and laughed. That is why our soldiers are not behaving in a friendly way towards you. We have ordered this; we have done this in order to save you, your children, and the whole world from another war. This will not always be the case. We are a Christian people, which gladly forgives; we like to smile and like to be friendly. But it is our aim to destroy the evil of the National Socialist system. It is too early yet to be certain that we have attained this aim. You are to read this to your children if they are old enough, and see that they understand it.

The Royal Warrant of 14 June 1945 had outlined the jurisdiction of the British Military Courts. The court would consist of a President and no less than two other officers. If the accused were officers, those sitting in judgment were expected to be of equal or higher rank (which was not an issue in the Elten case). In addition, if the accused belonged to the enemy Navy or Air Force, then the officer convening the court was required to appoint at least one naval or air force officer, as applicable, as a member of the court. In addition, a Judge Advocate could be appointed to assist the court to take an impartial stance and to advise the court on the law. However, this was not mandatory and a Legal Member could be appointed (as in the Elten case), who, as a member of the court, would be able to vote.

The British Military Courts still operated under the basic principle that the accused was innocent until proven guilty and that the prosecution had to prove its case beyond reasonable doubt. There was one important difference with respect to the rules of evidence, when comparing standard English courts with military courts. Normal English procedure would not allow the submission of some forms of evidence, such as written statements, if the respective people could take the stand and be examined verbally. There was a relaxation of this principle in war-crimes trials, owing to the difficulties of evidence gathering, and any document or oral statement that could help the court decide the case, and appeared to be genuine, could be allowed. Without such an allowance, a considerable amount of the evidence gathered in the Elten case would have been inadmissible.

A further regulation in the Royal Warrant concerned crimes committed by units of groups of men:

> Where there is evidence that a war crime has been the result of con-certed action upon the part of a unit or group of men, then evidence given upon any charge relating to that crime against any member of such unit or group may be received as prima facie evidence of the responsibility of each member of that unit or group for that crime. In any such case all or any members of any such unit or group may be charged and tried jointly in respect of any such war crime and no application by any of them to be tried separately shall be allowed by the Court.[1]

Between the dates of 17 September and 17 November 1945, at Luneburg, Josef Kramer, the 38-year-old Commandant of Belsen, who had also worked at Auschwitz, Mathausen and Dachau, and forty-four others stood trial in respect of the atrocities at Bergen-Belsen and the Auschwitz concentration camps; one of the first hearings concerning the 'lesser' war criminals in Germany. At one point in the trial Kramer was asked about his feelings when he had taken part in the gassing of eighty women at Auschwitz in August 1943: 'I had no feeling in carrying out these things because I had received an order. That, incidentally, is the way I was trained.' Kramer and ten of the other defendants, having been found guilty, were sentenced to death. Other defendants received various prison terms, and some were acquitted.

As the trial at Luneburg was drawing to a close, attention shifted towards the opening of the trial of the twenty-two 'major' war criminals before the International Military Tribunal at Nuremberg. Understandably, the trial of men such as Hermann Goering, Joachim von Ribbentrop and Rudolf Hess grabbed the media attention. Yet there were still less high-profile trials pending, both within Germany and in the liberated countries that had previously suffered under the tyranny of the Nazis. One such trial concerned the shooting of an airman and a Dutch civilian in Holland.

In March 1945 the SD had staged a night raid on a house in Holland, finding RAF evader Gerald Hood, who had been shot down in a

100 Squadron Lancaster on the night of 12/13 August 1944, and a member of the Dutch Resistance, Bote van der Wal. Hood was captured wearing civilian clothing. Both men were taken to Almelo prison. Hood was interrogated by Georg Sandrock, in charge of the SD unit, who then claimed that he had received orders that the British airman had been condemned to death. On 21 March Hood was driven to a wood by Sandrock and a Ludwig Schweinberger and told to get out of the car. Schweinburger would later recall:

> I knew before I got out of the car that I was going to shoot Flying Officer Gerald Hood. I was given that order at the *Dienstelle* [office] before we left. When we got out of the car we just went a few steps and then I shot him. I was perhaps one metre from him when I shot him in the top of the neck, at the base of the skull. I saw where the bullet had gone when I undressed the body afterwards. I had shot him from behind as he was walking away from me.

Sandrock dug the grave, and before burial Schweinburger took Hood's wristwatch. Bote van der Wal was similarly 'executed' a few days later.

Both Sandrock and Schweinberger and two other SD men implicated in the incidents were put on trial at the Court House at Almelo, Holland, between 24 and 26 November 1945. The prosecution made the analogy to a 'gangster crime', every member of the gang being responsible. The defendants claimed that they were under orders to shoot Hood, whom, they believed, had been condemned to death, and that the accused were in fear of the consequences for themselves and their families should they refuse to obey and that their judgement as to what was lawful was influenced by orders. All were found guilty, and Sandrock and Schweinberger sentenced to death. Both men had just over two weeks to live.

As in the Belsen and Almelo trials mentioned above, a common defence appearing in many cases, particularly with regard to shootings, was that the killings were carried out under orders. In the vast majority of trials judges were unsympathetic, unwilling to accept that in some cases those who fired the fatal shot defended themselves on the grounds of having no choice. At the International Military Tribunal at Nuremberg, Field Marshal Wilhelm Keitel, Chief of Staff of the Supreme Command of the Armed Forces, commented on the German military culture demanding compliance to superior orders: 'The traditional training and concept of duty of the German officers which taught unquestioning obedience to superiors who bore responsibility led to an attitude – regrettable in retrospect – which caused them to shrink from rebelling against these orders and these methods even when they recognised their illegality and inwardly refuted them.' Dictatorships provide a sound basis for the career development of 'yes' men.

The 'obedience' attitude was not just limited to the military. The Nazis similarly required a compliance to party doctrine at all levels of the leadership, split hierarchically, with Hitler, the Führer, at the top. Then came the *Reichsleiter*, the Party Directorate, making sure the will of Führer and National Socialism ideology was communicated along the chain, first through the *Gauleiter* (in 1945 there were forty-two *Gaue* in the Reich), then through the political leaders of the subdivisions of the *Gaue*, the *Kreisleiters*. The *Ortsgruppenleiters* then exercised the party ideals through their subdivision of a *Kreis*, followed by a *Zellenleiter*, and finally a *Blockleiter*, whose task was to ensure the political guidance and conformity of between forty and sixty households. With responsibility passing up the chain, each person at each level could rationalise his or her blind compliance, blaming the superiors. If such thinking is accepted, then there was only one man accountable in Germany: Adolf Hitler. His dictatorship, some argued, absolved them of any responsibility, and he could take the blame.

Others though, including some German Nationals, would argue to the contrary. On 24 April 1945 Matthew Halton of the CBC broadcast from Germany, reporting to the world on further horrors and providing an example of the ill feeling towards 'little Nazis'.

Within a radius of 30 miles of this north German town of Meppen there are six concentration camps and political prisons and several prisoner-of-war camps. In one prisoner-of-war camp there are two thousand Russians, and most of them are dying. We came too late to save them. They are diseased and starved and beaten. They are skin and bones. Quite literally there is no flesh on them. They are just bags of bones with swollen ghastly heads. In another camp, which I saw, there are twelve hundred Italians in the same condition . . . They are not human beings any longer to look at. They are grotesque monsters who make your blood run cold. I saw a boy of about 18 who had just died. Bones were sticking out of horrible holes in his skin. Then I saw some German civilians standing nearby. They looked like human beings and I wondered how this was possible. It was early morning. All round apple trees were in blossom and a dozen kinds of birds were singing. How could birds sing here? It seemed impossible, almost a blasphemy that birds should sing in this country of unspeakable evil . . . I walked down the street and saw three German policemen now working for our military government. They were talking to a woman who was crying. One policeman was a handsome young man. The second was a pleasant-faced middle-aged man, and the third was a smiling old fellow wearing glasses. The kind of policeman that children love and trust. I took these three German policemen into a house and questioned them for many hours. My first question was 'Why was that woman crying?' 'Because of one of those Polish devils,' said the young policeman eagerly. 'You know these Poles and Russians are acting like animals now that you have come. The woman's husband is a farmer. One of the Poles, who worked for him, hid a rifle in the farmer's house, then he went and told your military policeman that he was concealing arms, and the farmer was arrested. Awful.' 'But do you blame the Pole?' I asked. They looked at me with surprise. 'Of course we blame him; it was a dirty thing to do.' 'Listen,' I said, 'you Germans have murdered millions of people and now you are angry at one Pole for taking revenge.' They didn't reply. I said to them, 'What do you think of Hitler now?' At once they replied, 'We have no more use for Hitler.' 'Why?' 'Because he lied to us. He said there would be secret weapons that would win the war and we know now that he lied.' So that's why they dislike Hitler. Not for committing crimes that would make Caligula turn pale and draw away, but for failing to produce the goods. 'Do you believe', I went on, 'that you Germans murdered millions of Russians and Poles in gigantic death factories?' 'No,' they said, 'we naturally believed what we were told. We were told the Russians were doing that to us.' Then once more I tried to describe what the Americans had found in that hell hole of torture called Buchenwald. 'Do you believe me?' I asked. 'It's very hard to believe,' said the old policeman gravely. I showed them photographs in an English paper. Pictures worse than anything in the illustrations of Dante's inferno. They stared at them and one said, 'Of course we didn't know there were things like that.' I continued: 'Do you think it is a good thing then to take German civilians to see these horrors for themselves?' They thought it over and discussed it and then said, 'You should put the Nazis in concentration camps.' 'Hitler too?' I asked. That shook them; it almost shocked them. 'Not Hitler', they said 'but the little Nazis, they are the worst of all. The *kreisleiter*, the local Nazi leaders.'[2]

PART FOUR

A JUSTICE

Chapter 12

JUDGES

A t this point it is worth looking into the backgrounds of the men sitting in judgment in the Elten case, starting with three men who witnessed the fighting in Germany and the death throes of the Reich – three British officers, who were also heavily involved in the fight for the peace: William Yaldwyn Kington-Blair-Oliphant, of the 2nd Kensingtons, R. B. Sidgwick of the 111th Heavy Anti-Aircraft (HAA) regiment, and D. S. McNeill of the 62nd Anti-Tank Regiment Royal Artillery. An outline of the backgrounds of these men and the experiences of their respective units will provide an example of the conditions prevalent at the time.

William Yaldwyn Kington-Blair-Oliphant, born on 10 September 1906, was one of four children; he had one sister and two brothers. His father, Temporary Lieutenant Colonel Philip Laurence Kington-Blair-Oliphant, had died of wounds in April 1918, at the age of 50, serving with the Royal Irish Rifles during the First World War, having distinguished himself, being mentioned in dispatches four times and earning the Distinguished Service Order. Philip's sons would keep up the military tradition. Elder son Philip saw action in Warzistan and Iraq pre-war, becoming a Major in the Border Regiment in the Second World War. Youngest son David served with the Royal Air Force, becoming an officer in 1934. During the war he specialised as an armaments officer, serving in the Middle East and Africa. On return to England he helped direct weapons supply in the D-Day campaign and in the advance through Normandy, into Belgium and Holland.[1]

Middle son William was taught the art of war at the Royal Military College, Sandhurst, and fought in the North-West Frontier in 1930 and 1931. William saw further service in Palestine in 1936. During the Second World War he won the Military Cross in 1940, reported in *The Times* on 4 July: 'At Tournai between May 16 and 20 Major Kington-Blair-Oliphant's company held a difficult and dangerous position on the banks of the Escaut Canal. For three days and nights his position was subjected to incessant bombardment by air, mortar, and enemy artillery fire. No inch of ground was, at any time, yielded by his company.' William was honoured with the Officer Order of the British Empire in 1945 and achieved Lieutenant Colonel with the 2nd Battalion Border Regiment.[2]

After the war William took up command duties with the 2nd Kensingtons, as they endeavoured to maintain a semblance of law and order in the disarray of the social breakdown.

On 5 May the 2nd Kensingtons received the news that all German troops in Holland had surrendered, and the following day they, as part of 49 Division, were charged with helping concentrating, controlling, guarding and disarming the Germans in western Holland; their brigade was designated to disarm the 34 SS Division. On 7 May the unit war diary[3] recorded:

> The Bn [battalion] moved into Western Holland and was conc [concentrated] area Maarn. An extraordinary situation with own tps [troops], German tps and Dutch Resistance tps all walking about fully armed. A very tense situation but as a result of everybody's good sense and in particular the amazing discipline of the Dutch Resistance tps, there were no armed clashes of any size. On evening 7 May trouble was reported from Maarn, to which two tks and one MG Pl, A Coy, was sent and at Driebergen where Dutch SS tps were causing trouble, 4 pl A Co dealt with the latter and shot up a farm killing two Dutch SS and taking one prisoner.

Over the next few days the 2nd Kensingtons took charge of the disarming and concentrating of some of the SS troops. On 12 May: 'Day spent in planning Op Pied Piper – a sweep of the RA Bde area to clean out stragglers.' The next day's report: 'Total arrests for the Op was 53 assorted "rats".' The diary contained a summary of their duties.

> The end of the war against Germany saw the Bn engaged in an entirely novel operation: first, the occupation of territory with a capitulated enemy army still there, and still fully armed; secondly, the disarming of the enemy and his caging in the presence of an embittered local population and an armed Resistance Movement deeply conscious of years of persecution. No praise can be too high for the discipline and self-restraint of the Dutch Resistance in this ticklish situation. We found also with relief that the number of SS 'last ditchers' was far fewer than anticipated, and that their officers and NCOs retained control over their men throughout. The Bn's mobility and great fire-power made it an ideal instrument for this operation which, despite the very hard work entailed, was enjoyed by all ranks as a novel and gratifying experience.

Following a parade in front of HRH Princess Juliana in Nijmegen at the start of June, the battalion moved to Germany, Shwerte and Emst, to take up occupational duties, including the administration of prisoner-of-war and displaced persons camps, and quickly found itself overstretched, providing guards, carrying out patrols and making arrests of suspected war criminals.

The scale of the task facing the occupying troops cannot be underestimated. Hundreds of thousands of liberated forced workers roamed the countryside, and those from Eastern Europe were reluctant to return. A Colonel Paravicini, Chief of the Allied Liaison Section of the displaced persons branch, was reported on 29 May as saying that 'in general Poles were showing the greatest reluctance to go to the Russian zone, but Latvians, Lithuanians and others also seemed unwilling to go. As they could not be sent to the Russian zone against their wishes, they remain in the Anglo-American zone.'

On the same day estimates of the numbers of displaced persons ran to French, 1,200,000; Belgians, 200,000; Dutch, 200,000; Luxembourgers, 10,000; Russians, 1,500,000; Poles, 600,000; Yugoslavs, 100,000; Czechs, 60,000; Greeks, 10,000; Danes, 10,000; Norwegians, 10,000. There were also an estimated 350,000 Italians considered as former enemy nationals. Over four million former captives were now liberated from their Nazi enslavers.

Excerpts from the 2nd Kensingtons' war diary highlight examples of the breakdown of law and order.

9 June: A Coy went to a farm at Buchhulz on infm received that armed Russians were looting and had wounded a German girl. On arrival the looters had already disappeared. As a result of this and other cases of looting civ police and our own patrols instigated a system of farm protection.

14 June: B Coy arrested Wilhem Meeurath, who was known to have committed atrocities during the Nazi regime. At Vorhalle one Russian woman was wounded by a D Coy sentry after being warned to halt three times. She later died from the effects of the wounds.

30 June: Six Poles have died and two more seriously ill in Churchill Camp as a result of drinking methylated spirit, which they stole from a photographic store.

10 July: Farm at Ringdfenziegelei broken into by a band of 20 armed Russians. Band escaped before D Coy patrol arrived.

26 July: Standing patrol est. at farm. At 0100 hrs 4 Russians approached farm and attempted to attack it. All were armed and a fight ensued during which one escaped, the other three being captured. Handed over to Kabel Camp Jail. At 0130 hrs 6 Russians, one in offr's uniform, stole foodstuff from farm in Holthausen.

3 August: B Coy – A football match between Italian and Polish DPs at Kabel Camp was held. At 1900 hrs the referee's decision was disputed and a free fight ensued. Two Italians were knifed and taken to hospital.

In such conditions, on 21 September 1945 Lieutenant Colonel William Yaldwyn Kington-Blair-Oliphant, OBE, MC, joined the battalion and took over command. Towards the end of December he received notification that he would be needed to act as President in a war-crime trial.

R. B. Sidgwick was born on 3 August 1918. He was taken on strength by the 111th HAA regiment on 2 November 1942 and became a battery captain on 19 January 1943.

Early in 1943 batteries of the 111th HAA were in action against enemy aircraft bombing London and targets in the north. In September 1943 the regiment moved to the Canterbury area, and the guns of 111th were regularly engaging the Luftwaffe bombers. On 7 April 1944 their guns were positioned around Southampton, and on 15 May an enemy aircraft jettisoned two large bombs on 355 Bty (Battery), killing three men immediately, and wounding eleven others. Another man died from his injuries the following day.

Throughout the Normandy campaign the regiment stayed in Southampton, regularly sending shells up at flying bombs, with claims made. On 12 August 1944 Captain R. B. Sidgwick, with the 356 Bty, was given the powers of a Company Commander, and in September the unit moved to Cherbourg to protect the vital port facilities. In October the regiment was tasked with the protection of Antwerp, where it once again had to deal with the menace of the flying bomb, along with a new German secret weapon, the V2 rocket.

The regiment's war diary[4] recorded certain incidents.

13 October: Intermittent bombardment of Antwerp by enemy with as yet an unknown weapon.

25 October: The enemy continues to direct explosive missiles at Antwerp and a few flying bombs are arriving at intervals. One of these weapons caused casualties and damage near RHQ . . . The CO and personnel of the unit assisted in removing the dead and injured.

28 October: A flying bomb which fell in Schooten caused nearly fifty civilian casualties. A unit rescue party rendered first aid and unit transport evacuated some injured to hospital.

31 October: An enemy missile exploded near 'F' Troop 356 Bty and caused damage to property and casualties to civilians. The Troop Commander L. W. F. Davis RA immediately went to the scene of the incident and rendered assistance and first aid to the injured.

The following month the regiment had to deal with the aftermath of further German secret weapon revenge attacks. On 1 November an 'enemy explosive missile' fell on 'C' Troop of 355 Bty, and eight men were wounded. A week later another missile fell near the RHQ and injured two civilians. A rocket attack resulted in civilian casualties and injured one gunner on 12 November, and two days later the regiment's CO and Medical Officer did what they could for 'numerous civilian casualties'. On 29 November a rocket killed one serviceman, not from the regiment, and wounded eight others. Into December and the regiment's diary continued to record the matter-of-fact details of the V-weapon attacks, along with other incidents. The men of the regiment were witnessing first hand the shocking and dreadful events. The diary entries do not describe the blood, the shattered remains of a blasted body, the etched grief on the face of a mother, father, husband, wife, sister, brother, daughter, son. The diary does not record how the unit's men reacted when they saw the life snuffed from friends and colleagues. It does not record how the unit's men coped with the gruesome realities of Nazi revenge.

11 December: [Three gunners of 347 Bty] involved in an enemy land mine explosion which killed one of them, presumably killed the second (only small unidentifiable parts of a second human body have been found) and slightly injured the third.

17 December: 347 Bty reported that two Sgts had not returned from short leave to Antwerp – it is thought likely that they were involved in a V weapon incident in the city on the afternoon of the previous day.

18 December: One of the two Sgts reported missing . . . found dead in demolished cinema at Antwerp.

19 December: HQ notified by OC 347 Bty that portions of a soldier's body had been found and identified as being that of the second or [other ranks] previously reported missing following mine explosion on 11 December.

The rocket attack mentioned above on 16 December was a particularly devastating one: 567 people, including 296 Allied servicemen, had been killed when the Rex Cinema in Antwerp was hit, most killed beneath the collapsed balcony and ceiling. On 31 December the regiment diary closed the year stating: 'The enemy bombardment of Antwerp with PAC [pilot-less aircraft] and Rockets continues, this being the 90th consecutive day.'

Anti-aircraft and anti-diver (V1) duties continued at the start of 1945, with a redeployment to cover the south-eastern approaches to the Port facilities of Antwerp, but with the crossing of the Rhine and the advance into Germany, enemy incursions over Antwerp almost ceased and the regiment was occupied with a lot of trial firings and other activities. On 3 April the regiment actually managed to get in a soccer match, defeating another regiment 7–4, and on 11 April the CO called 'a meeting of musicians within unit to discuss the formation of unit dance band and concert party'. But a new responsibility was about to be placed on the regiment's personnel, when at the end of April it took up residence in the former SS barracks, at Fallingbostel, Germany, tasked with keeping order in the liberated Stalag Luft XIB and Stalag Luft 357. This was no easy task. There were problems daily, with extracts of the regiment's diary highlighting some of their problems.

2 May: Wooden barrack hut caught fire at east end of SS barracks. AFS were called in and the fire extinguished. 2 ORs of 356 Bty were admitted to hospital suffering from extensive burns.

3 May: A number of civilians reported that their village Bocholt was being pillaged and looted daily by Russian ex Ps.O.W and that the

culprits carried arms. A patrol was despatched and a number of weapons were confiscated. Further patrols of this area have been arranged and it appears reports were, in fact, true. Two Polish Officers living in the adjoining P.W.X Camp Stalag XIB reported that they had captured a leader of the Hitler Jugend and had brought him to the camp prior to handing over to the proper authorities. However, he committed suicide shortly after his arrival.

On 12 May 1,000 displaced and starving men, women and children, French, Belgian and Dutch, arrived, and the regiment set up mobile kitchens.

16 May: A displaced person accommodated in Stalag XIB and claiming to be a member of a German minority in the Ukraine reported that her lover had been murdered by a Russian P.W.X. The case was investigated and as her report appeared to be well founded the case was handed over to the SIB in order that a detailed investigation could be undertaken. It is believed that the dead man may have been employed by the Nazis to guard Russian POWs in a nearby camp.

21 May: Several Russians DPs and PWX have died or are seriously ill as the result of drinking self-concocted alcoholic liquid.

Following the deaths that were due to drinking binges, the stores of alcohol and methanol at a nearby factory were found, sealed and guarded. On 23 May 'the entire Fallingbostel Camp area was systematically searched by Russian authorities on orders from the CO and a small quantity of stills were confiscated and destroyed. A British officer is seriously ill and is believed to be suffering from alcoholic poisoning.'

Early in June the regiment moved to Berleburg for further 'garrison duties', including house searches and the arrests of Germans and Poles. But there were opportunities to escape the chaos. The regiment managed to get in a few cricket matches and a sports day, and on 23 September subjected a local German soccer team to a 19–1 thrashing. On 1 November Major Sidgwick actually took over as temporary CO of the regiment, and during his tenure Operation 'Butcher' was carried out, involving German civilians and *Forestmeisters*, in which some deer, a large boar and two foxes were 'bagged'. Security duties continued through December, but the situation was settling, with more soccer and the regiment enjoying the

Christmas and New Year festivities. A few days into 1946 Major Sidgwick
prepared to travel to Elten to judge a war-crime case.

On 9 June 1944 the diary of the 247th Battery of the 62nd Anti-Tank
Regiment Royal Artillery[5] recorded that 'Captain McNeill reported to Bty
HQ having landed the previous day'. The Regiment's guns blazed during
the fighting in Normandy, men were killed, men were wounded, and
some became sick with 'battle exhaustion'. In October 1944 the Regiment
had moved up into Belgium, and then followed up in the advance north
from Antwerp. At the end of the first week of November, Walcheren
Island fell to the Allies, and at last the Scheldt estuary route to Antwerp's
port facilities was opened to Allied shipping. But it had to be protected.
On 12 November 247 Bty took up defensive positions on Tholen Island,
and during December the Battery regularly opened up its guns on the
German positions across the water on Schouwen. On 28 December the
regiment received information that Schouwen had been reinforced and
that there was a garrison of 4,000 'young and fit German troops', with
the enemy threatening a landing on Tholen. Against such threats, in
January and February, the regiment's men maintained a defensive role,
protecting Tholen and the south bank of the river Maas. There were
occasional encounters with the enemy, with casualties, flying bombs were
seen, and the regiment's personnel witnessed Allied aircraft crash or
plunge into the water. Following a brief rest period in March, 247 Bty
moved to Raamsdonkveer, just to the south of the Bergse Maas River. On
19 April the Battery's 'H' troop opened up its Bren gun on a boat heading
its way. 'The party which turned out to be Russians gave themselves up to
246 Bty. There were two badly wounded.' Throughout April there would
be many incidents of Russians crossing the water and surrendering to the
regiment's batteries. On 3 May the men of 247 Bty received news that
there was a truce in operation and they looked on as their enemy cleared
mines and booby traps opposite their front. On 5 May a ceasefire came
into effect; 247 Bty's war was over.

Early in June the 62nd Anti-Tank Regiment RA moved up into the
Hamm–Kamen area to take up public security duties. The diary of 247 Bty
recorded their attempts to restore order.

11 June: At 0300 hrs this morning information was received that armed
Russians were in the vicinity of Holstrater Farm. Carrier patrol proceeded immediately to the farm and ascertained that armed Russians

had been there, also that two German civilians were missing. In carrying out a search of the area, the dead body of Johann Backes (a German) was found. Other civilians subsequently found, who stated that there were about 8 Russians in the party.

17 June: At 1420 hrs information received to the effect that two British soldiers would be calling at a farm . . . and endeavour to obtain farm produce under threats. Carrier patrol proceeded to this location with the result that the two men were intercepted, brought back to barracks and placed in close arrest.

During July further incidents of pillaging by Russians were recorded, and on 11 July the 62nd Anti-Tank Regiment's diary recorded: 'Two children killed on gun site. They had been hammering away at a 10.5 cm shell which exploded.'

At the end of August D. S. McNeill was promoted to A/Major and appointed 247 Battery Commander, and through the rest of the year oversaw his men's duties carrying out patrols, searching property, enforcing curfews, checking civilian identity cards and taking part in ceremonial marches. There were the occasional incidents – on 12 December, out of 250 civilians checked, 90 did not have identity cards – but, in general, a form of social order was being re-established. At the turn of the year Major McNeill received notification requiring his attendance at a war-crime trial in the village of Elten.

When the Allies overran the prisoner-of-war camps in Germany, one of the men liberated would go on to take up legal duties with the subsequent occupying forces. John Leicester-Warren's family history is entrenched within the British aristocracy. His *Times* obituary of 4 September 1975 described him as

the last of a long line of distinguished members of a Cheshire family, tracing its ancestry at least to the time of King John. The seeds of duty to God, to his country, to his fellow men, to the land with which he was entrusted and to his tenants, were sown in the early days of his boyhood. At Eton, and subsequently at Oxford those duties were clarified and he saw before him the life of public service to which he ultimately devoted his time and talents.

John had died unmarried in 1975, the last owner of Tabley House, Cheshire, and the direct descendant of Sir Peter Leicester, who had been imprisoned during the English Civil War and created a Baronet at the Restoration, and also of Sir Peter Byrne Leicester, 4th Baronet, who had built Tabley House in the 1760s. John's father, Cuthbert Leighton, was the son of Sir Baldwyn Leighton and Eleanor Leicester-Warren. Eleanor, the daughter of George Leicester, 6th Baronet and 2nd Baron de Tabley, had added the name of Warren under the terms of a relative's will. Cuthbert, who is remembered as not having a particularly strong constitution, had changed his name to Leicester-Warren. He had also had a daughter, John's sister, Margaret, who married General Sir Oliver Leese, who soldiered in North Africa and commanded the Eighth Army in Italy prior to a move to Burma, taking over as British Commander-in-Chief of Allied Land Forces, South-East Asia.

John Leicester-Warren had joined the Officer Training Corps at Eton, at which point Sir Oliver Leese was the adjutant. Following completion of an MA at Oxford, he looked to develop a legal career and was called to the Bar by the Inner Temple, although he still held military ambitions. His attempt to join the Coldstream Guards met with failure, but he did join the Cheshire Yeomanry, was mobilised at the outbreak of the Second World War and looked to develop his qualities at Staff College. Leicester-Warren travelled to the Middle East in 1940 and while in Palestine served as an intelligence officer with the Cavalry brigade. In October of that year he transferred to Greece with the 'Barbarity Force', initially serving with the RAF and then with the Army. In April 1941, with the situation in Greece deteriorating, the British Army began the evacuation, but John was captured, seeing out the rest of the war behind wire in Germany. While incarcerated he assisted fellow POWs who were looking to study law.

After the war Leicester-Warren would serve with the JAG Branch in Germany, then continue his service with the Cheshire Yeomanry, finally becoming Lieutenant Colonel Commanding, and retiring in 1958. The published history of the Cheshire Yeomanry records that his departure was 'to everyone's regret'.

From his early days he had always been keen on the Army and only an unfortunate stutter, now happily cured, prevented him from becoming a Regular soldier. The Army's loss was the Yeomanry's gain. His keenness was soon manifest . . . In the War he had the misfortune to be captured in Greece in the spring of 1941 when serving there on the

Staff. Later the story reached the Yeomanry in Palestine that he had last been seen pacing up and down the beach encouraging the tired and struggling troops and exhorting them to fight to the last while the rest of his Headquarters escaped by any means they could. Whether this story is true or not it typifies the man and his character.

He had been born and brought up to a high sense of public duty, and this characteristic had

dominated his attitude to life. It is not what he wants to do but what he feels he ought to do which has invariably prevailed.

As Commanding Officer some thought him rather too tolerant and easy going. Others knew that when aroused the reverse became the truth.[6]

To accompany the four men mentioned above, the Royal Australian Air Force detailed one of its officers to sit in judgment at the Elten trial. Atholl George James McLauchlan was born on 8 September 1917, the youngest of four children. He began school at Boonah Primary School in 1922, his diminutive stature earning him the nickname 'Bub'. After school Atholl worked as an assistant to a Boonah solicitor, completing the Junior Certificate of the solicitor's preliminary exam. He was not indentured, but by the time he enlisted Atholl had completed five years as an articled clerk. He enrolled with the Royal Australian Air Force Reserve in October 1941 and went through No. 3 Recruiting Centre, Brisbane, on 26 April 1942; his enlistment papers recorded him as Presbyterian and with the following physical characteristics: height – 5 foot 9½ inches, weight – 126lbs, chest – 33½/36 inches, complexion – fair, eyes – blue, hair – light brown.

Atholl's flying career would develop as an Air Observer/Navigator. In December 1942, having achieved the Air Observer's Badge, he was posted to No. 1 Air Navigation School, Parkes, New South Wales. Atholl's preparation for war service was similar to Bill Maloney's in that he sailed, from Sydney, to Canada in February 1943, and then enhanced his skills at No. 17 SFTS. On 13 September, by then a Flying Officer, he embarked for the UK, arriving six days later. It was not until 15 December 1943 that Atholl arrived at an operational unit, No. 547 Squadron, part of the Royal Air Force's Coastal Command, where he flew for sixteen and a half months on anti-submarine and anti-shipping duties in Liberators, attaining the rank of Flight Lieutenant, before a posting to No. 1647 Heavy Conversion Unit, less than two weeks prior to the end of the European war. It seems that McLauchlan's experience as an articled clerk was enough for his name to be put forward to act as a court member in the Elten case.

Chapter 13

TRIAL

The practical preparations for the Elten trial began on the first day of 1946. The four accused men were brought before the commanding officer at the No. 4 Civilian Internment Camp at Recklinghausen, remanded and presented with the charge sheet and copies of an abstract of the evidence. They were informed of who would be defending them, and arrangements were made for a British Medical Officer to see the defendants each morning of the trial and provide medical certificates on their state of health. All the witnesses were warned that the trial was imminent, and arrangements were made for Paul Barton, in a separate Internment Camp, to be taken to Elten and held in custody. The 53 (W) Infantry Division was charged with arranging accommodation and messing for the court members, though officers were instructed to bring their own bedding. Special accommodation arrangements were requested for two ATS Provost female searchers, as all women attending the trial had to be searched for concealed firearms. In addition the division had to arrange for a press area in the courtroom, provide directions along all the approach routes to Elten, provide sufficient car parking, and detail court orderlies and guards.

The Bahnhofs Hotel on the edge of Elten, and situated next to the first rail station in Germany following a crossing of the Dutch border, was just over a kilometre from the Bosmann farm. Its proximity to the scene of the incident and its spacious rooms made it ideal as a makeshift courthouse.

The case, in the Judge Advocate General's opinion, failed to warrant appointment of a judge advocate; it was sufficient to have one member of the court with legal qualifications. In addition, one member of the court should be from the Royal Australian Air Force. The men chosen certainly understood the military, they understood war, and they could draw on their experience of how they had seen men behave in such conditions.

President: Lieutenant Colonel W. Y. Kington-Blair-Oliphant, OBE, MC,
   2nd Kensingtons
Member: Major D. S. McNeill, 62 A/Tks
Member: Major R. B. Sidgwick, 111 Heavy A/A (RA)

Member: F/Lt A. G. J. McLauchlan, Royal Australian Air Force

Legal Member: Major J. L. B. Leicester-Warren, Cheshire Yeomanry,
Barrister-at-Law. Officer of the Staff of the Judge Advocate
General

Prosecutor: Captain H. Diamond, Pioneer Corps, Legal Staff,
Headquarters British Army of the Rhine

Defending Counsel (representing Hans Renoth): Dr W. Gobbels,
Barrister-at-Law[1]

Defending Officer (representing Hans Pelgrim, Friedrich Grabowski
and Paul Nieke): Lieutenant R. E. Milman, 1/5 Welch (Solicitor)

At 1030 hours the trial of the four men accused in the Elten case began.
With the court staff and interpreters sworn in, Kington-Blair-Oliphant
addressed the accused, confirming their names and reading out the
charge.

> German nationals in the charge of No. 4 Civilian Internment Camp
> Recklinghausen, pursuant to Regulation 4 of the Regulations for the
> Trial of War Criminals. You are jointly charged with committing a war
> crime, in that you at Elten, Germany, on 16 September 1944, in viol-
> ation of the laws and usages of war, were concerned in the killing of an
> unknown Allied airman, a prisoner of war. How say you, Hans Renoth,
> are you guilty or not guilty of the charge which you have heard read.

The 'unknown Allied airman' had still not officially been named as Bill
Maloney. Renoth replied 'Not guilty'. Pelgrim, Grabowski and Nieke,
when asked, gave the same response.

Prosecutor Captain Diamond made his opening statement, immediately conceding that much of the considerable evidence 'will be of a confused and possible conflicting nature; but the salient facts of the case are
essentially of a simple nature'.

> On a Saturday, 16 September 1944, an RAF single-seater plane crashed
> within a couple of miles of this courtroom. The pilot emerged from the
> plane apparently unhurt. The evidence is clear to this extent, that he
> emerged without any assistance and that there were no signs of blood
> or any other injury in the plane. He was arrested by the Accused Renoth
> without offering any resistance.

Subsequently the pilot was beaten by a number of people, including the other three Accused, Pelgrim, Grabowski and Nieke. Renoth appears to have stood aside while the beating took place. The beating started by the use of fists, then rifle butts were used and finally the pilot received a kick in the face.

Finally the Accused Renoth administered the *coup de grâce* by shooting the pilot with his rifle. It is by no means certain whether the pilot would have lived if he had been shot or if he would possibly have died as a result of the brutal beating he had already suffered. This much is certain, that the shot or shots fired by Renoth shortened his life.

In Diamond's view there was 'a common design in which all four Accused shared to commit a war crime' and that all were guilty in respect of the 'maltreatment and murder of this pilot'.

The prosecutor set out establishing the basis of the case, submitting into evidence previously sworn statements obtained from the Canadian War Crimes investigation team. Major John Blain was called to the stand to verify such statements: the record of Major Balfour's examination of the pilot's body at the Nordfriedhof, Düsseldorf, Karl Doll's testimony concerning the identification of the grave, and Captain Hunter's interrogation concerning the exhumation and examination of the body. In addition, the graphic and unpleasant photographs of the body, showing the extensive damage to the pilot's skull, were submitted. Finally a transcript of Wady Lehmann's interrogation relating his visit to the scene of the incident and finding the dental plate was circulated. Diamond handed to Blain Exhibit 'G', asking him if it was that which had been referred to in Wady Lehmann's statement. Blain replied: 'Yes this is Exhibit "G", the false teeth referred to; the one false tooth was broken from the plate at the time.' Dr Gobbels and Milman declined to question Blain. There really was nothing to contest, although Gobbels might have assisted his client by highlighting Balfour's inconclusive findings concerning gunshot wounds.

Diamond called his first German civilian witness, Peter Peters. Diamond's questioning initially established basic facts, and then Peters gave his own version of events.

On that morning I was ill and was lying in my bed, and then I heard firing and I got up and then I went down into the cellar. I stayed in the cellar for some time, and then I came out and I then looked outside and I saw a plane coming in, and then I told my wife, 'Hurry up, we have got to get into the cellar again', and then we were quite a time in the cellar, and after that I came out and then I looked outside and I saw at a distance of about 700 or 800 metres from our house a plane was lying on the ground. Then I entered the house again, and after about half-an-hour I went outside again and then I saw a crowd gathering and then I saw that the crowd was fighting.

Peters was sure there were three in the 'crowd', but they were too far away for recognition, though two of them were in field grey uniforms. (Interestingly this does differ from Peters's statement of 19 July 1945, when he said that he saw three or four men who were fighting, three coming from one side and one standing beside, three in field grey and one in darker attire.) Diamond ensured that Peters stated that soldiers, the army, policemen and customs officers wore field grey, but he could not state for certain the official position of the men he saw. (Nieke and Grabowski were actually in their party uniform, not field grey, having come from the funeral of an eminent local Nazi.) With respect to the third man, Peters could not see a uniform on him: 'I could not determine the colour of his clothes; it could have been black or blue – dark clothing . . . I saw two men going up to the third one . . . they had something in their hands and they were beating with the things that they had in their hands and they formed up in attack formation – they took on a fighting attitude.'

Whether the third man, in darker attire, was in a 'fighting attitude', Peters could not say, 'because the ground was much lower there'. When asked what the assailants had in their hands, Peters could not be certain, but he went on physically to demonstrate the body attitude of the attackers.

Diamond moved the questioning to Peters visiting the scene later that day, the witness stating that he saw the pilot about twenty-five paces from the plane, dead, with his face to the ground, black hair, and with a dark blue suit on; and Renoth was there, preventing Peters from getting any closer to the aircraft. Peters confirmed Renoth's identification, pointing him out to the court, and then stated that other people had been there when he had approached the aircraft but he could not confirm who.

After Dr Gobbels had declined to cross-examine, Lieutenant Milman sought to blur the witness's testimony about the number of people involved. Peters confirmed seeing two men in field grey fighting with another man in darker uniform, but he did admit that there might have been other people out of sight. Milman asked Peters if it was possible that he could have made a mistake about the colour of the uniform. 'No,' he replied. He did know the accused at the time, but was unable to state for sure if they were the men he had seen in the beating. Milman really should have emphasised that Peters had not seen anyone in brown, as worn by two of his clients that day.

When Gobbels then asked if Peters could clearly see the railway line and if he had seen a train stop that day, he replied that bushes blocked his view and he had not seen a train.

Kington-Blair-Oliphant finished Peters's questioning, confirming that his house was on the same side of the railway line as the crashed plane. The President then pointed to a Union Jack, asking if the pilot's clothing was as blue as that. 'Yes certainly as dark as that.'

Next to take the stand was Johann Bosmann, the key witness for the prosecution. Diamond's initial questioning placed Bosmann at his home witnessing the crash, 'about 1,200 to 1,300 metres' away. The farmer testified that he went back to his house to get his permit. 'Then I went to the plane. When I was at a distance of a few hundred yards I saw a car come and this car came to Johann Franken's on the road and four or five people got out of the car . . . I could not recognise them at that distance, it was too far away.'

When he had been about 300 metres from the plane Bosmann told Diamond he saw some people approaching the aircraft, the same people who had got out of the car. 'When I got nearer I saw some of them beating . . . Four men were there as far as I could see and one was standing apart.'

Captain Diamond. Did you recognise any of them at that time?
Johann Bosmann. Yes, then I recognised.
CD. Who did you recognise?
JB. Pelgrim and Renoth.
CD. Would you look round and see whether either of those men is in Court.
JB. That is Renoth and that is Pelgrim (indicating the Accused Renoth and Pelgrim).
CD. You say there were four men standing together and a fifth man standing apart. Where were Renoth and Pelgrim amongst these men?
JB. Pelgrim was with the four and Renoth was standing apart.

Bosmann had placed Pelgrim and Renoth directly at the scene of the killing. Captain Diamond re-emphasised the point ensuring Bosmann repeated his answers. Bosmann went on stating that Pelgrim and Renoth were in field grey uniform, two of the other three were wearing brown SA uniforms and the other was in a field grey, of a different hue, a darker grey, than the policemen's.

Captain Diamond. Was there anybody else there at all beside these four men standing together and Renoth standing apart.

Johann Bosmann. Later on I saw somebody in a dark blue uniform.

CD. What colour blue? Can you see the same sort of blue anywhere in Court?

JB. It resembles that kind of blue but it was a bit darker. (Indicating the uniform worn by Flight Lt McLauchlan, RAAF.)

Diamond extracted further damning testimony from Bosmann against the accused, particularly the two policemen.

The pilot was being pushed . . . but if they were all four pushing at the same moment I would not be able to say . . . Then they began beating . . . with their rifles . . . [the pilot] was walking in front of them and he was beaten the other side of the plane . . . At the other side of the plane I could only see the butts of the rifles over the plane and then they came round the plane to the place where I stood and then they went on beating and one of them kicked the man in the face with his boots . . . [the pilot] could hardly do anything because the whole side of his head was loose and was bleeding profusely . . . it was broken open . . . he was standing, bent.

Bosmann could not be sure who had kicked Maloney in the head, just that it was one of the men in field grey. He had not seen the faces of the men in the SA uniform. Diamond asked Bosmann what the pilot did after he was kicked. 'He could not do anything more, and then Renoth pointed the rifle at him and then I turned round and went home and I did not look back . . . I could not look at it any longer.'

Captain Diamond. Did you hear how many shots were fired?

Johann Bosmann. Yes.

CD. How many?

JB. Two shots.

CD. At what interval?

JB. I walked about ten metres and then I heard the second shot.

Diamond guided Bosmann through his recollections, returning to the scene later in the day; seeing a dead body, with a rosary lying on top, and the head clotted with blood: 'The skin was terribly torn.' Bosmann told the court that he had met Renoth at the scene, telling him he had been there earlier, with Renoth responding: 'In my excitement I did not see anybody at all.' Bosmann also crucially stated that Renoth said: 'It was high time that I gave him the *coup de grâce.*' With Diamond's examination concluded, the court closed for lunch.

On return Dr Gobbels somewhat surprisingly stated that he had no questions for Bosmann. So Lieutenant Milman began to cross-examine on behalf of Pelgrim, Nieke and Grabowski, and went straight on the offensive, attacking Bosmann's motives. Milman was in a difficult position. In representing three men, he had to be careful that in defending one man he was not undermining the defence of his other clients. If he emphasised that Bosmann had not seen Nieke and Grabowski, it focused the blame on Pelgrim.

Lieutenant Milman. You do not like Pelgrim, do you?

Johann Bosmann. No.

LM. You think he is a bad man?

JB. Yes, because he has done it.

LM. You thought that before this incident, did you not?

JB. No, not such a thing.

LM. But even before this incident you did not like him?

JB. No.

LM. Why did you not like him?

JB. We were not enemies but –

Milman cut Bosmann off and asked the farmer if he had known his clients before the incident and if he had lived in the town with the accused for many years. On receipt of the answer 'yes' in both cases, Milman then pressed Bosmann on why it was that he was able to recognise only Pelgrim and Renoth. 'It was such a mix up and I mainly looked at the pilot.' Milman talked Bosmann into agreeing that there might have been other men at the scene and then actually suggested that there could have been nine people, which the farmer was not prepared to concede. Milman attacked Bosmann's recall of the incident in that it 'was very confused and that you do not rightly remember very much of this at all'. And Bosmann was prepared to agree: 'I could not see it too clearly because it was such a mix up.' Milman tried to expose the inconsistency between Peter Peters's recollection of two people in field grey in 'a threatening attitude' and Bosmann seeing three men, but the farmer simply responded: 'It is possible that the third one was out of sight.' Milman asked Bosmann outright if he had seen Pelgrim actually hit the pilot: 'I have not seen it but I have seen him aiming at him.' And Milman asked if he had seen the two men in brown SA uniforms actually strike the pilot. The reply may not have been what he was after: 'Everybody was hitting; I could not see who.' Milman closed his cross-examination attacking Bosmann's motives.

> *Lieutenant Milman.* I put it to you that practically everything you have said has been a fabrication because of your dislike of these men.
> *Johann Bosmann.* No.
> *LM.* And that in fact at the time you saw very little and you have added to this from what your acquaintances have told you and from hearsay in the town and now you think that this is what happened.
> *JB.* No I am telling the truth.

Captain Diamond declined a re-examination, but Kington-Blair-Oliphant and Leicester-Warren had further questions, confirming that Bosmann had not been able to recognise Grabowski or Nieke at the scene. When asked what side of the head the wound was, Bosmann stated it was on the left, which in fact contradicted the physical evidence. After some further brief questions confirming what the pilot was wearing, Bosmann stood down.

Next to take the stand was Hubert Franken. Preliminary questions established he had been at his farm and seen the aircraft come down on the day in question: 'I was a member of the Home Guard and it was my duty to get hold of the pilot.' Franken set out to go to his sister's farm and passed Peter Peters in the yard of his house and had a conversation with him. He then carried on along the main road and met a car coming from Johann Franken's farm towards the main road. 'I saw four persons in the car . . . Two in SA uniform and two in Army uniform . . . I only recognised one . . . It was Grabowski.' After pointing out Grabowski, and that the

car was going too fast for him to identify anyone else, Franken testified
that he had cycled on to where Paul Barton's car was parked and then on
to the crash site, with Barton and Renoth there, 'and then I saw the dead
pilot lying there'.

Captain Diamond. How do you know he was a pilot?
Hubert Franken. I thought he was a pilot because he had a dark blue
    uniform.
CD. Had you ever seen that uniform before?
HF. No.
CD. What kind of blue was it?
HF. It was dark blue and woolly.
CD. You have told the Court that you saw the dead pilot. How do you
    know he was dead?
HF. I stood about and looked at him and it was awful and he did not
    move.
CD. Why was it terrible to look at him?
HF. The face of the man was terribly terror stricken.
CD. Was there anything else noticeable about him or his head?
HF. His teeth were next to him.

Franken related how after the war he had found the teeth with an
'English officer' (meaning Wady Lehmann), which he identified as the
exhibit previously submitted. Franken's testimony concluded by mentioning that 'Barton took a rosary and made a remark about Catholics and
I went off right away', and he confirmed that, of the accused, he had only
seen Grabowski and Renoth that day.

Dr Gobbels's cross-examination consisted of only five questions. When
asked what Renoth was like as an officer and a human being, Franken,
who said he had known Renoth for many years, stated: 'He was OK and
has not done any harm to anybody here in Elten.'

Lieutenant Milman's cross-examination was even shorter, asking
Franken if he had seen two men in the car in green uniform. Franken
said that he had not, although he could not be certain, as the car was
moving so fast.

Diamond carried out a brief re-examination, which added little more
until after his final question, when Franken asked if he could make
another remark, which the prosecutor allowed. 'When I went to the farm
of my sister,' Franken said, 'I saw two German soldiers walking around

about 400 metres away from the place where the plane came down.' Franken then withdrew. This last statement appears strange, and it is surprising that Diamond, who had the testimony he needed, allowed a voluntary contribution. Franken was clearly keen to place on the record the fact that two soldiers were in the area. He would have known his sisters were not going to appear as witnesses. He was undoubtedly aware that there were rumours of soldiers being involved, but they had not been apprehended and placed on trial. Was he trying, in a small way, to spread the blame?

Next to take the stand was Dr Jurist Otto Weyer, the *Bürgermeister* in Elten in 1944. Diamond was allowed to lead in the early questioning, establishing that Weyer had been away at the time of the incident, but on returning had received a report about the plane crash from Barton. He had then spoken to both Renoth and Pelgrim. Weyer identified the two policemen in the court, and, following some legal argument about the questioning, he testified: 'Renoth replied to my request why he fired at the pilot that he had been ordered to do so by Captain Kuehne. Moreover he said that the pilot was beforehand beaten up so badly that in order to prevent him from any more serious suffering he has given him the *coup de grâce*.' Weyer then began to say: 'Pursuant to that conversation he has produced a written declaration by Captain Kuehne . . .', but Leicester-Warren interrupted, asking whether this statement was going to be submitted? When Diamond responded 'No', Kington-Blair-Oliphant cut this line of questioning short: 'Then there is not much point in referring to it at all is there.' Diamond asked Weyer about his conversation with the other policeman:

> Pelgrim has declared to me that he has done no beating at all when the pilot came down. Furthermore he told me that in accordance with the report given me a few days before by Barton two Germans in the Army, a lance Corporal and a Corporal, jumped on top of the pilot who came down and beat him up with a rifle and that he was very badly injured.

Again Kington-Blair-Oliphant cut in, clearly not seeing any value in this line of questioning, asking Diamond if he wanted 'all this rather abstruse evidence'; the prosecutor claimed it was in the interests of fairness. Diamond closed by asking Weyer if he knew anything about Pelgrim's rifle, to which he responded 'No'.

Dr Gobbels developed the mentioning of the certificate, eliciting from Weyer that Renoth

> had the certificate on him, he showed it to me and after I read it he took it back. On top . . . was written 'Certificate. I, the undersigned Captain Kuehne have ordered the policeman Renoth to give the *coup* to the mortally wounded pilot.' I do not know exactly how it read but that is more or less how it read. I asked Mr Renoth if he had sent through that certificate to his boss, Captain of the Police Hamann in Wesel. As far as I remember he declared to me that Captain Hamann was in the picture and knew about the certificate.

Kington-Blair-Oliphant asked if indeed the certificate was going to be produced, or if Gobbels had it. Neither was the case. Gobbels finished by asking Weyer about Renoth's character: 'I think that Renoth is a man whose intelligence is below the average.' But Kington-Blair-Oliphant was not interested: 'The Court is not impressed by matters of opinion from the witness. What he thinks is not good evidence.'

Milman's questioning was brief, managing to draw out that the report Weyer received was that a Lance Corporal and Corporal of the *Wehrmacht* had beaten the pilot, and that Weyer had seen the aforementioned Captain Kuehne when he was billeted in Elten. Again Milman drew down Kington-Blair-Oliphant's ire when asking if the story about the soldiers was the generally accepted story in the neighbourhood, to which Weyer offered: 'Yes it was my personal opinion.' 'There again,' the President remarked, 'these are matters of opinion'. Before he left the stand Leicester-Warren had a couple of questions on the certificate, Weyer responding that it was a white sheet of paper, signed by a 'Kuehne Captain' and all in the same handwriting and ink.

Next to testify was Albertus Konning, the farmhand employed by Johann Franken. Initial questioning set the scene. Albertus had been living with Johann Franken, and had seen the plane crash, while working with some horses in the fields. Upon calming them, after about a quarter of an hour he went towards the plane and met Pelgrim in his police uniform near the crash site, and saw Grabowski and Nieke at a further distance in brown party uniform, all three of whom he identified in court. He also mentioned another person too far away to identify but in army uniform and confirmed that he had a conversation with Pelgrim. Konning testified that, on returning to the scene, between half an hour and three-quarters of an hour later, he was prevented from coming too close to the dead pilot by Renoth, whom he identified in court.

Dr Gobbels waived his cross-examination, and Milman ensured Konning agreed that there could have been others about that he had not seen. Indeed, Konning stated that, when he returned the second time, there was Renoth, two customs officials in grey, and two or three more men, and that neither Grabowski, Nieke nor Pelgrim was there.

Wilhelm Joseph van den Broek, the next witness, told the court of receiving the order 'to collect the body of an airman'. On arrival at the scene, among others he stated seeing Pelgrim, and identified him in court. Van den Broek went on to describe the condition of the pilot. 'The pilot was in between the engine and the plane . . . lying on his back . . . he was very badly injured in the back of his head . . . I have not looked so closely because I did not want to look at it, it looked so horrible. Parts of either his brain or the skin were on the ground as well.' Diamond wanted to show the witness the pictures from the pilot's autopsy, although Kington-Blair-Oliphant interjected, asking if it was really necessary and stating that 'there might be 300 bodies with similar wounds; it was taken some eight months afterwards'. Diamond dropped the matter. Van den Broek finished by stating that he took the body to 'the cemetery building', where he left it and went home. Van den Broek left the stand, and at 1620 hours the court closed for 55 minutes. Meanwhile, a man who had previously fought to ensure he was not one of the accused prepared to give testimony.

Reichswald Forest Commonwealth War Graves Cemetery, Germany, 10 March 2008. (Steve Darlow)

11 July 1945, Franken's field, near Elten, Germany.
Right to left: Johann Bosmann, 'Where physical violence against the airman commenced'; Wady Lehmann, 'Where the airman was located when he was shot'; Hubert Franken, 'Where Bosmann found the corpse'; Corporal A. Klassen, representing the position of a man currently in custody, 'when he fired at the airman'.
(The National Archives)

The church of St Vitus at Hoch Elten. (From Walter Axmacher, *Elten die letzten 100 Jahre*)

The Maloney Family at Rockmount, January 1938. Back row: Pop (Maurice), Clare (Sister Mary Audeon), Mum (Gertrude), Jose, Billy, Paddy, Kitty. Front: Sheila, Frances, Von.
(The Maloney family)

Left: A young Bill Maloney sporting his Rugby kit.
(The Maloney family)
Above: Bill Maloney, crouching on the right, at a dance.
(The Maloney family)

Top: Trainee pilot Bill Maloney, on the left.

Left: Bill Maloney in training in Canada.

Below: Bill Maloney in flying kit, crouching at the front.

(The Maloney family)

Above: 80 Squadron, with Spitfire IXs, in July 1944, Bill Maloney at the front crouching, second from the left, and Hugh Ross leaning against the trailing edge of the wing, second from the left. (Hugh Ross)

Below: 80 Squadron Tempest taking off from Volkel in October 1944. Bill Maloney's Tempest is likely to have had similar markings. (Chris Thomas)

Inset: Royal Australian Air Force pilot Bill Maloney (left). (The Maloney family)

Top: Witness Hubert Franken and family.
(The Franken family)

Right: Witness Johann Bosmann.
(The Bosmann family)

Below: The Franken family farm.
(The Franken family)

Top left and right:
German propaganda:
'The air terror continues.
Mothers, send your children
to safety!' and
'Be true to the Führer'.
(Courtesy of Randall
Bytwerk)

Above and right: Funeral of those
killed in Emmerich following
an American bombing raid on
14 June 1944.
(Emmerich Stadtarchiv)

Emmerich following the Bomber Command attack of 7 October 1944.
(Emmerich Stadtarchiv)

The grave of Frieda Schroder and Alfred Schroder killed by Allied bombing in 1944.
(Steve Darlow)

The liberation of Bergen-Belsen concentration camp, April 1945. A young woman photographed two days after the British entered the camp, her face still bearing the scars of a terrible beating by the SS guards. (IWM BU 3746)

Left: War-crime investigators Corporal A. Klassen (left) and Wing Commander 'Pat' Durdin (right). (Wady Lehmann)
Right: War-crime investigator Captain Wady Lehmann. (Wady Lehmann)

Right: Vehicle of the North-West Europe detachment No. 1 Canadian War Crimes Investigation Unit at a Dutch border crossing. (Wady Lehmann)

North-West Europe detachment No. 1 Canadian War Crimes Investigation Unit at Bad Salzuflen July 1945; left to right: John Blain, Private A. Klassen, Wady Lehmann, Neil Fraser, George Drynan. (R. Robichaud)

Right: Wing Commander 'Pat' Durdin, head of North-West Europe detachment No. 1 Canadian War Crimes Investigation Unit. (Oliver 'Pat' Durdin archive)

Above: Wady Lehmann.
Right: War-crimes investigators Wady Lehmann (left) and George Drynan (right).
(Wady Lehmann)

A photograph dated before 1920 of Bavarian foresters from the area around Berchtesgaden. Hans Renoth is third from the left at the back. (Monika Kersjes)

Above left: Hans Renoth's son Erasmus, who was injured on the Eastern Front and captured.
Above centre: Elten policeman Hans Renoth.
Above right: Maria Kersjes née Renoth in her early twenties.
Below left: The Renoth family in the late 1920s.
Below right: Hans and Anna Renoth at their wedding in 1922. (All photos Monika Kersjes)

Right: Customs official Friedrich Grabowski. (The National Archives).

Below: Customs official Paul Nieke. (The Nieke family)

Below: Meister der Gendarmerie in Elten Paul Barton. (The National Archives)

Elten policeman Hans Pelgrim. (The National Archives)

The Bahnhofs Hotel in Elten, scene of the trial. (Bahnhofs Hotel)

Above: Hans Renoth's defence counsel, Doctor Walter Göbel. (From Walter Axmacher, Elten die letzten 100 Jahre)

Right: Lieutenant Colonel John Leicester-Warren, legal member in the Elten trial, in 1951. (Cheshire Military Museum)

Gnadenbild „Unsere Liebe Frau von Werl"
13. Jahrhundert

Werl, den 30. Mai 1946

Liebes Frl. Renoth!

      Dass Sie immer noch ohne
Nachricht sind, kann ich nicht be -
greifen. Auf meine Anfrage antwortete
der Pfarrer von Hameln am 16.4.:
" Ich war der Ansicht, dass den Ange -
hörigen bereits von amtlicher Seite
über die am 8. März im hiesigen Zuchthaus erfolgte Hinrichtung Nachricht
gegeben sei. Da dieses Ihrem Schreiben
nach nicht geschah, habe ich nunmehr
postwendend den betreffenden Pfarrämter
Mitteilung gemacht mit der Bitte, es
den Angehörigen schonend beibringen
zu wollen."
Ich bin erstaunt, dass Sie von Ihrem
Pfarrer keine Nachricht bekommen haben.
Obigem Schreiben nach, ist Ihr Vater
schon in der Ewigkeit und wird sicher
einen gnädigen Richter gefunden haben.
Ich bete für seine Seelenruhe und
auch, dass Gott Sie und Ihre Mutter
in Ihrem Leid trösten möge.
      Meiner innigen Teilnahme dürfen
Sie gewiss sein. Grüsse Sie die Mutter
und seien Sie selbst gegrüsst

The note from the priest at Werl to Anna Renoth, informing her of her husband's death. The photograph of the statue of Our Lady of Werl, Consoler of the Sorrowful, was on the reverse of the card. (Monika Kersjes)

A modern view from the former location of Peter Peters's house (no longer in existence). Bill Maloney's Tempest came down in the field just beyond the tree-lined ditch. The spire of St Vitus can be seen in the distance. The train line and the main road are to the left. (Steve Darlow)

A modern view from the edge of the ditch near to the scene of the incident back towards Johann Bosmann's farm in the distance. (Steve Darlow)

Top: Hameln Zuchthaus in 1960.
(Stadtarchiv Hameln)

Right: The mass grave of the
executed war criminals at the
Friedhof Am Wehl, Hameln, in
1985. (Bernard Gelderblom)

Below: The mass grave of the
executed war criminals at the
Friedhof Am Wehl, Hameln,
in 2008. (Steve Darlow)

PILOT OFFICER
W. E. MALONEY
ROYAL AUSTRALIAN AIR FORCE
16TH SEPTEMBER 1944   AGE 23

MY JESUS, MERCY

The grave of W. E. Maloney at the Reichswald CWGC cemetery. (Steve Darlow)

Chapter 14

FREE HUNTING

Gendarmerie Kreisführer Dietrich Hamann had been in hospital at the time of the killing in Franken's field, having fractured his right foot in a motorcycle accident. Hamann held the position of district super-intendent of the Rees district, with thirty-three constables, including some Gendarmerie reservists. In Elten, the northernmost part of Hamann's district, were Meister der Gendarmerie Barton, Oberwacht-meister Pelgrim and Gendarmerie Reservist Renoth. Everything Hamann knew about the incident came to him second hand. His deputy informed him Renoth had shot an Allied airman, who had made a forced landing. Hamann insisted Renoth went to see him while he was in hospital, and after Renoth had given his account of the incident, that a *Wehrmacht* Hauptmann had ordered him to shoot the pilot, Hamann rebuked his subordinate. All this was recorded in two post-war statements to investi-gators. (In this first statement, on 14 November 1945, Hamann referred to 'Renoth' as 'Porschke', correcting it in the subsequent second state-ment on 17 November 1945.)

14 November statement: I reproached him for having acted in non-accordance with the law and told him that he would be brought to account for it one day. He had known that captured Allied airmen were to be sent to the nearest *Wehrmacht* headquarters. He was in no way subordinate to the *Wehrmacht* Hptm, and the latter could never give him orders. He replied that it had happened, there was nothing he could do about it, he would have to bear the consequences. As he did not even know the name and unit of the Hauptmann in question I ordered him to go and ascertain them at once.

17 November statement: The instructions for the constabulary stated that in case of forced landing of aircraft the constable had to proceed at once to the spot in order to take the necessary security measures, until *Wehrmacht* arrived. If the *Wehrmacht* was on the spot it was from the start their responsibility to take all measures.

Hamann makes it clear in his statements that Renoth had not acted in accordance with stated policy, but other comments in his 17 November statement suggest that he may also have been covering his own back. Hamann was after all in captivity, and he was no doubt keen to distance himself from any responsibility: 'I ordered Gendarmerie Reservist Renoth . . . to come to the hospital to see me. I did this merely out of pure humanity although officially I had nothing to do with the matter since during my illness a deputy was carrying out my duties . . . If Meister der Gendarmerie Barton states in proceedings that I took affidavits in this affair, then he is mistaken. The truth is that at our first meeting and also later I merely talked with him about the incident and strongly condemned Renoth's action.' Hamann also commented on Renoth's character.

> *14 November statement:* On duty he was less capable of acting independently, and he worked under orders and instructions of Gendarmerie Meister Barton in Elten. Generally speaking Porschke [Renoth] is the typical yes-man who carried out any order without thought.

Hamann had also seen to it that after the event Renoth was posted away to continue police duties elsewhere. Hamann was quite clear in his statements that Barton had authority over Pelgrim and Renoth, something that Barton had desperately fought to deny when he had been questioned by Canadian Wing Commander 'Pat' Durdin.

'Pat' Durdin passed away in 2004 and left behind a 'trunk' filled with his wartime memorabilia: hundreds of photographs of him participating in war-crimes trials, many pictures taken at German concentration camps, which he had seen liberated, and numerous newspaper clippings. One described how he had walked away from the crash of a 435 Squadron Dakota on 13 February 1946, in which eight people had been killed. Another told how he had been injured surviving another crash.

Described as 'tougher than nails' and a 'hard-nosed legal advocate', Oliver William 'Pat' Durdin, MBE, QC had been 96 years old when he died in his home city of London, Ontario. Despite his well-earned reputation as a determined and forceful lawyer, he was clearly well respected and loved. People close to him described him as 'a very generous man', doing 'many wonderful things for less fortunate people'. Even those who came across Pat as a 'formidable opponent' developed a 'very deep respect and affection' for him. Pat's obituary described him as being 'from humble beginnings, growing up in a blue-collar London family', but he clearly had drive and aptitude. 'Durdin was a self made man who put himself through the University of Western Ontario and Osgoode Hall law school by doing a variety of jobs.'[1]

Pat had been called to the Bar in 1931, and had acted as an Alderman of London prior to the outbreak of war and in the early years of the conflict. He resigned his position to enlist with the Royal Canadian Air Force and assisted in the establishment of bombing and gunnery schools in Canada, where the potential bomb aimers and air gunners could hone their skills prior to a posting to Europe.

When Pat transferred to the UK, his legal background was put to use in the defence of fellow Canadian airmen accused of wrongdoings. Pat went on to serve with the RAF's 2nd Tactical Air Force's 83 Group during the Overlord campaign, driving a jeep ashore on D-Day itself to set about establishing airstrips in Normandy, a crucial element in the developing battle. There is a story that Pat actually pulled out a gun to persuade the driver of his landing craft to get closer to the beaches. Pat was 'Mentioned in Dispatches' twice, awards effective 1 January 1945, and 1 January 1946 respectively, for his 'Distinguished Service', and his membership of the Military Division of the Most Excellent Order of the British Empire appeared in the *London Gazette* of 13 June 1946.

Wing Commander Durdin's excellent qualifications and the capable manner in which he had previously performed his duties, together with the confidence of his superiors in his ability to be just, fair and thoroughly conscientious in his responsibilities to Canada, led to his appointment as Officer Commanding No. 1 Canadian War Crimes Investigation Unit, over a large number of superior but less qualified officers. During the many months it has taken in the tracing, locating and apprehension of war criminals, who will by Wing Commander Durdin's unstinted efforts be brought to trial to face charges of offences against the Royal Canadian Air Force personnel, his enthusiasm and zeal for the most minute details in considering every possible method of detection and justice has been an inspiration to everyone connected with the unit. Faced with numerous language and transportation problems, he has dispensed his duties in the atmosphere of a defeated and occupied nation with a courage and efficiency that reflects great credit to himself and to Canada.

At the end of the war Pat Durdin's legal training was put to good use investigating alleged war atrocities against Canadian servicemen. Indeed, Durdin was the prosecutor when some of these went to trial. He had witnessed the heat of battle and could bring that experience to interrogations and courtrooms. The prosecution in the Elten case trial would be a purely British affair, but Pat Durdin had been involved in the lengthy investigation. He had been the man who had confronted Paul Barton shortly after he was taken into custody.

The arrest of Paul Barton took place on 15 August 1945 at 1930 hours in Westkirchen, Kreis Warendorf, because he was 'wanted by 1 Cdn War Crimes Investigation Unit as an accessory to the murder of an unknown allied pilot on 16 September 1944'. Further details on Barton were noted in his arrest report,

Rank: A/2Lieut of Gendarmerie (Elten Gendarmerie)
Born 8 Jun 1891 in Leobschutz Ober-Schelsien (Upper Silesia)
Left Protestant Church 15 Dec 38, now G.L.
Married
Lived: Elten, Zevenaer Str 80. Former place of residence: Scharmbeck
Member of: S.A. Received the S.A. Bronze Athletic Medal 27 Jul 37
    from S.A. Standerte 57 in Heselm 1 Mar 39.
Also of: *NSDAP* 1 May 1933, Party No. 3565122
Served in the Army from 3 Oct 1911–1 Oct 1920
Received E.K. II Class (Iron Cross 2nd Class), D.A. II Class, Frontfighter
    Cross of Honour, Police Medal of Honour in Gold, Colonial Medal.

At 0930 hours on 21 August at Bad Salzuflen, the investigation team headed by the then Squadron Leader Pat Durdin sat down with Barton. Initial questioning confirmed that he was Meister of the Gendarmerie in Elten. But when Durdin tried to establish whom he was Meister of, whom he had superiority over, he had a little more difficulty. Barton conceded that Pelgrim and Renoth were under his control, but he would go no further.

Squadron Leader Durdin. So you were then the senior policeman at Elten with Pelgrim and Renoth under you. Is that correct?
Paul Barton. But I wasn't their superior.
SLD. Why do you say you were not their superior, did they not take instructions from you in their police duties?

PB. No sir, I wasn't – we have duty orders and prescriptions and according to these each gendarme, that is policeman, is to work on his own.

SLD. But is it not true that they were responsible to you for carrying out their duties as policemen?

PB No sir, each man is responsible for his own work and doings.

SLD. Are you telling me that they were not responsible to you in any way for the manner in which they carried out their duties?

PB. No.

Barton was preparing to cover his back. He knew the seriousness of the situation. Durdin was having none of it and tried a different tack.

Squadron Leader Durdin. If they were absent from their duties did you have any responsibility to bring the matter to the attention of higher authority?

Paul Barton. If that should have been the case I tried to establish what happened but it is the responsibility of these policemen to report themselves in writing or otherwise to the next higher authority.

SLD. But you none the less would have to report it and investigate it?

PB. Yes, I would establish the fact but the officers would have to report it themselves.

SLD. Would you as part of your duty ensure that they did so report it?

PB. I had to go there and see if they were sick in case they didn't report themselves and I made the report to the Landrat to that effect.

SLD. But if in fact they didn't make a report it is true is it not that you would have investigated the situation and reported it to your superior?

PB. Yes, that would have been my duty.

SLD. I take it the same procedure would have prevailed if you found them drunk on duty or something to that effect?

PB. Well, one doesn't report everything right away after all had it been very bad however I would have had to report it.

SLD. That is, regardless whether they reported it or not, if anything of importance happened you would report it?

PB. If anything of importance happened I would have to report it, in which case Kreisführer Hamann would have arrived to take evidence but I would not have taken evidence myself.

SLD. And before making your report intelligently I presume you would have thoroughly investigated the situation which you were reporting?

PB. Well if something very important had happened I would have telephoned Hauptmann Hamann and he would have come to make the necessary investigation.

It is not difficult to read between the lines of Durdin's questioning. He was clearly getting a little frustrated, and there is a sense of disbelief throughout, highlighted with the occasional injection of sarcasm. Durdin obtained a lengthy description of Hamann and Bergmann before moving on to questioning Barton about the events of 16 September. Barton was doing his best to distance himself from the incident. He stated he arrived at the crash scene at around 1230 hours, and Durdin asked him who was there.

Paul Barton. Two *Wehrmacht* officers, Krause and Werner, the two Party officials, Grabowski and Nicke [i.e. Nieke] and a *Wehrmacht* private and the two policemen, Renoth and Pelgrim, otherwise there was no one there.

Barton gave a description of one of the officers, Hauptmann Krause, small, solid build, approximately 40 to 45, no glasses, clean shaven, a Captain in the *Wehrmacht*, about 130 to 140 pounds, height approximately 170, billeted in the Kurhotel in Hochelten.

Squadron Leader Durdin. What colour were the uniforms worn by Werner, Grabowski and Nicke?

Paul Barton. Field grey, Werner wore field grey, Grabowski was a Political *Leiter* and wore brown trousers, brown coat or shirt, Nicke also brown trousers and shirt or coat, the private wore field grey and the police officials Pelgrim and Renoth wore grey green.

Barton related that on arrival at the scene he had seen the pilot lying 5 metres to the right, and 4 or 5 metres ahead of the aircraft's right wing. Durdin asked Barton what weapons the men at the scene carried:

the only ones I know are the two policemen who each had a rifle and a pistol, I do assume that the officers wore pistols but I cannot remember to have observed them wearing them, the soldier left shortly after I arrived and I don't know what he carried, the Party officers may have been wearing weapons with their uniforms but I didn't observe it.

After a description of 'Nicke', Barton went on to tell Durdin what he was told had happened at the scene.

The two *Wehrmacht* officers never told me anything at all, the two political officials never said anything either, the *Wehrmacht* private didn't say anything, he left shortly after I arrived. The police officer, Renoth, told me the *Wehrmacht* soldier had beaten the flyer and had beaten so long till he broke down, after which the *Wehrmacht* officer, Hauptmann Krause ordered Renoth to shoot the pilot and Renoth replied 'you do that yourself' after which Hauptmann Krause said, 'I am giving you an order to shoot this man', the police officer Renoth then shot the pilot. On hearing this I turned about, went straight home and reported the incident to the Landrat and Kreisfeuhrer.

Durdin, of course, had statements from other witnesses that Barton had not immediately left the scene and that he had gone to the morgue later in the day. Durdin asked Barton if Renoth had told him what the soldier had used to strike the pilot.

Paul Barton. First he tackled by hand and then he took the rifle from Pelgrim and started to beat him with the rifle.
Squadron Leader Durdin. Did he tell you with what part of the rifle he beat him with?
PB. I don't know exactly, I just assume he used the butt of the rifle.
SLD. Why do you assume that?
PB. Well, I don't know really, I didn't see it, I just assumed it.

Barton told Durdin that he had not touched the pilot, but could see the 'large hole' in his head, 'but I couldn't say whether it was the point where the bullet had left his head'.

Squadron Leader Durdin. Did you see the rifle that Pelgrim had with him when he was at the crash?
Paul Barton. Yes, I have seen it.
SLD. Did you notice its condition?

PB. Yes sir, near the butt end it was broken, I added that because of the damage to the rifle Pelgrim would have to report this to his Captain.

SLD. Did you learn what rifle the soldier had used to beat the pilot?

PB. He used Pelgrim's rifle.

SLD. Did Pelgrim or Renoth make any explanation as to why the soldier had been permitted to beat the pilot?

PB. When I came there I noticed that Pelgrim's rifle was broken and I asked him how that happened and Pelgrim explained that the soldier had grabbed his rifle and started to beat the pilot with it.

SLD. Did you ask Pelgrim or Renoth or anyone else if any attempt had been made to stop the soldier?

PB. No I have not asked, we didn't even discuss it, I have however later discussed it and inquired why it had been permitted, but it all had happened so fast that there was no chance, I replied, 'One could always have prevented it' and the reply of Pelgrim and Renoth was that it had all gone too fast.

Barton believed the only one involved in the beating was the soldier, and that shortly after his arrival he saw the soldier 'manipulating the rubber dinghy' and told him to leave. Durdin asked Barton: 'Can you give any reason why Pelgrim or Renoth permitted the soldier to leave when they knew what he had done?' 'No, that I cannot say,' replied Barton, 'because the two knew what happened they could have held him.' Barton was of the opinion that Pelgrim had not been involved in the beating. But Durdin had Johann Bosmann's statement.

Squadron Leader Durdin. Do you recall having a conversation with one Johann Bosmann in the Landwache about a missing rifle and Pelgrim's broken rifle, sometime after the pilot was killed?

Paul Barton. Yes, I have spoken to the sentry, Johann Bosmann, who was guarding the aircraft.

SLD. Do you recall telling him that the rifle had been broken in the Pelgrim affair?

PB. That can be but I do not remember word by word what I said.

SLD. Do you recall using these words to him when referring to the broken rifle, 'It happened that time when Pelgrim was in on the beating, you know the story, don't you?'

PB. It could easily have been.

SLD. So that, in fact, you did believe Pelgrim had participated in the beating?

PB. Oh yes, I mean that when Pelgrim was there, he was present at the beating, that is what I mean.

SLD. Did you state that Pelgrim was in on the beating?

PB. I didn't say that he had been beating.

SLD. What did you mean then when you said, 'He was in on the beating'?

PB. That he was present when the beating took place.

SLD. Did you not consider Pelgrim partially responsible for the pilot's death?

PB. Pelgrim was that day the senior . . . man on duty.

SLD. My question to you is, did you consider him partially responsible for the pilot's death?

PB. As the police officer was there he could have stopped it, if I had been there I would have stopped it and would have stated, this man is under the protection of the police.

After establishing what had happened, Barton claimed to have reported the incident to the Landrat, von Werder, and to Hauptmann Hamann, who had come to Elten to speak to Renoth and Pelgrim. Barton told Durdin 'I only arrived in the course of the interrogation and Hauptmann Hamann said to me when I came in, "Pelgrim, from what I see, could have prevented the incident and Renoth would not have needed to fire, that wasn't necessary," and Renoth was later on reposted away to continue his police duties elsewhere.' Barton was fighting hard, doing his best not to incriminate himself and trying hard not to incriminate his subordinates. There is no doubt that Barton arrived at the murder scene after the killing had taken place. He had to make sure that he had not, in any way, authorised the killing of airmen.

Durdin questioned Barton over the 'certificate', the Meister of the Gendarmerie responding: 'Hauptmann Hamann gave orders to Renoth that he was to go to Hauptmann Krause to get a certificate in writing to prove that Renoth had been acting on the orders of Hauptmann Krause when he shot the pilot and this certificate he brought back.' Barton recalled seeing the certificate: 'I cannot remember the wording of it, I did see however from its content that Renoth had acted on the explicit order of Hauptmann Krause . . . I have [seen] the signature. It was very badly written but I did know the name of the Captain was Krause.'

Durdin's questioning now jumped about as he tied up loose ends. Barton told him that the pilot wore a slightly darker blue uniform than the RCAF one worn by Durdin, that Captain Krause was billeted in the Kurhotel in Hochelten, run by a Wilhelm Heiting, and that he had not seen any bloodstains in the aircraft, but that when he had seen the pilot, 'the face was all bloody'.

Captain Blain took up a so-called cross-examination, establishing that Barton claimed being in Emmerich at the time of the crash. Barton also stated that orders with respect to crashed aircraft came from the government via the Kreisführer:

In the case of a crashed aircraft it is the duty of the policeman on receipt of the message to proceed to the place of the crash . . . all those who parachuted from the aircraft had to be captured, we also had cases like this and we caught them, but where the army arrived first they were the masters on the scene and pushed the police out of the way. For that reason there was an order stating that if the army arrived on the scene first it was an army matter and the police had nothing to do with it.

Blain was not satisfied. Who had authority?

Captain Blain. Who arrived first at the scene of this accident?
Paul Barton. That I don't know, I assume however that the military arrived first because they have a car whereas the policemen only have bicycles.
CB. If, in fact, the police and military arrived at the same time who would be in charge?
PB. Either they would cooperate or they would not, I never had a case where the army interfered, as often as I recovered crashed aircraft I never had any sort of an incident.
CB. In such a case would the army probably take charge?
PB It says in the order should the army arrive on the scene first the army will take over complete control of the recovery. There is nothing we can do against the *Wehrmacht*.
CB. In view of the situation in this case do you think Renoth would feel himself bound by the order of the *Wehrmacht* officer to shoot the pilot?
PB. Yes I assume so. He is a timid type.

CB. Would you yourself, if you had been in Renoth's position felt bound by such an order?

PB. So help my God if I had of been there it would never have happened, I would never have done it, no.

CB. Do you know if Renoth and Pelgrim were afraid of the *Wehrmacht* at the time?

PB. Yes, I definitely have that feeling.

Blain asked Barton if he had done anything to identify the body, to which he replied: 'No for that purpose we have Bergungs Kommando, I merely had the body placed in a coffin then waited for the Bergungs Kommando to arrive and search for documents and identify him.' Barton also told Blain that he had not searched the body, which he reconfirmed to Durdin when he conducted a short re-examination.

Squadron Leader Durdin. Did you see Hubert Franken at the scene of the crash?

Paul Barton. No, he wasn't on the scene of the crash, he was further back.

SLD. Do you know whether or not the pilot had any money in his clothing?

PB. No, I merely had the man placed in the coffin and taken to the morgue.

SLD. Are you sure you didn't examine his pockets, take any money out of them or take a rosary out of his pocket?

PB. No I have never touched any of the bodies, that has all been done by the Bergungs Kommando.

On the latter point Durdin had witness statements to the contrary, but the interview closed and Barton returned to his prison cell. With nothing directly implicating Barton in the murder, he would not face charges, but he would still appear at the trial of his junior policemen.

On the afternoon of 8 January 1946 Paul Barton was called by the prosecution in the Elten case, to provide testimony about the conduct of the men he was superior to, yet for whom he had not been prepared to accept responsibility. Captain Diamond's initial questioning established Barton's apparent authority over Renoth and Pelgrim, and that he went to the scene of the incident after hearing about it first from a town-hall clerk and then from his wife. At Franken's meadow he initially came across two *Wehrmacht* officers, whom he named as a 'Captain Wermat' and a 'Captain Krausa', and Grabowski and Nieke. Then at the plane were Pelgrim, Renoth and a soldier. 'When I came to the plane I saw the German soldier do something about this plane and I asked him: "What are you doing here?" He replied: "Nothing" and then I told him: "Get away from here".' Diamond also ensured that Barton mentioned not seeing any bloodstains in the aircraft, suggesting of course that the injuries to the pilot were sustained after the crash landing. The prosecutor pressed Barton on the conversations he had with Pelgrim and Renoth at the aircraft, the others having left the scene: 'Renoth looked at me back and was laughing and told me: "I have found the pilot in the bushes near the water". . . . Renoth told me that he asked the pilot to come out of the bushes and come to the plane.' Barton explained that, when he stated to Renoth that the pilot was dead, Renoth responded: 'That has been done by the *Wehrmacht* . . . The *Wehrmacht* has beaten the pilot until he broke down, in the presence of the officers [Wermat and Krausa].' Diamond asked Barton what Captain Krausa then told Renoth.

'Shoot the pilot dead; he is suffering very much.' Renoth refused it and said: 'Do it yourself.' Captain Krausa repeated his order and told him for the second time: 'Shoot him dead,' and Renoth refused it again. Captain Krausa repeated for the last time and told him: 'I give you officially an order: shoot him dead' and then Renoth told me: 'Then I was answerable, I received the order and I have shot.'

Diamond asked Barton about his conversation with Pelgrim: 'I turned around to Pelgrim and told him: "What happened with your rifle". . . he had the rifle in his hand and the wooden part of it was broken off. . . Pelgrim said: "The soldier has taken off the rifle from me and has beaten the pilot until the butt broke off."' Each of the judges, as military men, had handled rifles. They would have had some idea of how ferocious the attack must have been to break the butt.

Diamond now tried to explore the authority of the policemen at the scene.

Captain Diamond. Can you tell the Court what were the orders which existed as far as the police were concerned in connection with any pilots who landed?

Paul Barton. The police were ordered to fence the plane where a plane came down, either German or British.

CD. What were the instructions with regard to enemy pilots or fliers?

PB. Pilots should be taken into custody as long as they did not defend themselves with arms. Further instructions had come from the Government and were that the population had free hunting for pilots.

CD. What exactly do you mean by 'free hunting'?

PB. The Government has brought to the notice of the population that airmen that fall into their hands can be killed or lynched.

CD. What was the duty of the police in such a case?

PB. Airmen caught alive stay in our custody and are taken to the nearest air force unit.

CD. What were the instructions of the police if there was such a lynching as you have already referred to in the presence of the police?

PB. Then the policemen had no power whatsoever when many people were around; with a few it was not so difficult.

CD. In the case of a small lynching party what were the instructions given to the police?

PB. In that case the official should have taken with him the airman.

Diamond tried, but failed, to force a definite answer from Barton over who had authority when the police were in the presence of political leaders, but he did try to deflect any responsibility from his subordinates.

Captain Diamond. Who is regarded as superior, the political leaders or the police?

Paul Barton. The police is by itself, and the political leaders are in the Party or for the Party.

CD. Given a situation where you have, say, Nieke, Grabowski, Pelgrim and Renoth all together, who would be in charge?

PB. Here it was as follows: the police were in charge, and because the army officers were over there the police were under the impression that the *Wehrmacht* was in charge. In case the *Wehrmacht* had not been there I am absolutely convinced that the pilot would still be alive.

Barton's defence of his men concluded Diamond's examination. Gobbels asked only two questions, eliciting from Barton that, if the police arrived at the scene of an aircraft crash after the *Wehrmacht*, then, if the Army said they were in charge, 'then there is no task for the police'. It seems quite extraordinary that Gobbels did not bring up the certificate Renoth claimed to have obtained from Kuehne/Krausa. It seems that he was not going to challenge testimony stating that Renoth did shoot at the pilot. A major part of Renoth's defence was that he was ordered. Gobbels must have known that. Barton claimed to have known about the certificate, yet Gobbels failed to raise the matter with the witness. Perhaps Kington-Blair-Oliphant's dismissal of Weyer's testimony about the certificate held him back. Nevertheless, surely he should have tried again. As it was, the certificate issue would be raised again.

Milman's questioning was almost as brief, eliciting that Barton had not seen Hubert Franken at the scene, that he had seen the two captains on the way from the plane to their car and spoken to them, and that he believed the soldier was in field grey. He also reconfirmed that Pelgrim had said the rifle was broken by a soldier.

Under re-examination from Diamond, Barton stated that there was only a brief conversation with the two officers. Leicester-Warren asked if he had seen this 'Captain Krausa' before, Barton responding that either the captain told him his name or he had seen it on the certificate. This sparked off a lengthy discussion about the certificate. Kington-Blair-Oliphant and Leicester-Warren pressed Barton on the matter; he had seen it the next day, in the police station: 'As far as I can remember it said that the Captain had to detail repeatedly Renoth to give the *coup de grâce* to that airman.' The certificate, including the signature, according to Barton, appeared to be all in the same handwriting, and it was then posted to Captain Hamann. Diamond asked Barton: 'When Captain Hamann came to Elten following the report which he got, what instructions did he give to Renoth?' Barton replied: 'He asked Renoth and Pelgrim: "How did it happen? Tell me."' But Kington-Blair-Oliphant cut the questioning short as 'more hearsay', and Barton left the witness stand.

The Meister of the Elten Gendarmerie was Diamond's last witness, and he now sought to put into evidence three statements 'purporting' to be signed by Renoth, Pelgrim and Grabowski. But he had a problem. He could not present the officers who had attended when the statements were made. Leicester-Warren and Kington-Blair-Oliphant had concerns.

Captain Diamond. Under Regulation 8(i): At any hearing before a Military Court convened under these Regulations the Court may take into consideration any oral statement or any document appearing on the face of it to be authentic, provided the statement or document appears to the Court to be of assistance in proving or disproving the charge.

Leicester-Warren. Are you submitting that that abrogates the ordinary rule of evidence that it is on the Prosecution to prove that a statement made by an accused person is taken freely and voluntarily and not under duress?

CD. Yes. The question of the weight to be attached to the statements will under the provision of Paragraph 8 be a matter for the Court to decide.

Kington-Blair-Oliphant. The Court takes the view at the present moment that in view of the words 'the Court may', the Court feels that those documents will be of such a prejudicial nature that it is difficult to assess prejudice with the amount of weight that they are going to give to them; so before we make the decision whether we are going to accept those documents under those terms, the Court will retire to consider it. Meanwhile I should like to know before I retire: are you in a position to call an officer or any other person who can produce the statements?

CD. I am not in a position to call any such person.

LW. How do you argue that a statement made by an accused person, which, let us assume for the purpose of the argument, is prejudicial, is admissible under this Army Order 8(i)?

Diamond repeated the respective regulation: 'the terms . . . are clear and unmistakable.' Leicester-Warren still had reservations. How could the statement be submitted, 'without any evidence that in fact it had been signed by the Accused'? If the defence challenged the authenticity, Diamond countered, it was for the court to decide if the documents were authentic. The Legal Member of the Court remained unhappy: 'Surely the normal procedure . . . [is] to have an affidavit from the officer who took the statement.' Diamond stood firm. These statements were central to his case. 'Although the production of such an affidavit or oral evidence is the ideal state of affairs, where there is no such affidavit . . . ' Kington-Blair-Oliphant cut the prosecutor short: 'Unless you have any fresh light . . . the Court will retire and consider this point.' Diamond added that, if there was no challenge of authenticity from the defence, then the statements were admissible. If there was any doubt in the court's mind, Milman responded, as to the admissibility of the statements, 'I suggest it should be given to the Accused.' Surely Milman had seen the statements, and it is surprising that he did not fight harder for exclusion.

At 1830 hours the court closed. Just 10 minutes later the members returned, and Kington-Blair-Oliphant voiced the decision: 'the Court . . . is to use the wide powers given to it and to accept these statements as evidence by the Prosecution'. Following a check by interpreters, the statements of Renoth, Pelgrim and Grabowski were presented to the court, and read by Diamond in English. It was not deemed necessary to read them also in German, as written German translations were provided. Just before half past seven on the evening of 9 January 1946 Captain Diamond stated: 'That concludes the case for the Prosecution', and the court adjourned until the following morning.

Chapter 15

UNDER ORDERS

It was not just the sight of her father on trial that Maria Renoth found traumatic. It was also the sense of public humiliation, compounded by the fact that she, along with Agnes Pelgrim, had been made to clean the courtroom.

Maria Renoth, born in 1923, grew up in the Elten area. Her father, Hans, was originally from Berchtesgaden in the Bavarian Alps, where he learned his trade as a forester. Hans moved to Elten in the early 1920s, having been successful in applying for a forester position advertised in a hunting magazine. Hans, with his wife, Anna, settled in to the 'Six Corner House' and began to raise his family. A year after Maria's birth a brother, Erasmus, was born. Maria always held fond memories of her father, especially the times Hans took her and Erasmus into the forest to share his knowledge of the trees, the plants and the animals. During the war Erasmus was called up for service with the German infantry, serving on the Eastern Front, where he became hospitalised owing to shrapnel wounds to his lungs. A return to front-line duties resulted in his capture by the Russians.

Owing to his public responsibilities, Hans avoided military service, although he did take over local policing duties, when the regular police in the area were drafted into the army. Such a position required membership of the Nazi party, but Hans was not a political man. He held Catholic convictions, which resulted in occasional difficulties. At one time he had been asked to report on the activities of the parish priest at the church in Hüthum, between Emmerich and Elten. Hans, seeking to avoid conflict, decided to exclude himself from that particular congregation, and he began to go to the church in Elten. Hans's superiors would describe him as quite a simple and straightforward man, but his official duties first as a forester and then as a policeman did not necessarily endear him to some of the locals. Some photographs exist of Hans in his police uniform, the expression on his face one of uncertainty, a slight smile somewhat forced. He does not appear comfortable. When compared to pictures of Paul Barton, looking confident and proud of his position, Renoth appears uneasy and unsure.

Shortly after the incident in Franken's field, Hans was posted away to the Leipzig area, leaving his family behind. At the end of the war he returned to Elten and, because of the rumour and the gossip, he gave himself up. The paperwork recording his initial arrest and detainment clearly records his acceptance of giving the pilot the *coup de grâce*. He made no attempt to deny it. Quite probably he believed that, in acting under orders, he had done nothing untoward.

On the morning of 10 January 1946 Maria Renoth's father and Anna Renoth's husband took to the stand. The statement he had given on 12 July 1945 had already been read to the court.

Hans Renoth's statement: I have been warned that this is a voluntary statement and that it can be used as evidence in court.

At the beginning of September 1944 a farmer reported by telephone that an aircraft (single engine bomber) had crashed in Grondstein Elten. I was at the office in Elten as *Wachtmeister* on the Gendarmerie Reserve. I informed Wachtmeister Pelgrim, who was also at the office, two captains of the Signals staff who were stationed in Hoch-Elten in the Kurhaus (I think that one was called Koernkes, exact spelling unknown); it was the latter who later gave me the order to give the pilot the *coup de grâce*. We then drove in the captains' army car to the aircraft. In the car were in addition to the captains, two political leaders by name Grabowski and Nicke [*sic*], who were employed as Customs Officials, and Oberwachtmeister Pelgrim (*Oberwachtmeister* of the Gendarmerie) and myself. I had a service rifle (type 9B) and a pistol (type O8), as did also Oberwachtmeister Pelgrim. I assume that the officers also had small calibre weapons. I think that the political leaders had no weapons of their own with them. We left the car just past the railway tracks in the side road leading to the farm of Johannes Franken. We went on foot toward the aircraft. We saw the fallen aircraft but the pilot was not to be seen.

During the search for the latter we had to take cover as other aircraft were flying over. After these aircraft had flown past, we continued our search for the pilot. The pilot was located in a ditch about 50 meters from the aircraft in the direction of the AA site. I told him to come with me, which he immediately did. I searched him first but I found no weapons. I went with the pilot in the direction of the aircraft towards the captains. On the way the pilot was taken from me by two soldiers, the political leaders and Pelgrim, with the remark 'You want to be friendly with the dog who has murdered our women and children'. I assume that the soldier came from the railway (or the main road).

A beating ensued. The following were present: two soldiers, the two political leaders and Pelgrim. The pilot was beaten nearly to death. I took no part in the beating, but withdrew and went to the captains. We conversed briefly: I can no longer remember the subject of the conversation. I saw that the rifle model 9B was broken in 2 pieces. (It was Pelgrim's rifle.) It is my opinion that the pilot had been beaten so severely that the rifle broke. Captain Koerkes [actually spelt differently from above in the statement] ordered me to give the pilot the *coup de grâce* and I carried out this order. In accordance with my oath, I had to carry out the order. I made no protest. I received a written order from Captain Koerkes, I passed this on to the Kreisfuhrer of the Gendarmerie Harmann [*sic*] by name in Wesel at the office of the Landrat. I fired a shot into the pilot's chest from a range 5 to 7 meters. The pilot died immediately without uttering a sound. A second shot went off by accident and grazed the pilot's skull. About half an hour later Barton, Meister of the Gendarmerie and Chief of Elten Police, came from Elten and took charge of the affair. He gathered up the pilot's belongings, Pelgrim assisted him. Among the objects I saw: money, iron rations, maps. Immediately after the shot had been fired, the two captains had gone away, along with the two customs officials, in the automobile. Then the two Gendarmes, Pelgrim and Barton, went away with the pilot's belongings in the direction of their Service vehicle, which was apparently parked on the road leading to Johann Franken's. Before they left I was given the task of standing guard at the scene until I was relieved. My period of guard duty passed without further incident, although a number of people came to look on. Between 18 and 19 [hundred] hours I was relieved by Landwachtmann Boshmann [*sic*]. On the following morning between 8 and 9 o'clock I returned to the scene and saw that the corpse was no longer there. I do not know what later happened to the body. Fallen aircraft were usually taken away by a Fliegerkommando (Air Force Detachment) 'Boeningshardt'. Meister Barton forwarded a report to Kreisfuhrer Harmann [*sic*] at Wesel, who was under the jurisdiction of the Landrat Von Werder. I noticed no insignia on the aircraft other than the English national emblem.

I declare that my statements are true
Mil Gov Prison, Bedburg
12 July 1945
(Signed) *Hans Renoth*

At 10 a.m. on 10 January the court reassembled to hear the testimony of Hans Renoth. His counsel, so far, had done little to counter the damning testimony of Bosmann and the submission of the similarly powerful evidence of his statement. Gobbels's initial questions established, indeed reaffirmed, basic facts: that Renoth had gone to the scene of the crash in the company of the two captains, Grabowski and Nieke, and Pelgrim; that there were two rifles in the car; that the *Wehrmacht* officer was in charge and had told them to search the area, and that he, Renoth, had found the pilot. 'I called out to him to come out from where he was,' testified Renoth. 'I searched him for arms, which I did not find . . . I took him in the direction of the captains and the plane . . . On the way and at a certain distance from the plane – at what distance I cannot say – two soldiers met us and one had a truncheon and he pushed me away from the pilot and took the pilot away from me with the remark, "You want to be friendly with the swine who murders women and children?"' The policeman tried to make it clear that he had no right to intervene. The captains, he claimed, were 30–40 metres away and 'at quite a long distance behind [the soldiers] there were the two political leaders and Pelgrim'. Renoth was trying to distance his co-defendants from the actual beating, contrary to his statement. The beating then started and Renoth went to speak with the two captains, 'with my back turned to the pilot . . . When I turned round I saw the pilot with his head beaten in and he was supporting himself near the plane, he was standing bent . . . While the pilot was standing there Captain Kuehne [Koernkes in his statement] told me to give him the *coup de grâce*.' At first Renoth stated he could do nothing; he was in shock. Then the captain 'shoved his revolver up to the front along his belt', and repeated the order.

> *Kington-Blair-Oliphant.* Is the Court to understand that the captain threatened you with his revolver?
> *Hans Renoth.* Yes, because a superior officer had the right to make use of his arms if an order was not obeyed.
> *Dr Gobbels.* What did you do then?
> *HR.* Then I shot at the pilot while he was still standing but if I had waited another second perhaps he would have fallen to the ground anyhow.
> *DG.* Was there a second shot?
> *HR.* Yes.
> *DG.* How did that happen?
> *HR.* By not very careful loading of the rifle it went off by accident.

DG. Did this shot hit the pilot?

HR. No, the shot went over the head of the pilot and threw up the dirt over his head.

This 'accidental' second shot registered with Diamond, which he would challenge when his chance came.

Dr Gobbels moved on to the certificate, his client stating that he had spoken to Hamann, who had advised that, 'if Hauptmann Kuehne is killed in the war I have no proof that he gave the order'. Renoth followed this up, stating he had gone to see Kuehne, who had written an order on a letter headed 'Headquarters of the Luftwaffe Signals'. He showed it to Barton, Weyer and a few others prior to mailing it to Hamann. Renoth's testimony about the certificate does bring into question why Gobbels had not questioned Barton on the matter, when Renoth's superior had been in the witness stand. It was a major facet of his client's defence.

Gobbels, having his client's testimony that he had not been involved in the beating, that he had been ordered, with a direct threat, to shoot the pilot, and that he had obtained a written order backing up the circumstance, sat down, giving way to Lieutenant Milman.

Grabowski, Nieke and Pelgrim's counsel immediately set about diverting blame for the beating, ensuring Renoth reaffirmed the presence of the two soldiers and that, while the beating was taking place, his clients were behind the captains and at no time did they strike the pilot. Milman moved on to Renoth's statement.

Lieutenant Milman. In that statement you say, 'On the way the pilot was taken away from me by two soldiers, the two political leaders and Pelgrim'?

Hans Renoth. There is a slight mistake in this. A girl wrote this and perhaps she forgot the words 'at the back'.

This was, of course, crucial to Milman's defence, as it distanced the other accused from the scene of the beating. There then followed some lengthy debate between Milman, Diamond and Kington-Blair-Oliphant concerning the serving of the original statements in English and German to Renoth.

Kington-Blair-Oliphant. The English translation is perfectly clear and says: 'On the way the pilot was taken away from me by two soldiers, the two political leaders and Pelgrim with the remark' and so on. He is now trying to add to that something which was never in the original. (To the witness) All that the Court is trying to find out now is: Do you admit that this statement is the statement that you yourself gave at the time you were in Bedburg prison? The Court is not now trying to find out whether you disagree with what you wrote; all the Court is trying to find out is, do you agree that this is the statement that you gave then? The fact that you disagree with what you wrote is another question which will be dealt with in due course?

Hans Renoth. This is the same as I made at Bedburg but something has been left out in these statements.

KBO. I take it that what has been left out is that the two political leaders were a large distance away?

The Interpreter. Yes.

KBO. He maintains that at the time he gave that statement those words were in?

The Interpreter. Yes.

KBO. Did you read it through before you signed it?

HR. The girl read it out to me.

KBO. Then why did you not point out this mistake at the time?

HR. I do not know.

KBO. Mr Milman, the position is that the witness has agreed that that is the statement that he made, subject to the fact that he now alleges that something was left out which he did not notice at the time the statement was read out. Whether the Court accepts that or not is immaterial at the moment; that is what he says.

Renoth was trying hard to defend his co-accused. As he had admitted actually killing Bill Maloney, it might have served his personal defence better if he had taken the line that they had in fact beaten the pilot to a point at which he could continue to live only for a matter of seconds.

Milman closed his questioning, with a statement from Renoth that he had not seen Bosmann at the scene of the incident, when the beating and shooting took place.

Diamond immediately attacked Renoth over his claim that words had been left out of the original statement, but Kington-Blair-Oliphant was not prepared to prolong the matter. 'We know what is in the document and if he now disagrees he is at liberty to tell the Court how he disagrees and there that matter will close.' Diamond moved on, challenging Renoth that, if he had his back to the pilot, how could he say the other accused had not been involved in the beating. Renoth's answer was confused.

Captain Diamond. Then I repeat my question: is it not possible that while you were standing talking to the captains, Grabowski and Nieke were beating the pilot?

Hans Renoth. I cannot see at the back of my head, but these three men were not at the back of me as far as I could see.

CD. Can you say that they were in front of you?

HR. No, they did not stand in front of me either; before me were the captains.

CD. So they did not stand behind you and they did not stand in front of you; is that right?

HR They could have stood to the left or to the right of me.

CD. How do you know they were not behind you?

HR. I cannot answer that question because I did not notice it.

CD. Does an oath mean anything to you?

HR. Yes.

CD. Then will you remember that you are on your oath?

HR. Yes.

CD. I put the question a third time. Was it possible that these three men behind you were beating the pilot when you were talking to the captain?

HR. I could not say at all.

Diamond let the matter rest, but clearly Renoth continued to do his best not to incriminate the other accused. After a short inconclusive exchange concerning who had authority in this situation, the police or the soldiers, Diamond raised the actual shooting itself.

Captain Diamond. Where did your first shot hit the pilot?

Hans Renoth. In the chest.

CD. Would you point on your chest?

HR. About *here* (indicating centre of chest).

CD. Was he standing up when you fired the shot?

HR. He was just at the point of breaking down.

CD. Was he standing up or was he lying down or was he sitting down – in what position was he?

HR. He was still standing, but he was at the point of breaking down.

A small but crucial point. As Bill Maloney was still standing, he was therefore still alive. You cannot murder a dead man.

> *Captain Diamond*. Will you explain to the Court – I am sure they will be very interested from their knowledge of firearms – just how the second shot went off on account of faulty loading?
>
> *Hans Renoth*. I put in a round and I pushed it to the front; I could not push the round in the whole way, and then I shoved the bolt up to the front and the shot went off.
>
> *Kington-Blair-Oliphant*. Why were you pushing in a round?
>
> *HR*. As soon as you fire a round you always put in another round; that is usual.
>
> *Captain Diamond*. Did you always have your rifle loaded at all times?
>
> *HR*. Yes, while on duty you always have it loaded.
>
> *CD*. You are quite sure you did not fire the second shot deliberately?
>
> *HR*. No, I did not fire; it was just carelessness.
>
> *CD*. If Pelgrim says that you fired a second shot into the pilot's head, that you went right up to the pilot –

Kington-Blair-Oliphant interrupted the prosecutor sharply: 'Pelgrim has not said that.' Diamond was referring to Pelgrim's statement, which had been read to the court but not yet verified by the respective defendant. The President would not allow questioning on what was, at this stage, an alleged statement.

> *Captain Diamond*. At any rate, you are quite sure the second shot was not aimed?
>
> *Hans Renoth*. No, it was not aimed; certainly not, it was only carelessness in loading; it was an accident.
>
> *CD*. And you are equally certain that the second shot never entered the pilot's head.
>
> *HR*. At first I thought the pilot had grazed his head because the dirt was thrown up just at the back of his head and after that while I was standing guard I walked around the pilot, then I saw that the shot had entered the ground about a metre from the head of the pilot.
>
> *CD*. But you said in your statement, did you not, in July that the second shot did graze the pilot's skull.

HR. Yes I thought so.

CD. What has made you change your mind since July?

HR. When I came back from Leipzig and I came back to my family, then they told me they were looking for me, and then I gave my-self up to the police.

CD. Will you answer the question: what has made you change your mind about the effect of the second shot since July?

HR. I was just trying to explain. Then I was arrested and I was a bit out of my mind because I was arrested and was sitting there in my cell, because I had never been arrested before, I was a bit out of my mind, and then I told this to the best of my knowledge; and now after I have been in prison for seven or eight months I had time enough to think about everything, how it actually happened.

Diamond showed Renoth the autopsy photographs: 'Is it possible that your second shot made that hole in the skull?' 'That is no shot', Renoth responded, 'and this has been beaten in with a blow.' Renoth remained adamant that 'a shot never entered his head; I never saw a shot enter his head'. Diamond had to move on. He had no medical proof that a bullet pierced the pilot's head – the pathologist's report was inconclusive.

Captain Diamond. You said in your first statement that the pilot died immediately as a result of the first shot; is that right?

Hans Renoth. No, the pilot was almost dead when I fired.

CD. Although he was standing up?

HR. He was at the point of death because he was just breaking down. If I had waited another second the pilot would have fallen with-out a shot and would have been dead.

Kington-Blair-Oliphant. Then why did you not wait another second?

HR. It is not easy to say; you cannot say it; I should not be able to say why. If I had waited another second he would have fallen down.

CD. How do you know he would have died?

HR. Because his skull was beaten in.

CD. Who had beaten his skull in?

HR. The soldiers.

CD. Were they still standing round him when you fired?

HR. Yes the soldiers were still there.

KBO. Where?

HR. In the neighbourhood; they were to the left or to the right, but I

173

cannot say exactly where they were standing.

CD. Were you not afraid of hitting one of them with your shot?

HR. Yes, perhaps they were at such a distance, and in any case I could shoot the pilot without having to be afraid of hitting one of the soldiers.

Diamond switched tack, trying to establish why Renoth had not intervened on the pilot's behalf. 'There was an order of the Government', Renoth responded, 'that if one of these "terror" pilots were taken by the population, the *Wehrmacht* or the SS or the police were not allowed to protect them.' Renoth reaffirmed his position that the captains were in charge anyway and 'we [the police] cannot do anything if the *Wehrmacht* is there'. Diamond concluded his cross-examination of the police officer, challenging his defence that the captain had threatened him with the pistol.

Captain Diamond. Have you any idea why the captain did not use his own pistol to shoot him?

Hans Renoth. I do not know; I have no idea at all why he did that; I cannot get into the mind of another man, and moreover he was a superior, he was an officer; I was just a *gefreiter*.

CD. When he moved his pistol round to the front of his belt, do you not think it possible that he did that with the intention of himself shooting the pilot?

HR. No, he wanted to shoot me, I think, if I refused to obey the order.

CD. How long had you been in the German Army?

HR. Since 1939.

CD. Have you ever known of anybody being shot for disobeying orders?

HR. I do not know.

Kington-Blair-Oliphant. You must answer the question. Do you know of anyone being shot or do you not know?

HR. I do not know anybody who was shot because it never happened while I was around.

KBO. Then say no when you are asked the question. Answer the questions properly.

Dr Gobbels declined to re-examine his client, but Leicester-Warren had further questions, asking Renoth about his conversation later in the day with Bosmann: 'He has sworn that you said to him, "It was high time that I gave him the *coup de grâce*."' Renoth claimed he could not remember what he had said, 'but it is probable that I said that'. Kington-Blair-Oliphant finished off Renoth's ordeal, following up on his defence that it was 'an act of war', and if so then why did he get the certificate. The President, very briefly, became the prosecutor. Renoth responded that, if the captain was killed, he wanted a written order.

Kington-Blair-Oliphant. I put it to you that you had done something very wrong and that you were afraid.

Hans Renoth. No.

KBO. Can you describe the dress that the pilot wore?

HR. He had the same kind of blue uniform as the man sitting over there (indicating RAAF officer).

KBO. Were there any marks or badges on it?

HR. I saw 'Australia' written on the shoulder; I though it was 'Canada' and afterwards I knew it was 'Australia'. It was just like a civilian suit because he had torn everything from his uniform himself.

It was probably not a good decision on Renoth's part to associate further one of the men sitting in judgment, Atholl McLauchlan, with the victim. Dr Gobbels declared that he would not be calling any further witnesses.

Milman set about the defence of his clients, informing the court that all would be taking the stand. Milman's situation was problematic. In representing Pelgrim, Grabowski and Nieke, he had to be very careful that testimony by one of his clients did not incriminate one of his co-defendants. A modern viewpoint of the trial would suggest that Pelgrim, Grabowski and Nieke would have been better represented individually, each one's representative focusing on each client's specific defence and possibly leading to what is called a 'cut-throat' defence. Nieke, for one, could easily have assigned blame to the others; he had not had an incriminating statement presented, and there was little direct evidence, so far, of his actual involvement in the beating. Whether each man was offered individual counsel is not in the record.

Pelgrim. Hans, Johann, Jacob, Bezirks Ober Wachtmeister (Sjt) of the Gendarmerie, Elten

I know that the statements I am about to make may be used in court and I declare that they have been made voluntarily.

In September 1944 I was on duty at the town hall in Elten. As I left one of the rooms on the ground floor, Wachtmeister of the Gendarmerie

Renoth came and said to me. 'It is a good thing that you are here because a call has come in from Grondstein to say that an aircraft had come down. There are two captains here with a vehicle who are also going there. We can go along in the vehicle.' Oberzollsekretär (Customs Lt.) Grabowski and Zollsekretär Nicke [*sic*], who also happened to be present at the town hall, came along to Grondstein. We passed my home on the way and picked up two service rifles there. One of the Captains carried a pistol. I do not know what the other one carried. In addition Renoth and I carried pistols type 08. We left the car just past the railway crossing on the side road which leads from Highway 8 to Johann Franken's farm. We arrived at the aircraft which lay in the meadow 300 meters away from the road to the right. Lights were still burning in the aircraft and the sound of an electric motor was still audible. The pilot's seat was empty. We decided to search the wood and the surroundings. About 200 meters away I saw a farmhand by the name of Batje Könnemann [probably Konning] running away. I called him over and asked him whether he had seen the pilot which he denied. Thereupon we searched the area. Renoth proceeded to the left, as seen from the aircraft. I proceeded towards the right, jumped over a small brook and proceeded in the direction of the coniferous wood ahead of me. I assume that Nicke came with me. I cannot remember whether Grabowski came along. I do not know whether I had my service rifle with me or my pistol while searching the woods. I think Nicke had my service rifle. I heard someone shouting and returned. When I reached the open I saw Renoth coming from the left as seen from the aircraft. He was being followed by two apparently unarmed soldiers. They looked like MT drivers. These two men grabbed the pilot and beat him with their fists. I was about 2[00]–300 meters from the spot. The three men moved from the left to the right of the aircraft. The soldiers were beating the pilot continuously. When I came closer I said to the Captain, 'Can't you see what is going on, why don't you do something about it? Our duty has been performed and I hereby turn the pilot over to you.' The captain did not reply. Instead he jumped back and I saw one of the soldiers twisting a rifle out of the pilot's hands. It was my service rifle. The soldiers hit the pilot over the head with the butt, breaking the rifle in two. I jumped forward and picked up the rifle. I do not know how the pilot got possession of the rifle. I assume he took it off me or Nicke in his desperation. At the same moment the first shot was fired. It hit the pilot in the abdomen causing him to fall over.

I turned about and exclaimed: 'Renoth, what are you doing?' to which Renoth replied that the captain had ordered him to do it. I said to the captain, 'Capt., but haven't you your own pistol?' In the meantime Renoth fired a shot into the pilot's head. During the first shot Renoth stood behind me. For the second shot he came right up to the pilot and fired an aimed shot at his head. Before receiving the blow with the rifle butt the pilot was still standing on his feet, although he was bleeding from the head. The condition of the corpse was as follows: I think the corpse lay on its back, blood was visible from the abdominal wound. The last shot had torn the back of the head apart. The man wore his blue uniform, blue blouse and long blue trousers, black low shoes and black socks.

I think that the officers and soldiers left. Furthermore I think that Grabowski and Nicke drove back with the officers. Our Section/ Station Chief Barton appeared at the same time. Whether the officers and soldiers were still present at the time I am not certain. Barton recorded everything in his notes. I assume he searched the corpse because he exclaimed, 'The man has no papers on him.' With Renoth I searched the spot where the pilot was found. There we found several scraps of paper – which had been cut up into very small pieces. We collected the largest of these and placed them in an envelope which Barton later took with him. I am unable to say anything about the pilot's belongings. I think Renoth said to me 'A soldier took his wristwatch along.' Normally the belongings are removed by the GAF detachment along with the corpse. I think that Fliegerhorst Kommando 'Boenning-hardt' operated here at the time. The Muenster-Hantau or Duesseldorf detachments could also have been involved. Barton ordered Renoth to remain on guard. I do not know whether I was at the aircraft twice with Barton, but before I left with Barton, the town labourer, Ruetten took the shoes and socks.* I left the scene of the crime with Barton during the afternoon. On the same day the pilot's corpse was taken to the morgue. One or two days later it was taken to what I assume was Boenninghardt in a lorry of a recovery section of the nearest Fliegerhorst.

Barton informed me that the recovery section insisted on having the pilot's shoes and socks back. I retrieved the shoes and socks from the town labourer Ruetten. I gave them to the recovery section at the morgue. They forgot them there. When we went to get them they had disappeared.

The name of one of the captains present was Kuehne.

I declare that the above statements are the truth.

Mil Gov Prison
Bedburg
12 Jul 45
Signed *Hans Pelgrim*

* Ruetten, remarked, 'The man wears a good pair of shoes.'
Barton said, 'if you like them, take them off and keep them.'

Pelgrim's opening answers to his counsel's questions established that he was at the office of the *Bürgermeister* in Elten when Renoth informed him that 'an aeroplane has crashed in Grondstein . . . There are two officers of the *Wehrmacht* from Elten with a car and they want to go down and we can go with them.' Pelgrim then hinted at the basis of his defence, claiming he told Renoth: 'Let the officers go there themselves, because it is the concern of the *Wehrmacht* and we have got nothing to do with it.' Nevertheless he had gone, asserting that Renoth said the officers asked for him as they did not know the way. Pelgrim added the following contradicting part of Renoth's statement concerning the type of aircraft:

Grabowski and Nieke came from a funeral and had no arms on them. Renoth had not asked whether it was a four-engined bomber or a fighter plane or something else; we did not know what kind of plane it was. Because we did not know that – I never experienced that airmen offered any resistance, but it might have been a four-engined bomber – I said: 'If we go down that way we will come up in the neighbourhood of my house, because I live in Bahnhofstrasse.' Then I went on my push bike to my house and took two rifles and I took some rounds of ammunition and after that I drove in the car to the place where the plane had crashed.

At the plane Pelgrim recalled that 'the radio was still on and the orders of the commander were still coming through'. Pelgrim confirmed that they had only two rifles, adding that both he and Renoth had a pistol, and then, 'Hauptmann Kuehne gave us the order to search the surroundings.' Stating that he carried the rifle to the plane, Pelgrim was then keen to get it out of his hands. 'I left my rifle near the plane . . . because I had taken the rifle along with me for Grabowski or Nieke.' The butt of Pelgrim's rifle had been broken in the assault on Maloney, so the policeman added that he had not seen either of his co-defendants actually carrying a rifle.

Pelgrim confirmed that he went to search, spoke briefly with Konning, and then onto the railway line, at which point he heard shouting and turned to go back.

Hans Pelgrim. I did not see anything on the way back, but as soon as I got a clear sight without any bushes standing around, then I just saw at the same moment that Renoth was pushed away by the two soldiers and that the soldiers began to beat the pilot.

Lieutenant Milman. How far away were you from the beating when you first saw it?

HP. About 250 metres; that was about 30 metres behind the plane where the soldiers were beating the airman.

LM. Can you show us roughly on this diagram where the beating was taking place?

HP. They were coming down in the direction of the plane 25 to 30 metres from the plane. (Witness marks position on diagram.)

LM. At this time how was the pilot being beaten?

HP. I did not look at it long; I only thought: 'What can I do now', and as fast as I could I ran to the officers. I went up to Captain Kuehne – I did not know his name at the time, I only heard it later – and told him – I do not know the precise words I used – 'Why do not you do anything about this? Our work as policemen is finished now. Hereby the pilot has been given into your charge, into the charge of the *Wehrmacht*.'

LM. Did Captain Kuehne do anything about it?

HP. No.

LM. During that while, what was happening to the pilot?

HP. It happened so quickly, it happened in the twinkling of an eye; it happened so very quickly while I was speaking to Captain Kuehne. I saw that the pilot had got hold of the rifle and the soldier had also got hold of the rifle.

LM. What happened?

HP. I intervened and I wanted to stop him.

LM. How did you intervene?

HP. I jumped between them and tried to get the rifle.

LM. Did you succeed?

HP. No, I came somewhat too late.

LM. What happened?

HP. The soldier beat the pilot's skull in.

LM. With one blow?

HP. With one blow.

LM. Meanwhile what was happening to Renoth and Grabowski and Nieke; where were they?

HP. I did not notice that, I did not look that way, because I was so busy with the rifle and with the pilot.

LM. What was the next thing that happened?

HP. With this blow the butt broke off the rifle. The soldier still had the barrel in his hand and I took it away from him, the butt was lying on the ground and it was still connected with the strap of the rifle. I picked up the butt and then I heard a shot.

LM. What happened when the shot was fired?

HP. Then the pilot fell on his back.

Pelgrim continued the defence of Grabowski and Nieke, with a confirmation that he had not seen any of the accused hit the pilot, 'only the two soldiers'. And Pelgrim made sure the court was aware that he did not consider himself in charge at the scene. Milman's examination drew to a conclusion.

Lieutenant Milman. Have you during this war had custody of large numbers of prisoners of war?

Hans Pelgrim. We had much to do with them because they were all near or trying to get to the Dutch border; they were French, British and Dutch.

LM. Have there ever been any allegations of this type against you before?

HP. Such a thing has never happened here in Elten or in the neighbourhood, and I know that if the soldiers had not come down nothing would have happened.

After a 50-minute recess Dr Gobbels declined to cross-examine, and Captain Diamond, armed with inconsistencies, took to the floor. On presentation of his statement, Pelgrim admitted that it was his signature, 'Yes I made it willingly . . . it is not the truth; I have to cancel a few things.'

Captain Diamond. Will you tell the Court in what respects it is not the truth?

Hans Pelgrim. In one respect I know that it is not right, about the rifles. I could not state at the time who had carried the rifles, if it was Grabowski or Nieke, and I believe I have stated Grabowski, or whether I carried it myself. I did not know if Grabowski or Nieke was walking next to me.

CD. I will read out the passage as I have it in the statement: 'I do not know whether I had my Service rifle with me or my pistol while searching the woods. I think Nieke had my service rifle.' Do you say that that is untrue?

HP. The British interrogation officers told me I should think it over for some time, they would come back and would ask me again about this, but they never did come back.

CD. Why did you sign it if it was not true?

HP. I have not said that it was Nieke that carried the rifle, but I said I assumed that Nieke carried the rifle.

Kington-Blair-Oliphant. In the English text it says: 'I think Nieke had my Service rifle.'

CD. Now are you quite sure that you left your rifles near the aeroplane?

HP. One rifle.

CD. Did you give it to anybody.

HP. No, I left it at the plane.

CD. Did you ask anybody to look after it?

HP. I have thought some time about it, and the officers were standing near the plane; all of us from the car went to the aircraft.

CD. Was it a loaded rifle?

HP. No, it was not.

CD. You heard Renoth say this morning that on duty it is customary always to have your rifle loaded?

HP. Yes, I took the rifle with me not for myself but . . .

KBO. That is not an answer.

CD. Did you hear Renoth say this morning that it was customary when on duty always to have your rifle loaded?

HP. Yes.

CD. Is that correct?

HP. Yes, but while on duty we have the revolvers 08.

CD. If you brought the rifles along for Nieke and Grabowski, why did you not give them to them?

HP. I took the rifles with me because it might be a four-engined bomber with 13, 14 or 15 crew.

KBO. That is not an answer to the question that was asked.

CD. I will repeat the question. If you brought the rifles along for Nieke and Grabowski why did you not give them the rifles?

HP. That did not happen.

KBO. Why?

HP. I will make a picture of what happened again. All six of us went from the vehicle to the aircraft. After receiving instructions from Captain Kuehne to search the land around, we made up parties to search the land. Then I saw Kuehne . . .

KBO. The Court has heard all this before. You were asked why you did not give the rifles to the people for whom you have said you brought them?

HP. I wanted to explain it this way. The rifle was left near the plane and I went to Kuehne and did not go back to the plane.

Pelgrim simply had to keep the rifle, the bludgeon, out of his hands. Diamond was not going to back down on the policeman's change, repeating an excerpt from Pelgrim's statement: 'I do not know how the pilot got possession of the rifle. I assume he took it off me or Nieke in his desperation.' Pelgrim reaffirmed that he assumed that Nieke had the rifle.

Leicester-Warren. Are we to understand that today you are saying that you left the rifle standing up against the aeroplane?

Hans Pelgrim. Yes.

LW. Whereas on the 12 July you said that you assumed the pilot took the rifle off you or Nieke?

HP. I could not say anything definite on the 12 July.

LW. But surely on the 12 July you would have remembered what happened better than you do today?

HP. No; later on, on thinking it over it came back to my mind on account of the questions put to me.

LW. But this statement was read over to you and you signed it, was it not?

HP. Yes, but they are not definite.

Pelgrim's last statement is somewhat ambiguous. It is not clear who or what 'they' are. Diamond, however, moved on quickly and intimated through his questioning that since 12 July Pelgrim had had a chance to speak with Nieke to establish a new story. Diamond asked how he knew it was his rifle used to beat the pilot, Pelgrim replying that he recognised it on account of the light coloured wood, from about 10 metres away. Diamond looked to question Pelgrim over the actual shooting, but Kington-Blair-Oliphant jumped in, trying to clarify Pelgrim's story concerning where he had left the rifle.

Kington-Blair-Oliphant. Before you go on, there is a point about the evidence which has just been given. (To the witness) How do you explain now that the pilot got possession of your rifle?

Hans Pelgrim. I have not seen if the rifle was taken at first off the pilot or off the soldier.

KBO. Did you ever see these two soldiers near the aircraft where you left your rifle?

HP. I have taken the rifle off the soldier near the plane.

Captain Diamond. Before the beating started or while the beating was on did you see either of the two soldiers go near the plane.

HP. No.

CD. Do you think that one of the soldiers stopped beating in order to go to the plane and get your rifle?

HP. I have not seen who first of all took the rifle. While they were beating the pilot moved towards the plane where the rifle was.

CD. Did the beating stop at all or was it continuous?

HP. It was continuous until the hit with the rifle took place, and afterwards the pilot fell.

CD. Then if your story is correct it means that either one of the two soldiers or else the pilot had your rifle all the time?

HP. No, they had their hands and later on they had a stick and later when they came near the captains they have beaten with their hands and their feet.

Milman came to his client's aid: 'What he is trying to say, I think, is that whilst when this beating first started they were a little way away from the plane – that mark on the diagram is where the beating started – they then proceeded towards the plane.' 'That point was understood', stated the President, 'and furthermore he has said that neither of the people detached themselves from the fight'. Milman again tried to support his client; the fight was continuous until they came near the plane, 'where one of them picked up the rifle'. But Kington-Blair-Oliphant was quick to retort that Pelgrim had not stated that the fight was continuous.

Captain Diamond. You say you did not see anyone pick up your rifle?

Hans Pelgrim. No. When I asked the captain why he did not interfere, the captain pointed with both hands to the pilot, and then I looked and the pilot was near the plane. Both the soldiers and the pilot had their hands on the rifle. Then I jumped in between, but came late.

Pelgrim sought a further amendment to his statement. He had said that Renoth had gone right up to the pilot, aimed and fired into his head. But in court, if not before, Pelgrim had heard Renoth claim that the second shot had gone off by accident. It was an inconsistency he tried to explain away, saying he had not seen the second shot.

Captain Diamond. Did you see him fire a second shot?

Hans Pelgrim. No; he just took a few paces forward and then the second shot was fired.

CD. How do you know he came forward?

HP. I have seen it that he came a few paces forward.

CD. And then you very conveniently looked the other way?

HP. I got frightened when a shot was fired and I looked around and then Renoth came on a few paces.

CD. Then what did you do when Renoth went a few paces forward?

HP. I asked Renoth what he did and why he did it. He told me the captain has ordered him.

CD. What were you doing when the second shot was fired?

HP. I do not know what I did.

CD. You were looking at Renoth and talking to him immediately before it, were you not?

HP. Yes, and I looked and the shot went past me at a distance of about 30 centimetres.

CD. The second shot?

HP. The first shot.

CD. The first shot went past you about 30 centimetres away?

HP. Yes.

CD. Then Renoth came forward?

HP. No, immediately after the second shot, then Renoth came forward.

CD. Where were you looking when the second shot was fired?

HP. I do not remember. I saw the pilot fall down.

CD. When you say in your statement, 'For the second shot he came right up to the pilot and fired an aimed shot at his head', you were only guessing, were you?

HP. I assumed the shot went in the direction of the head of the pilot and I saw the pilot fall down.

Leicester-Warren. But when you [say] an 'aimed shot' what do you mean?

HP. I thought that Renoth wanted to make sure and gave a shot to the head of the pilot.

Captain Diamond. When did the pilot fall?

HP. Right after the first shot.

Kington-Blair-Oliphant. Did you see Renoth fire the second shot?

HP. No, I was looking at the pilot; I assumed that because I looked at the pilot.

Captain Diamond. Then how do you know it was a head shot?

HP. I assumed it because some dust went up near the head.

CD. You are assuming a great deal in your evidence, are you not?

HP. It is possible that the head has been hit.

CD. This cloud of dust you mentioned, had you ever heard of it or thought of it until you heard it mentioned in the witness-box this morning?

HP. Yes, I had thought of it before.

Having exposed serious inconsistencies in Pelgrim's account, Diamond gave way to Milman.

Lieutenant Milman. I do not wish to re-examine unless you are not yet clear how the soldiers got possession of Pelgrim's rifle. Is that now clear?

Kington-Blair-Oliphant. It is not at all clear. I am not convinced that they had possession of it at the moment. If you can make that point clear to the Court I shall be very grateful.

LM. When you went away to search you told us that you left your rifle by the plane?

Hans Pelgrim. Yes.

LM. Can you explain exactly where you left it?

HP. Yes I left the rifle in the corner of the wing and the body of the plane.

LM. Will you mark in this sketch map where you left the rifle? (Witness marks position in the corner formed by the rear part of the right wing and the body of the aircraft.)

LM. Whilst the fighting was going on how did the pilot move?

HP. He moved from the place where he was first hit by the soldiers in the direction of the plane.

LM. Did the fighting move towards the place where you left the rifle?

HP. Yes, towards the aircraft.

LM. Which side of the aircraft did the fighting move to?

HP. Before the aircraft and afterwards they went around the wings and over the wings of the plane; I do not know that exactly, but the wings were right on the ground.

LM. Where did you see the soldier with your rifle first?

HP. At the wing of the plane.

LM. Which wing?

HP. The right wing if you are looking in the direction of the movement of the plane.

LM. Where would that be in relation to your rifle?

HP. They went over the wings of the plane or round the plane while I was talking to the captain.

LM. Will you mark on this diagram where you first saw the soldier with your rifle? (The witness marks on the diagram the position of the *Wehrmacht* soldier with the rifle as just behind the right wing of the aircraft, about halfway between the wing tip and the fuselage.)

KBO. When you saw the *Wehrmacht* soldier with the rifle near the aeroplane, was that before the beating and fighting or during it?

HP. During the beating.

Pelgrim, when asked by Leicester-Warren, stated that he, Grabowski and Renoth had not spoken since seeing the English translation of their statements, which had been read to them in German.

Leicester-Warren. A witness has stated on oath that he saw you pushing and beating the pilot. Is that correct or not?

Hans Pelgrim. No, it is not possible that the witness has seen it.

LW. Is the Court to understand that you say you took no part in the fighting at all?

HP. I have not beaten and I have not kicked; on the contrary, I have tried to prevent it. (The Accused Pelgrim leaves the place from which he has given evidence.)

Chapter 16

AN ABSENCE
OF HUMAN FEELING

Following Hans Pelgrim's ordeal at the trial, Friedrich Grabowski prepared to take the stand and offer his defence. It is worthwhile, at this point, providing some background to Grabowski's involvement in the incident, and the aftermath. The year 1941 had been a tragic one for the Grabowskis. Friedrich's wife died – the cause of death officially registered as tuberculosis of the lungs – and he lost a young daughter. The family had moved to Elten, from East Prussia, in 1933, so that Friedrich could take up customs official duties. Prior to the move Friedrich had completed twelve years of military service. Before the war's end, Friedrich would remarry, to Elisabeth, almost eighteen years his junior, and together they brought up the two boys and one girl from the first marriage, Hilmar, Manfred and Ingeborg, all born in Elten. It would seem that Elisabeth and her stepchildren did not get on. To this day Manfred will not refer to Elisabeth as 'mother', just as his father's second wife.

As required for the new position in Elten, Friedrich joined the *NSDAP* party, and he left the Protestant Church because of his Nazi affiliations. On the morning of the incident in Franken's field on 16 September 1944, accompanied by Paul Nieke, he had been at the funeral of local retired police officer and *NSDAP* member Heinrich Heinemann, who had died of natural causes three days earlier. A few days before, his two sons had endured an experience that may well have influenced Friedrich's mindset on the fateful day.

Manfred and Hilmar both recall that a short time before the 17 September 1944 Allied landings at Arnhem, and therefore just before the incident involving their father in Franken's field, they had been sent home from school by their teachers because of an Allied air attack. They were walking home, separately, when they heard the sound of an aircraft overhead. Realising that it was not German, Manfred dived into a ditch, cowering as the aircraft flew on. Hilmar recalled: 'I was on my way home from school on Zevenaarer Strasse, very near to the railway tracks, where a train was standing. A fighter came in at low-level, flew directly over and shot at me. I leapt into the ditch next to the road. I could clearly see the head of the pilot.' Hilmar was sure the pilot had not shot at the train, although 'may be there was machine gun fire from the train at the fighter'. When the aircraft, which made only one pass, disappeared, Hilmar climbed out of the ditch, finding numerous empty cartridges. Terribly shaken by the whole incident, he would develop a stutter. He ran home and told his father.

Elisabeth and the children were evacuated to a farm north-east of Hanover towards the end of 1944; Friedrich remained in Elten. When the fighting ended Friedrich rejoined them and they headed back west, returning to Elten, setting off the day before the Russians arrived to take over from Allied forces. They were going to survive the peace; other members of Friedrich's family were not. His first wife's mother froze to death on a train, when the family fled from the advancing Soviet Army early in 1945. In 1946 Friedrich's mother would die of starvation in a camp in the Russian zone of occupation.

On his return to Elten, 'wanted' posters informed Friedrich of the Canadian investigators' desire to know his whereabouts. He wasted little time approaching the local representatives of the occupying power, was promptly arrested and put in gaol.

Grabowski, Friedrich Wilhelm
Oberzoelsekretav, Abteilungsfuhrer in Zolegrenzschutz (Customs Lt in charge of a customs border control in the sector)
I know that the following statement, which I am about to make voluntarily, can be used in court.

One morning in September 1944 I was in the town hall of Elten. A message was received there from two border control stations to the effect that an aircraft had come down in the direction of Babberich. Two officers were in the town hall at the time presumably to see Ortsgruppenleiter Holtkamp. The names of the two officers are unknown to me. As the officer had the intention of inspecting the crashed aircraft, my comrades, Nicke [sic] and Gendarme Renoth, and I joined them. Pelgrim joined us in the car en route. Pelgrim stopped at his house to pick up some weapons. Thereupon the following weapons were in the car: two service rifles and presumably the weapons of the officers and gendarmes. I personally carried no weapon. We then proceeded to the scene of the accident and left the car about 200 metres from the aircraft on the road leading to Franken's farm. From there we walked to the aircraft. A second aircraft was flying low overhead, forcing us to take cover. Most of those present at the scene took cover to the right of the aircraft while I took cover to the left. The two gendarmes Pelgrim and Renoth were over 100 meters apart, Renoth in front and Pelgrim behind. Nicke was with Pelgrim. After the aircraft had left, the pre-arranged search for the pilot began. Renoth found the pilot while taking cover in a shallow ditch near the country road which leads to the AA site. Renoth approached the aircraft with the pilot. I was about 80 to 100 meters away, walking toward the aircraft. The others were also gathering around. Suddenly two German soldiers appeared, apparently from the train which had been forced to stop by the fighter-bomber. The bigger of the two soldiers shouted, 'So this is how you treat our enemies here.' Foaming at the mouth he ran towards the pilot and the gendarme, shouting, 'He has shot my wife and child.' Thereupon he shoved the Gendarme Renoth aside, grabbed the pilot, whom Renoth was leading by the arm, and began to beat him with his fists. While fighting they moved towards the aircraft, where the others had already gathered. Renoth was also joined by the officers. At first the fighting took place to the right of the aircraft. When they arrived in the centre of the group the fighting turned off to the left. No one intervened actively on behalf of the pilot. I saw Pelgrim speaking to one of the officers. As the fighting turned off to the left, I noticed that one of the soldiers had a rifle in his hand. What was done with the rifle I do not know I assume the pilot was given a blow with it because he bled from nose and mouth and the rifle lay broken on the ground. Gendarme Pelgrim tried to pick up the rifle. The pilot was standing. Suddenly there was a rifle shot, which Renoth fired at the pilot from a distance of about 8 to 10 meters. At that moment I was standing 15 meters from the pilot and about 10 meters from Renoth. Near the latter stood the captains. I can no longer remember the positions where the others who were present stood. I only heard one shot fired, saw the pilot fall and left the group. I went to the car and drove back to Elten in the company of the two officers and Nicke. The two gendarmes and the two soldiers remained on the scene. Barton had appeared in the meantime. During the early afternoon I saw a lorry proceed to the site with the coffin which was presumably intended for the corpse.

To justify my having refrained from interceding for the pilot I give the following reasons: (a) I had no authority as the Gendarmerie and the *Wehrmacht* representatives were present, (b) according to the law in force at the time German officials were forbidden to take part, (c) I declare not to have beaten the pilot personally.

I declare that the above statements are true.

Mil Gov Prison

Bedburg

12 Jul 45

(signed) *Friedrich Grabowski*

Grabowski took the stand and again Milman's initial questioning set out basic facts. His client had been at a funeral that morning in his political leader uniform. He had gone to the town hall to collect his pushbike and while there heard of the crash and the two *Wehrmacht* officers expressed their desire for him to accompany them to the crash site. Grabowski confirmed he had gone in the car with the two *Wehrmacht* and the other accused.

> *Friedrich Grabowski*. We had a look at the aircraft and discussed where the pilot could be. Pelgrim asked a farmhand of Franken's if he knew anything about the pilot. During the time that Pelgrim asked that farmhand more fighter planes were in the air. They were circling round low getting near to a train that was standing on the railway track. As they came down very low to us we had to seek shelter from the planes. Before we had spread to search the country around and we dispersed. Pelgrim and Nieke left in a south easterly direction and Renoth . . . went north and I went west. The two officers stayed quite near the plane.
>
> *Lieutenant Milman*. How far did you proceed from the plane?
>
> *FG*. It was about sixty or seventy metres from the plane.
>
> *LM*. What was the next thing you saw?
>
> *FG*. When the fighters had left us we all got up and then we heard shouting; I believe it was Nieke who said 'I believe we have got the pilot'. I turned round and saw Renoth had the pilot.
>
> *LM*. At that time how far away were you from the plane?
>
> *FG*. I was away from the plane about fifty to sixty metres. And Renoth and the pilot at least eighty metres, in the northern direction from the plane moving towards the plane.
>
> *LM*. What was the next thing you saw?
>
> *FG*. Then I went over to the plane where the two officers were and then two German soldiers came running close past me.
>
> *LM*. Going in which direction?

FG. They came from the railway, from an easterly direction.

LM. Did these soldiers pass near you?

FG. Yes they passed quite near me.

Leicester-Warren. How near?

FG. Five metres.

LW. In which direction were they going?

FG. Running north to the place where Renoth and the pilot were standing.

LM. Where were you standing when they ran past you?

FG. I was standing at the plane, at the tail end of the plane.

LM. Where was Renoth and the pilot at this time?

FG. Renoth had gone with the pilot already towards the plane; possibly he was forty or fifty metres away from the plane.

LM. Meanwhile where were Pelgrim and Nieke?

FG. Pelgrim and Nieke were for this time a little over 100 metres away from the plane.

As they passed, Grabowski claimed hearing the soldiers shout: 'That way our enemies are treated here, who kill our wives and children'; they then took the pilot from Renoth and began beating him with their fists and a small 'truncheon'.

Lieutenant Milman. Did you up to this point see a rifle lying around anywhere?

Friedrich Grabowski. I have seen two rifles. One was carried by Renoth and the second one was carried by Pelgrim from the car to the plane.

LM. While you were standing when these soldiers passed you, did you see any rifle lying about there?

FG. There was no rifle there as long as the soldiers came to the aircraft with the pilot.

LM. Will you tell us in your own words what happened after the soldiers started hitting the pilot?

FG. When the soldiers started hitting the pilot he moved backwards towards the plane where the other people were standing. When the three men approached the nose of the aircraft, the place where the engine is fitted, Pelgrim and Nieke had arrived as well.

LM. At that time did you notice whether Pelgrim was carrying a rifle or not?

FG. No, I had not seen it.

Kington-Blair-Oliphant. Do you mean that Pelgrim was not carrying a rifle?

FG. Not carrying a rifle; as far as I remember no rifle. Pelgrim immediately went to the two officers and spoke with one captain. When I looked at the group the rifle was in the centre of it.

KBO. What group?

FG. The two soldiers and the pilot.

How had the soldiers got hold of the rifle? Grabowski could not say: 'I have seen that several hands were gripping the rifle and they fought for possession of it and moved about.' According to Grabowski, none of the other accused was involved in the beating, but Pelgrim did jump in among them and grab the long end of the rifle, at which point the butt had been broken and 'the pilot was standing with blood running over his face'. Then, 'everything went very quickly, a matter of seconds; I heard a shot, the pilot was hit and collapsed down to the ground'. Finally Milman asked Grabowski why he had not prevented the beating. 'I was not allowed to do so and I could not because the *Wehrmacht* and the police were over there.' Dr Gobbels declined to cross-examine. The court closed for 40 minutes.

Diamond immediately attacked a weakness in Grabowski's defence when asking why he had even gone to the scene. Grabowski answered: 'I must declare that I did not go as a political leader but as a customs official.' Taking contraband into enemy territory was not the usual practice of Allied fighter pilots. Diamond followed on, sarcastically: 'Did you think this pilot was smuggling something in to the country apart from bombs!' Grabowski responded: 'No not that, but I had special orders for that type of aircraft . . . I was leader of a customs border patrol and in that capacity I have been called by the post that noticed the plane crash down to go over there.'

Captain Diamond. What duty did you have to do when you got there?

Friedrich Grabowski. Our instructions were to take in custody all baled-out pilots, prisoners of war etcetera. I thought in this case that it concerned taking into custody the pilot of a plane that had crashed down, or more pilots.

CD. Was it still the duty of the customs officers to do this when the Army was represented or the police?

FG. When the *Wehrmacht* or the police were over there it was not my order.

CD. Then why did you go together with the police and the *Wehrmacht* officers?

FG. Because it was not quite sure what happened; when, for instance, in case of death or injury of people of the Customs Border patrol it is my duty and not the duty of the *Wehrmacht* or police to look after them.

CD. Had you any reason to believe there had been any injury or death to members of the organisation you referred to?

FG. I had no reason to believe that one of the men was killed or injured. If one of my men had taken the pilot into custody it was my duty to hand him over against a receipt to the *Wehrmacht* or the police.

CD. Would it not be true to say that the main reason you went along was to join in a lynching party?

FG. No, because I as a political leader never was called up or 'phoned up when a plane came down.

CD. Is this a case of split personality, that as a political leader you were never told and as a customs official you were always told?

FG. As a political leader I was never called up, but as a customs official I always was; the Party had nothing to do with it.

Diamond was not prepared to let the matter rest, and shortly after Grabowski was again trying to distance himself from any responsibility at the scene.

> *Captain Diamond.* Were you prepared to go searching for a pilot who might possibly have been armed?
> *Friedrich Grabowski.* It could be possible, but I assumed that the people of the Customs were standing near the plane.
> CD. When you got to the plane and found that they were not there were you still prepared to go looking for a possible armed pilot still without being armed yourself?
> FG. When I arrived at the scene where the plane came down and I did not find any Customs officials, then my job was finished and I was just an on-looker.

A mere on-looker? Diamond remained cynical. Then why had Grabowski not remained at the aircraft, or returned to the car?

Captain Diamond. But you were given an order to go searching in a
    particular direction, were you not?
Friedrich Grabowski. I was not ordered.
CD. Did you go on your own accord then?
FG. I went because the fighters were still circling around and I went
    to lay down in the meadow.
CD. Did you take no part in the search at all?
FG. No, the affair was finished because when we got up the pilot was
    there already.
CD. It would be untrue then to say that you, Nieke, Pelgrim and
    Renoth all got orders to go off in various directions to search for
    the pilot?
FG. It is not untrue, because we were standing together, and the
    officers said that it was not an order for me, it did not apply to me,
    I had nothing to do with it; I was a private person over there.

Grabowski accepted that his written statement was mostly accurate but
that he had seen Pelgrim with a rifle only from the car to the aircraft, 'but
afterwards not'. And when questioned on when he had seen Pelgrim try
to take the rifle, he answered 'when Pelgrim approached to get hold of
the rifle, then the blow had been given already and the rifle was broken'.

Captain Diamond. You did not see the blow yourself?
Friedrich Grabowski. No, not at that moment; I must have looked some-
    where else.
CD. It was a very convenient time to look somewhere else, was it not?
FG. No, I was just changing my place and walked around the plane
    and around the group and have not seen anything.
CD. Why did you not try to help the pilot?
FG. I could not do that.
CD. Why not?
FG. Because it was a matter for officers, and I was over there as a
    private person.
CD. There was murder being committed before your eyes, was there
    not?
FG. It did not look that way, and none of the people expected that it
    would turn out to be so bad.
CD. Please answer as to what you yourself expected. Murder was being
    committed in front of your eyes, was it not?

FG. I could not say that; there was a beating going on but no murdering.

CD. But the pilot is not alive today, is he?

FG. No.

CD. And because you were a private citizen murder was no affair of yours?

FG. I was a private person, I had no right to intervene in matters of the *Wehrmacht*.

CD. You are a human being, are you not, or are you?

FG. Yes, I am a human being.

CD. Do you not think it is up to you to prevent murder if you see it being committed?

FG Yes, not only in my case but in the case of all the other Accused human feelings rose up.

CD. But you managed to suppress them, did you not?

FG. One could not suppress his feelings and one did not want to do so; you had to subject yourself to the rules and regulations of the country.

CD. I suppose it was breaking your heart to watch this pilot being murdered?

FG. I must say that I was not indifferent in this killing. Intervening for my part was impossible.

Grabowski confirmed hearing Renoth fire, but one shot only. He had not heard any order to shoot, but had 'assumed it'. Diamond read back part of Grabowski's statement: 'To justify my having refrained from interceding for the pilot I give the following reasons: (a) I had no authority as the Gendarmerie and *Wehrmacht* representatives were present. (b) According to the law in force at the time, German officials were forbidden to take part.' 'Exactly what do you mean by that?' asked Diamond.

Friedrich Grabowski. I mean that supposing I had entered the scene and taken it up with the pilot, I would have been liable to punishment according to the law then in existence.

Captain Diamond. Punishment for what?

FG. That would be called treason to the population.

CD. You say that according to the regulations German officials are forbidden to take part. Forbidden to take part in what?

FG. That means taking part for the pilot or intervening on behalf of the pilot.

CD. They were forbidden to intervene on behalf of the pilot?

FG. Yes that was forbidden.

CD. Was that forbidden to you as a Customs officer or as a Party leader or what?

FG. As a Customs officer; the Party had nothing to do with it.

CD. As a human being did you have no obligation at all?

FG. The law was made to suppress human feelings.

CD. You say in your evidence: 'When I looked at the group a rifle was in the middle'?

FG. Yes.

CD. Whereabouts in the middle?

FG. In between the two soldiers and the pilot.

CD. On the ground?

FG. In the air, about the height of the heads.

CD. Was it forbidden to you to intervene on behalf of the lynching party?

FG. In a general case more people were about, they could not have intervened either.

CD. You told the Court that you are forbidden as a Customs official to intervene on behalf of the pilot?

FG. As an official and generally.

CD. Supposing you saw the pilot getting the better of the people who were attacking him, are you equally forbidden to interfere on their behalf?

FG. That case would never have happened.

CD. Was it forbidden to you in such a case to help against the pilot?

FG. I do not understand.

CD. Were you forbidden to take part in the ill-treatment of the pilot yourself?

FG. In case there had been a group of civilians it would have been different. Here it was a matter of soldiers and police.

CD. Will you answer the question. Was it forbidden to you to take any part in the ill-treatment of pilots?

FG. No, it was not forbidden me to ill-treat pilots. On the contrary when other men have got hold of a pilot then we were obliged to look after his life as long as they were handed over to a *Wehrmacht* or police station.

CD. Perhaps I can clear that up. Is it not correct to say that you were encouraged to ill-treat pilots?

FG.   No, the instruction I had just spoken about is right, and before that we have handled more airmen.

There seemed to be an impasse, yet Diamond persevered. 'Is it not correct to say that if you had a pilot in your custody you had to look after him, but if anybody tried to lynch a pilot you were forbidden to interfere?' Grabowski persisted with his 'on-looker' defence; when it concerned soldiers he could not do anything. 'What', asked an unsatisfied Kington-Blair-Oliphant, 'were the orders that you received as a Customs official about enemy pilots?'

> *Friedrich Grabowski.* The order was as follows: all men who got hold of a pilot had to call me up by telephone.
> *Kington-Blair-Oliphant.* Are you refusing to answer the questions?
> FG.   No.
> KBO.   Once more I ask you: what were the orders that you received as a Customs official about what you had to do or had not to do with enemy pilots?
> FG.   I have said that all pilots we got hold of were searched for weapons, the material they carried put together, and handed over to the police or to the *Wehrmacht* in case there was a *Wehrmacht* unit in the place, the handing over had to take place against a receipt.

Captain Diamond's patience ran out, telling the court he did not 'intend to pursue this somewhat fruitless line of questioning'. Diamond asked Grabowski if, after the pilot had been shot, he had returned in the car, with Nieke, 'because your morning's work was done?'

> *Friedrich Grabowski.* No, I wanted to go away before.
> *Captain Diamond.* Why did you not?
> FG.   Because I had nothing to do over there; I could not intervene, I could not do anything.
> CD.   You said you wanted to go away; why did you not?
> FG.   The last phase of this business, when the shot had not been fired, I would not have been a witness of this.

Once again Kington-Blair-Oliphant jumped in: 'I want a straight answer to that question.' Diamond tried again: 'You said you wanted to go earlier.

Why did you not go?' To which Grabowski replied: 'Because I was not over there yet for a long time.' Kington-Blair-Oliphant's frustration boiled over. 'Answer the questions that are put to you. You have told the Court that you had no duty at the scene at all?'

Friedrich Grabowski. Yes.

Kington-Blair-Oliphant. You have told the Court that you did not want to stay there?

FG. Yes.

KBO. Then why did you stay there?

FG. I had nothing to do over there because my men were not over there.

KBO. Why did you stay there? Why did you not go away at once?

FG. I wanted to see if the pilot was taken into custody and taken with us in the car.

Diamond took on the questioning. 'Were you satisfied with what you saw?'

Friedrich Grabowski. I was not satisfied.

Captain Diamond. I put it to you that you went there with one object, that was to assist in a lynching which you knew was going to take place?

FG. I did not go there with that intention, I simply went on duty.

The confrontation was over. Diamond's cross-examination concluded. Milman decided not to re-examine.

Chapter 17

'TO BE OR NOT TO BE'

Paul Nieke was the last of the defendants to take the stand at the trial in Elten. Shortly after the incident in Franken's field on 16 September 1944 Nieke and his close family had left the Elten area. Seven months later his family had been subject to an atrocity. But, in January 1946, he was defending himself against the accusation of a war crime.

Paul was born on 17 October 1903 in Köpenick, Berlin, and grew up in Saxonia, near the Polish border. At the age of 21 he joined the German army, completing twelve years of service before taking up the offer of a customs officer position in 1937 – a position that required membership of the *NSDAP*. His father held the same profession. On 17 April 1942 Paul moved with his close family to Elten, living in a house provided by the customs authorities on von Lochnerstrasse, near to the house of his superior, Friedrich Grabowski. The rest of his family remained in the Berlin area. It is not known if any of the family experienced first hand the Allied bombing campaign against the city during the winter of 1943–4, but they were undoubtedly aware of the scale of the attack and the suffering of the local population. Paul left Elten, with his family, in October 1944, for a new posting, to Torgelow, near Stettin, on the Baltic coast.

The Soviet army took Stettin in April 1945 and began exacting their own form of humiliating revenge upon the local population, including the Niekes. When soldiers took hold of Paul's wife and set about repeatedly raping her, there was little he could do with a gun pressed firmly to his head. When they reported the assault and brutal humiliation to the Russian commanding officer, he questioned his men, but nothing came of it.

Shortly after the rape incident the Niekes discussed leaving the area, to return to Elten and the British zone of occupation. Paul's wife was fearful that her husband might have to account for his involvement in the death of the pilot in September 1944. Paul reassured her that there would be no problems; he had nothing to feel guilty about.

But on their return to Elten, Paul was indeed arrested and taken to Recklinghausen prison, where, undernourished and weak, he claims to have been assaulted by Polish guards. There is no evidence of Paul ever making a statement concerning the incident in Franken's field. It appears that the trial was his first opportunity officially to present his defence.

Paul Nieke's opening questioning added little that was not already in evidence. Renoth and Pelgrim carried a rifle to the plane, and, after taking cover from the aircraft that were still flying overhead, Nieke had seen Renoth with the pilot. He called to Pelgrim, although he had not seen a rifle on him. 'Will you tell us when you first saw anything happening to the pilot?' asked Milman.

Paul Nieke. I had turned around to Pelgrim and waited till Pelgrim was coming my way, and when I turned around I saw that two soldiers were just there and pushed aside Pelgrim.

Lieutenant Milman. Do you mean Pelgrim? Are you sure that it was Pelgrim they pushed aside?

PN. Renoth.

LM. What else did you see?

PN. Then the two soldiers started beating the pilot.

LM. What were they beating him with?

PN. With fists.

LM. How far away from the aeroplane was this beating taking place?

PN. The place where the pilot was taken from Renoth was about 50 to 60 paces from the plane.

Nieke told how the beating had carried on all the way to the plane. Meanwhile, Pelgrim was 'speaking excitedly' to the officer.

Paul Nieke. By that time the pilot had reached the place behind the wings, somewhere in the middle of the plane; he always went backwards that way.

Lieutenant Milman. What happened there?

PN. Then I looked at Pelgrim and the officers and saw that Pelgrim turned around abruptly and sprang to the group. One of the soldiers had a rifle. The pilot gripped the butt and the soldier took the rifle out of the pilot's hands. The butt of the rifle went up. At that moment Renoth – I mean Pelgrim – sprang in the direction of them, but he came too late.

LM. Did you see Renoth do anything after that?

PN. Renoth was standing near the officers. After that affair with the rifle I saw that Renoth moved a few paces towards the plane and then all of a sudden a shot was fired and the pilot collapsed, fell down to the ground and lay on his back.

Nieke added that he had not struck the pilot; indeed none of the six men in the car had; that Renoth fired a second shot and that he could not intervene, 'What could I do all by myself? It was a purely *Wehrmacht* affair.'

Dr Gobbels declined to cross-examine, and Diamond stood to confront Nieke. After reconfirming that the defendant had seen Renoth fire two shots, Diamond challenged Nieke on who had possession of the rifle used in the assault.

> *Paul Nieke.* When we were at the Town Hall and it was clear that we were to go down to that place I, as Border Control man, said: 'We do not know what will be up near the plane. If there is a bomber plane there with a large crew we will only be a few men ourselves and we would be without any arms'; but after that time we did not speak of it at all, and when we came to the place and saw that it was a fighter plane, then we knew that there could only be one pilot.
>
> *Captain Diamond.* When you were told to go searching for the pilot did you go?
>
> *PN.* Yes, I went; I walked alongside of Pelgrim.
>
> *CD.* How near to him?
>
> *PN.* The distance varied; it could have been 50 metres or 80 metres or it could have been even less than 50.
>
> *CD.* Were you keeping near to Pelgrim so as to have the benefit of protection from his weapon?
>
> *PN.* Yes, but that would not have been necessary because there was only one pilot.

Nieke, perhaps inadvertently, had admitted that Pelgrim was armed when he moved away from the aircraft. He had not stated, however, whether it was with a pistol or a rifle. Diamond may have missed an opportunity to counter Pelgrim's claim of leaving the rifle at the plane.

> *Captain Diamond.* But he might have been armed, might he not, that one pilot?
>
> *Paul Nieke.* Yes, but one man alone would never have started anything against six other people.
>
> *CD.* But there is no objection to six starting against one, is there?
>
> *PN.* There were so many prisoners of war in this neighbourhood and so many airmen came down and nothing ever happened here.

CD. Except this one time?

PN. Yes. I often was on a recovery party of several airmen and also several injured airmen who came down, and we treated them all the same, we made no difference at all whether they were German airmen or Allied airmen.

CD. In that case German pilots must have been treated very roughly, must they not?

PN. How must I take that?

CD. You said in your evidence: 'The officers told us to search the surroundings as the pilot might be injured'?

PN. I assume that; I think that is what he meant.

CD. They did not actually say that?

PN. I assume that he meant that.

Diamond asked: 'Is it not extraordinary how everybody in this case seems ready to assume so many things?', but Leicester-Warren rebuked the prosecutor, before the witness had a chance to respond, as having passed 'comment'. Diamond moved on to the rifle, asking Nieke if he had seen Pelgrim put it down.

Paul Nieke. I only knew that Pelgrim carried his rifle up to the plane, and after that when he went up to Konnen [Konning] that he had not a rifle any longer, and after that time I never saw him with a rifle.

Captain Diamond. Did you see him put it down?

PN. No. We all took a look at the plane and then I did not notice that.

CD. Did you not think it strange that when Pelgrim brought a rifle for your benefit it was not given to you?

PN. Yes, it was not necessary because it was only a plane with one pilot.

Nieke claimed that the soldiers had the stick prior to being at the plane, and that he had seen the butt of a rifle come down, and he reconfirmed that Pelgrim had sprung into the group after the butt had been broken. Diamond questioned Nieke on Renoth's actions.

Captain Diamond. Did you hear Renoth being given an order to shoot?

Paul Nieke. I heard one of the captains calling out something more than once to Renoth.

CD. Do you know what he called out?

PN. No.

CD. How do you know he called out more than once?

PN. I heard it; the captain got more excited every moment.

CD. How far away were you from the captain?

PN. That varied; sometimes it was 8 metres, sometimes it was 50 metres.

CD. How far away were you standing when you heard this captain shout something which you could not hear?

PN. It would be too strong to say that he called out; he said something to him.

CD. How far away were you from the captain when he said something to him?

PN. 10 metres.

CD. Was anybody else standing nearer to the captain than you were?

PN. Yes.

CD. Who?

PN. Pelgrim.

CD. How far was Pelgrim from the captain?

PN. Three or four metres.

CD. Do you think he can have failed to hear what the captain said to Renoth?

PN. He really should have heard it.

CD. Whatever it was that the captain said to Renoth, was this immediately before Renoth fired?

PN. Then Renoth moved away some paces and shot.

CD. Did you see the captain reach for his own pistol?

PN. No.

CD. But you were watching him the whole time that he was talking to Renoth?

PN. No, I only heard the voices.

Diamond's cross-examination drew to a close with him accusing Nieke of going to the crash to take part in a lynching. He simply replied 'No'.

Captain Diamond. Do you think it would have been better to walk than stand and witness a murder?

Paul Nieke. With such an ending to the case, we never thought the thing would end in such a way. We all expected that when the group with the soldiers should come nearer to the officers that the officers would at least know their duty and would do something to their own people.

CD. How do you know what the others were expecting?

PN. Nothing has ever happened here.

CD. You are telling the Court that you were all expecting such-and-such would happen. How do you know what the others were expecting?

PN. I know my other three comrades as far as that. I know no one of them could commit such an act.

CD. But you can all stand by and watch it being committed, can you not?

PN. It all happened in such a very short time that you never knew what to say or what to do, because it had already happened.

CD. And one of these comrades who would not do such a thing did in fact shoot the pilot?

PN. So far as I heard from him he had been ordered to do that. I saw this order from Captain Kuehne himself.

Diamond's cross-examination concluded, and, after Milman had declined to re-examine, Kington-Blair Oliphant had questions of his own, asking Nieke, 'When did you see this order?'

Paul Nieke. It could be about eight days later, but I cannot say for sure that it was eight days.

Kington-Blair Oliphant. Where was this?

PN. That was at my office, and I think that Barton ordered Renoth to send it to the Landrats at Wesel.

KBO. Why should this order be in your office?

PN. Renoth lives at Mordyke, and the road leading from his house to the Town Hall passes my house, and then he came in and showed me this order.

KBO. Did he make any comment about it when he showed it to you?

PN. He told me that he had got the order to see to it that he got a written order, and now showed me that he had the order.

Nieke left that stand at 1945 hours and the court closed for the night.

The following morning Milman brought his defence to a conclusion, introducing a number of witnesses who claimed to have spoken to soldiers who had bragged about their involvement in the incident. A Maria Schamschat told the court that at about four o'clock on the afternoon of 16 September she had been standing with her father and mother, several soldiers and a small 9-year-old girl, looking at the crashed aircraft.

> Then a soldier came up to us and he spoke to us about the plane, about where they were going to bomb and things like that. Then he told us without being asked, I think, 'This morning I beat one up' . . . He told us, 'I came from Holland and while I was on the road I saw the plane landing. I went up to the plane, took away a rifle from a Customs official and beat him down with the butt of the rifle'. . . My father told him, 'You have not done an honourable thing by that.' After that he told us, 'We never take prisoners.'

When Diamond had his chance to put his questions, he asked, 'Are you sure this soldier said that he took a rifle away from a Customs official?' 'Yes,' she replied. Diamond asked, 'Did he say how he knew it was a Customs official?', 'No,' Maria replied, 'he did not say.'

Bernhard Jansen, Maria Schamschat's father, next gave evidence, backing up his daughter's testimony.

> While we were standing there he [the soldier] came up the hill . . . and he said, 'I beat one up today.' He came from Holland and he saw that the plane landed there and then he took a rifle away from a Customs official and then he beat him down with it. . . . I told him he did not get any honour by this . . . He said, 'I never take prisoners', and after that I went away because I did not want anything to do with him.

Diamond had only a few brief questions, Jansen testifying that the soldier wore black uniform and that in his opinion he was from a panzer unit and wore the *Totenkopf*.

Next to give evidence for the defence was physician Dr Hans Uhlenbrock, who had practised in Elten for the past forty-eight years; he stated that he had known Pelgrim since his youth: 'I was born here at Elten and Pelgrim too.' But all he added to the defence was that he considered Pelgrim 'a good and a cheery fellow'. Neither Gobbels nor Diamond had any questions.

Milman next sought to call Dr Weyer, and, following some legal debate on whether he was allowed to call someone who had already been a prosecution witness, to which Diamond did not object, Weyer once more stood to give evidence. Weyer commented on the character of Grabowski, whom he had known as *Postenführer* during the previous war and come to know as 'a man with a sense of duty. Further personal contact with him I did not have, but the impression I received of him of the work together between soldier and Customs official and *Burgomeister* was a good one.'

With the defence case closed, Dr Gobbels was first given the opportunity to sum up and address the court.

The Accused Renoth has said that he did not feel himself guilty. That question was put to his conscience and was answered by that. You, however, have to decide in accordance with the laws of the Allied Nations if he is guilty of a war crime. I in my defence are subject to those laws.

Renoth is a simple man. His intelligence is little developed. He is used to obey. He is not used to giving orders. The war makes out of the forester with petty duties a policeman with a greater responsibility.[1]

The Prosecution says that the Accused have acted together. To begin with it is a question if they went to the place of the landing with a previously made up plan. I believe that such was not the case. The improvised way in which the passengers were collected proves my opinion that every one in his own way wanted to perform his duty over there.

I cannot come to the conclusion that a plan was made up at the landing place. Anyhow, Renoth went all by himself searching for the pilot of the single-seater. He took prisoner the pilot, ascertained that he was without weapons and he took him in a correct manner to the aircraft. It seems that the pilot and he even talked to one another. There can be no doubt about it that on the way to the plane he committed no ill-treatment. It is also sure that he took no part in the bad ill-treatment which took place immediately afterwards. You have heard it from the witness named Bosmann. That he did not deliver the blow with the butt end of the rifle is clear because not his but the second rifle was broken.

I ask myself more as a human being than as a lawyer if the further things that happened, including the blow with the rifle, could have been prevented by personal action against those that took part in it. The answer is difficult. But I think of the possibility that from a certain distance things happened so quickly that he could not make a proper decision and that the act had taken place already before he could intervene. Perhaps he too thought that the *Wehrmacht* officers had taken over the responsibility from him for subsequent events.

Renoth approached the group around the aircraft when the blow with the rifle butt had been already given. We all know how beaten and injured the head of the unknown airman was at that time. Harder natures than the Accused Renoth could not stand the sight of it. Major Balfour has established the complete absence of the right side of the skull. It has been crushed in. Furthermore he says that the cause of death was the blow on the head, which completely shattered the skull. The blow on the head was in itself the cause of the death. To the question whether injuries of this nature to a live man would result in his death, he answers: 'Instantaneous death, yes.'

It was key to Renoth's defence. A dead man cannot be murdered. Gobbels was trying to show that Maloney was dead before he was shot. Gobbels might have better served his client by further developing the argument that essentially the pilot was beaten to death, with no evidence of Renoth taking part in the beating. The pilot was going to die as a result of an assault by others. And that, perhaps, is why he did not divert blame, as he would have been focusing guilt on the other defendants. 'At this moment, the last act of the tragedy, Captain Kuehne gives Renoth the order to shoot at the pilot. This order is repeated, and then Renoth fires. A second shot leaves his rifle. I do believe that the second shot was an accident.'

Gobbels could have developed the premiss that this was a mercy killing. Something abhorrent, the vicious beating, had already happened, and the pilot was clearly in a terrible condition. There was no direct evidence presented of Renoth bearing any ill will to the pilot, backed by his actions on finding Maloney. It was the others present who had ferociously attacked a defenceless prisoner. Describing Renoth's actions as an 'act of mercy', however small, might have helped his case, but again it would have shifted blame to the other defendants.

Gobbels continued his summation, speculating: 'But what may have happened in his [Renoth's] conscience? We do not know.' Surely that was something he could have made clear when examining his client.

Pity, blind obedience; anyhow, it was not revenge and brutality. We do not know if his 'not guilty' will be confirmed by God. You know the words of the King in Hamlet: 'But it is not so above, There is no shuffling, there the action lies in his true nature; and we ourselves compelled even to the teeth and forehead of our faults to give in evidence.' You decide as his earthly judges in accordance with law, order and justice. You decided for Renoth the question: 'To be or not to be.'

Milman summed up the defence of Pelgrim, Grabowski and Nieke, in English, without a translation, as accepted by Gobbels. Milman began by attacking Bosmann's testimony, which he believed was at the heart of the case.

The Prosecution allege that the three Accused with Renoth went to the scene of the crash and there proceeded to commit a foul murder. To substantiate this they produce one man, the most important witness. On his word, in the submission of the Defence, depends the whole case for and against the Accused. That witness is Johann Bosmann. He says that he went across the fields, he was in the area of the crashed aircraft and he only recognised Pelgrim, a man who he admits to not liking, and Renoth. He did not recognise two other men who must have been well-known to him. He does not see there anything of two *Wehrmacht* captains. Yet all the Accused state quite fairly that they were there, and Franken's evidence tends to corroborate this. He sees a beating going on with a rifle. He says that three or four rifles were used. I think it must be abundantly clear that only one rifle was used in this attack.

It is the submission of the Defence that this man Bosmann went to the scene, he saw fighting going on, but either through his lack of memory or his fear of looking at the scene he did not see clearly what was taking place, but he has picked out these various details from his friends and from what he believes happened, and it is my submission that his evidence should be viewed with a very great amount of suspicion.

Barton himself saw a soldier there, and he again confirms that there were in fact these two *Wehrmacht* officers there, whereas the witness Bosmann says he did not see them at all. On this man's evidence must to a large degree depend the fate of all the Accused. Having made these suggestions as to his defence on these points, I would like to say that I myself cannot think that this evidence is sufficient.

Throughout this hearing and right from the time of the scene the Accused have maintained the story that there were two soldiers there who did the actual beating of the pilot, and you have heard today two witnesses come and testify that they spoke to a soldier in this area who admitted that he had beaten a pilot. It is always possible to make one witness contradict another in minor degree; but throughout all this time and throughout this hearing the Accused have maintained at all times the same fact, that these two soldiers were there and they [i.e. the Accused] were not in any way responsible for this.

However, there can be no doubt that concerted action could have done something to save the pilot, that the Accused were present and that they witnessed this beating and they took no active part to stop it or to help the pilot. That is morally culpable, I agree; but does it as such constitute a crime? It is my submission that it does not. To prove an offence against these men on that ground it is essential that the Prosecution should have proved that the Accused acted in concert with the persons who committed the offence and aided and abetted them to commit that offence. Mere presence as such is not sufficient to find a man guilty of the crime of being a principal in the second degree.

The weight of the burden of proof in this case is always on the Prosecution, and it is my submission that the Prosecution have failed to discharge their duty, and that if any doubt remains in your mind that doubt must be exercised on behalf of the Accused in accordance with the principles of English law. In weighing the evidence you will no doubt be well advised as to the value of certain evidence which has been admitted and the proper weight to be attached to it.

Diamond prepared to make his closing arguments, again to be in English without translation and accepted by both Milman and Gobbels. He opened, clarifying that the burden of proof did indeed rest with the prosecution, beyond reasonable doubt, 'the sort of doubt to which you as ordinary men would lend weight in the normal conduct of your everyday affairs, the sort of doubt which would influence your actions one way or another'.

In my submission on the evidence there can be no doubt that a war crime was committed. Here you have an Allied pilot, probably an Australian, escaping unhurt from a crashed aircraft, surrendering himself or being captured without resistance by a German policeman, going with him without resistance and then set upon and brutally murdered. That is contrary to all the laws and usages of war with regard to the treatment of prisoners of war . . . and that undoubtedly amounted to a war crime . . .

Let me first of all deal with Renoth, who perhaps stands in rather a different category from the others. There is not the slightest doubt that Renoth fired a shot at the pilot, that the pilot was standing before the shot was fired and that when the shot was fired the pilot collapsed, apparently dead.

Renoth's answer to that is two-fold. Firstly he says: 'This was a dying man.' Secondly he says: 'I was given orders by a superior officer which I had to obey.'

Diamond referred to an extract from *The Manual of Military Law*:

A court confronted with the plea of superior orders adduced in justification of a war crime is bound to take into consideration the fact that obedience to military orders, not obviously unlawful, is the duty of every member of the armed forces and that the latter cannot, in conditions of war discipline, be expected to weigh scrupulously the legal merits of the order received. The question, however, is governed by the major principle that members of the armed forces are bound to obey lawful orders only and that they cannot therefore escape liability if, in obedience to a command, they commit acts which both violate unchallenged rules of warfare and outrage the general sentiment of humanity.

Diamond was clear, in his opinion, that 'there can be no doubt that shooting at a pilot in this case was an act which violated beyond doubt both the rules of warfare and outraged the general feelings of humanity'. Diamond drew on precedent to bolster his position, referring to the *Llandovery Castle* case, 'which was tried at Leipzig before a German court', at which the court found that 'the defence that an accused acted on superior orders was no defence if the order was obviously an unlawful and criminal one'. Diamond closed that point of his summation succinctly – 'So much for that line of defence' – and moved on to the claim that the pilot was already dying. Gobbels had tried to defend his client on the basis that the beating had been the cause of death. Diamond's response was simple. In that Maloney was standing at the time the rifle trigger was pulled; he was still alive.

There is the evidence that the man was standing on his feet at the time when the shot was fired, and further that Renoth was ordered to fire. According to his own story Renoth said, 'I was ordered to fire. I was so shaken that I did nothing and I was ordered again', and as far as he could recall no further beating took place during that time – I think that is on the record – and throughout all that time the victim was still standing on his feet.

Diamond quoted from Archbold, the leading English and Welsh criminal lawyer's text.

There is a proposition which in my submission covers this case: 'If a man is suffering from a disease, which in all likelihood would terminate his life in a short time, and another gives him a wound or hurt which hastens his death, this is such a killing as constitutes murder (according to Hale) or at the least manslaughter.' If Renoth by his shot shortened the life of the pilot, even if only by a matter of seconds, then that is such an act as constitutes murder in English criminal law, and in my submission this was such an act as constitutes a war crime under the laws and usages of war. In addition it might not be unprofitable to consider the story of the second shot that was fired . . . Renoth said that the second one was an accident due to faulty loading. Asked why he was loading his rifle after having shot the pilot he said: 'We always go round with our rifles loaded when on duty.' If that carries conviction, you may wonder if faulty loading is likely to cause a rifle to explode; and you may also wonder how much truth there was in the statement made by Pelgrim on the 12 July in which he said: 'During the first shot Renoth was behind me. For the second shot he came right up to the pilot and fired an aimed shot at his head', and then goes on to say: 'The last shot had torn the back of the head apart.'

The prosecutor dismissed the defendants' attempts to make changes to their original statements.

I would remind the Court that all these three Accused who made these statements, when confronted with them in the box made various amendments. Pelgrim with regard to this statement said: 'I only assumed that he had gone up and fired an aimed shot', in the same way as so many of the Accused have assumed so many things. The statements were made before the three Accused had had an opportunity of getting together and discussing things whereas, as you heard in the box, they have been together since November, and it is not unlikely that they should have decided that it is better to hang together rather than separately.

Diamond sought to address an apparent inconsistency in Major Balfour's medical evidence: that the blow that caused the injuries to the skull, revealed at post-mortem, would be fatal and death instantaneous. Yet the pilot had been shot while standing.

> I would suggest this for the consideration of the Court that it is not impossible that some of the more extensive injuries to the skull might have taken place after the shot was fired, because it passes the bounds of comprehension how a man with injuries of that sort to his skull could be still on his feet. However, that is merely a matter of conjecture; unfortunately Major Balfour is not available to make clear his evidence. He did also make a statement in his evidence that the body when he examined it was in such a state of decomposition that there might very easily have been a shot wound in the body without him being able to discern it, presumably provided it did not touch any bone structure.

Diamond finished his summation against Renoth. He could find no reasonable doubt, and the policeman was guilty as charged: 'He fired and he hit the pilot. The pilot was still alive at the time he fired. Although he may have received orders from his superior officer, it is no defence, although the pilot might have been dying at that time.'

Diamond turned his attention to Pelgrim, Nieke and Grabowski, beginning with the crucial testimony of Johann Bosmann. 'In my submission Johann Bosmann was a good and frank witness and his evidence was clear.' Diamond referred back to Bosmann's testimony when asked about whom he had seen at the scene of the incident, when the beating was taking place. The shorthand writer read back from the trial transcript.

Captain Diamond. Did you recognise any of them at that time?
Johann Bosmann. Yes, then I recognised.
CD.   Who did you recognise?
JB.   Pelgrim and Renoth.
CD.   Would you look round and see whether either of those men is in Court?
JB.   *That* is Renoth and *that* is Pelgrim. (Indicating the Accused Renoth and Pelgrim.)

CD.   You say there were four men standing together and a fifth man standing apart. Where were Renoth and Pelgrim amongst these men?

JB.   Pelgrim was with the four and Renoth was standing apart.

CD.   Do you mean Pelgrim was one of the four.

JB.   Yes.

CD.   Pelgrim was one of the four that were standing together and Renoth was the one who was standing aside?

JB.   Yes.

CD.   What clothes were Renoth and Pelgrim wearing?

JB.   They were wearing field grey uniforms.

CD.   What were the other three people wearing?

JB.   Two were wearing SA uniforms and the other one was wearing field grey.

CD.   What colour is the SA uniform?

JB.   Brown.

Captain Diamond once again addressed the court.

The Court will remember that police uniform and *Wehrmacht* uniform are identical, the only difference being in the hat. Grabowski himself said there was nobody else present in brown uniform except he and Nieke, and therefore when Bosmann refers to two men in SA uniform there can be no doubt that the two men are Grabowski and Nieke.

Diamond again asked the shorthand writer to read back two specific excerpts from the trial transcript. The first was during Diamond's questioning.

Captain Diamond. You say you saw pushing. Who was pushing and who was pushed?

Johann Bosmann. The pilot was being pushed but, who was pushing him I could not say.

CD.   You saw four men together and the pilot with them and you saw pushing. Why cannot you say who did the pushing?

JB.   Yes, they were pushing at the pilot.

CD.   Who – all of them?

JB.   Yes; but if they were all four of them pushing at the same moment I would not be able to say.

Kington-Blair-Oliphant. Let me get this clear. This group of four people
    included the Accused Pelgrim?
JB.   Yes.
KBO. And all these four people including the Accused Pelgrim were
    pushing the pilot?
JB.   If all of them at the same moment were pushing the pilot I could
    not say.
KBO. But you have said that Pelgrim was one of the four and you have
    said that all the four were pushing and you have said that you
    will tell the whole truth and you are on oath?
JB.   Yes, Pelgrim beat too.

The second excerpt came from Milman's cross-examination.

Lieutenant Milman. Did you see Pelgrim actually hit the pilot?
Johann Bosmann. I have said he actually hit him; I have not seen it but
    I have seen him aiming at him.
LM.   With regard to the other two, the two people who you saw in SA
    uniform, in brown uniform, did you see them actually strike the
    pilot?
JB.   Everybody was hitting; I could not see who.

Diamond continued his summation.

That evidence in my submission was clear enough and was not effectively challenged in cross-examination. Against that you have the
evidence given by the Accused themselves, who all seemed to have seen
exactly the same things and missed seeing exactly the same things. You
heard a great deal about the rifle which was broken, the rifle which was
seen in the possession of the Accused Pelgrim. Does it not strike you as
extraordinary that all the Accused should remember so well that Pelgrim carried a rifle as far as the plane and after he left the place he was
not carrying it, and yet nobody saw him put it down? You may wonder
whether that is an extraordinary community of memory which existed
or whether, as I submit, it is simply the result of a thrashed out story.

Let me recall to the Court again part of the statement of the Accused
Pelgrim: 'I do not know how the pilot got possession of the rifle. I
assume' – again an assumption – 'he took it off me or Nieke in his
desperations'. There can be only one implication from that, that at the

time when the pilot was in desperation – and God knows he had good cause to be in desperation – he was near enough both to Nieke and Pelgrim to be able to take the rifle from one of them. The Accused Pelgrim now says that was not so.

Diamond moved on to the defence of superior orders, attacking the premiss from a number of angles.

Nobody thought it was their duty to interfere because the *Wehrmacht* officers were present. Yet is it not a strange thing, if this was a purely *Wehrmacht* affair, that the moment the crime was committed the two *Wehrmacht* officers went off with Grabowski and Nieke, leaving the police in charge?

You heard of the lynching orders, the orders that officials were not to interfere if the righteously indignant mob got hold of a pilot and took matters in their own hands. Grabowski said: 'That is why I did nothing, although it hurt me to see it.' One wonders whether possibly the effect of this painful scene on all of the Accused was to make them turn round; they could not bear to see it, so what did they do? They closed their eyes.

There is another point in that. Despite all this respect for superior orders and the Accused saying that it would have been grossly improper on their part to interfere, both on account of these orders that existed and the presence of the *Wehrmacht*, you have heard that Pelgrim goes dashing off to the *Wehrmacht* officers to ask them to intercede on behalf of the pilot and then rushes from there into the midst of the fray to get back his rifle. Whether it was concern for his rifle or concern for the pilot is a matter of some doubt; but it seems entirely inconsistent with a state of affairs such as the various Accused have stated existed in which they were powerless to interfere in any way.

Diamond made it clear to the court he believed Pelgrim, Grabowski and Nieke were actively involved in the beating that led to the pilot's death, but that if the court did have some doubt on this matter then even if they had not had an active involvement they were still guilty of the crime, and he quoted from Archbold:

It is not necessary, however, to prove that the party actually aided in the commission of the offence; if he watched his companions in order to

215

prevent surprise, or remained at a convenient distance, in order to favour their escape, if necessary, or was in such a situation as to be able readily to come to their assistance, the knowledge of which was calculated to give additional confidence to his companions, he was, in contemplation of law, present aiding and abetting.

Diamond then asked the court 'to consider the situation'.

Here we have two captains in the *Wehrmacht*, two representatives of the police, the guardians of law and order, Renoth and Pelgrim, and two customs officials cum party leaders in their Party uniform – the representatives of the three mainstays of the Nazi State, the Army, the Police and the Party – all there in their official capacities, standing by watching two *Wehrmacht* soldiers beating up a pilot and doing nothing. Can it be suggested for a moment that that would not give moral encouragement to the two soldiers to go further with their activity? What better encouragement could they have than the presence of these six men, silent, tacitly agreeing with what was being done. Even if the Accused's story is accepted that they did nothing active, then in my submission that is enough to damn them.

Diamond dismissed the importance of evidence, 'of a somewhat novel nature', relating that a member of the SS Death's Head Battalions had admitted to having beaten up a pilot with a rifle taken from a Customs official.

How did he know he took it from a customs official? A customs official's uniform is field grey. The only customs officials who were there were wearing brown uniform. The two customs officials in brown uniform did not know who the soldier was; presumably therefore the soldier did not know that these two were customs officials. In my submission that story is one which does not help in any way in the investigation of the case and merely serves to make confusion worse confounded. You would have thought that if one of the soldiers concerned had been in black uniform that would not have escaped the attention of all the various witnesses who had been called previously.

Diamond, having concluded his closing argument, stated to the court that overwhelming evidence had been produced and that he had met the onus of proof required of the prosecution: 'There is no room left for any form of reasonable doubt but that the Accused are all guilty of participation in this particularly brutal crime.'

With summations concluded, Kington-Blair-Oliphant closed the court, at 20 minutes past midday, 'to consider the finding'. After just 50 minutes of deliberation, word came through that a verdict had been reached, and the court reassembled. The four Accused stood. Kington-Blair-Oliphant addressed each individually.

Hans Renoth, the Court finds you guilty of the charge.
Hans Pelgrim, the Court finds you guilty of the charge.
Friedrich Wilhelm Grabowski, the Court finds you guilty of the charge.
Paul Herman Nieke, the Court finds you guilty of the charge.

Diamond declined to produce any evidence concerning sentencing and Dr Gobbels addressed the court in German.

You have declared Renoth as being guilty. I ask you to take into consideration all the reasons which might make the sentence lighter. He has been found guilty as he has participated in that act, and he must be punished for it; but kindly consider that up till now he has never done anything wrong and in the past he had a very unhappy time. At home he has a wife and a child; his son is a prisoner of war in Russia. I believe that his character is such that the mercy of the Court can be applied to him.

Lieutenant Milman then made a short statement on behalf of his clients.

I only wish to say now that as far as my three prisoners are concerned, I wish to appeal for clemency on their behalf on the grounds that although they were there and were concerned, as this Court has found, they may not have been actually the perpetrators of the crime.

This was a somewhat odd appeal, since the court had just found them guilty as perpetrators of the crime.

Kington-Blair-Oliphant closed the court for consideration of the sentence, and just 20 minutes later the Accused returned to learn their fate.

Paul Herman Nieke, the sentence of the Court is that you be imprisoned for 10 years.

Friedrich Wilhelm Grabowski, the sentence of the Court is that you be imprisoned for 10 years.

Hans Pelgrim, the sentence of the Court is that you are to be imprisoned for 15 years.

Hans Renoth, the Court sentences you to death by hanging.

The sentences are subject to confirmation by the Confirming Authority.

Kington-Blair-Oliphant informed the defence counsel that, should they wish, they had fourteen days to petition against the court's finding, and, following an expression of thanks to both Lieutenant Milman and Dr Gobbels, the court closed.

PART FIVE

A KILLING

Chapter 18

DEATH OF A POLICE OFFICER

Immediately following the trial proceedings, Friedrich Grabowski submitted his petition against the finding: 'I took no part in the beating and I consider the punishment too heavy.' Nieke and Pelgrim submitted similar petitions, using almost the same wording. Hans Renoth claimed that, as he had been acting on the order of a superior authority, 'a lesser punishment should have been inflicted'. In the days that followed further petitions were made in a desperate attempt to reduce Hans Renoth's sentence. On 21 January 1946 Anna Renoth wrote to 'the high Military Court'. Here, with the original spelling mistakes, is the literal translation of her letter, as contained in the Judge Advocate General's Branch files.

As his wife and the mother of our two children I address the high Military Court for my husband's sake, the forester Jack Renoth, with the intimate and hearty request once more to try in the office for appeal the reasons which he was sentenced to on January 10 1946.

So far as I know he did not participate in the cruelties. It was also ascertained that it wasn't he who struck the deadly blow with the butend. Therefore I assume that he was sentenced because he had fired the shot at the pilote. I know my husband whom I am living with in happy marriage and who is sticking to his children with a true father's love so well and distinctly that I can confirm by an oath that he only acted in this way because it was a matter of fact to him that he had to obey the order of his Military superior. Also yet at that moment he was a soldier as he only received the pay of a soldier and he was only ordered for rendering services at the police. My husband is a simple man in whom the belief in the autority of the superior was developed in a large measure. At the bottom of his heart he is kind and can neither do any haren to an animal nor especially to a man. If he nevertheless, fired the shot then it is proved that he was so puzzled by the aspect of the pilote, wounds offering to him as well as by Captain Kühne's repeated orders that independent thinking was shut off at all.

Please, consider that he himself treated the pilote in a kind and human manner so long until the man was suatched away from him by others. If this had not happened the unknown pilote would still be alife to-day thanks to the treatment by my husband who also honours and esteems the enemy soldiers out of his general and natural humanity.

Please, consider that he is the father of a son whom we didn't hear anything of for a long time after being put into action in the last. During his imprisonment we received the news that our son is still living in a Russian prison Camp. He doesn't know anything of all this and is hoping and longing for seeing us again. Please give the father a chance that this hope is realised. A short time ago I read in a paper that particularly in those cases when the deed leading to punishment was ordered by a superior commander, an alleviation of the punishment can take place. I believe that this point of view can just be applied to my husband's case.

I speak to you as the wife and the mother. Grant my request! Our life is depending on it.

Many other petitions were submitted, coordinated by Dr Gobbels, most being joint statements commenting on Renoth's good nature, with numerous signatures appended. It does make one wonder, however, why so many people were prepared to appeal on behalf of Renoth at this late stage. Only a few people had actually appeared at the trial itself to provide a character reference. Perhaps the death sentence had finally shocked them into action.

A document in the case files reveals that, in considering the findings, the relevant British authorities first established that the proceedings had been conducted in a proper and legal fashion. With respect to Grabowski and Nieke, it was conceded that 'the evidence fails to prove clearly that they did take any active part in the beating up, but, as DJAG points out, they were "aiding and abetting" by their presence and failure to interfere on the victim's behalf'. It was recommended that the sentence be confirmed. Against Pelgrim it was found that 'there was considerable evidence of physical participation in the beating up and he might indeed be considered fortunate to escape with a sentence of 15 years imprisonment'. Again, the recommendation was that the sentence be confirmed.

Renoth, on first examination, appeared to have some grounds for leniency, 'He acted on the orders of his superior officers to administer the *coup de grâce*; He took no part whatever in the beating up; the victim had already received fatal injuries, as proved by the medical evidence.'

'Superior Orders' are no defence to a War Crimes charge although they may be taken into consideration when deciding sentences, and although the victim was dying Renoth clearly committed murder. Nevertheless, you may consider that the worst criminals in this case were those who took part in the beating up, that the disparity between Renoth's sentence and the sentence of the others does not fairly reflect their relative guilt, and that in all the circumstances it would be reasonable to commute Renoth's sentence to one of life imprisonment.

The above point of view has been advanced by an experienced member of my staff and I think it right to put it before you. I do NOT however, support it. I consider that Renoth is clearly guilty of murder and should pay the full penalty. The fact that Pelgrim may be lucky should not affect this decision. The Court were in a better position than any reviewing authority to gauge mitigating circumstances in his case.

The recommendation was made to confirm Renoth's sentence.

Another document records: 'I think there was justification for the death sentence on Renoth, but I should have felt happier about it had Pelgrim also been sentenced to death. You will note that a permanent president was not employed.' All the petitions were dismissed and sentences confirmed.

Renoth's nephew made one further appeal, a translation of which is held in the Judge Advocate General's Branch files.

Let me beseech your Excellency for mercy, in the name of a large group of acquaintances and on behalf of an uncle of mine.

I have already submitted my letter of grace through the lawyer Dr Goebel [*sic*], Elten, together with other petitions, on behalf of my uncle Hans Renoth, who was sentenced to death on 10.1.1946. Meanwhile I have had the opportunity to meet my uncle in the prison at Werl, which gave me anew the full knowledge, Sir, that this man became an innocent victim of an unfortunate conjunction of circumstances.

I beg you kindly but firmly, Sir, to form a notion of my uncle's character on the basis of the different letters of grace and certificates forwarded to you or still to be sent, and to look into the whole matter.

All my acquaintances and myself cannot understand this terrible sentence because we know my uncle as a tender father who as good Christian disliked every violent action.

During his long career as a forester, my uncle has never been sentenced and has a good reputation in his acquaintances circles. He did not only love human beings but also helpless creatures. I have often noticed myself that in his great love for little animals, he took them prudently in his hands to give them freedom and life.

Allow me, Sir, that I explain once more the occasion and the circumstances of the tragedy in which my uncle was mixed and in which he became a victim. The High Court has already established that such a fact would never have happened if my uncle would have stayed along with the lamentable victim of this tragedy, the unknown Australian pilot. Human as always, after having found the pilot, he came in a friendly companionable contact with him. The pilot offered him cigarettes and he accepted them. The pilot was snatched away from him by the crowd, without having bad intentions himself.

In this confusion the pilot received a mortal blow on his head from an unknown. It was established by the English doctor-expert after a post-mortem that this blow caused death and not the finishing shot.

My uncle received the oral order and afterwards the written order from his officer commanding, Capt Kuhne belonging to a Luftwaffe Reporters Unit to give the dying man the finishing shot in order to liberate him from his death agony.

Witnesses, declared credible by the High Court itself, stated under oath that he received a written order. My uncle refused the order several times and obeyed only after that Capt Kuhne had put his hand on his pistol. My uncle only obeyed the order under this symbolic threat. Those who know the German Army and its obedience know that the non-execution of such an order means refusal to obey the order which would certainly have cost him his life.

The fatal wounds of the bleeding pilot certainly made such an impression on his soft mind that he was convinced that the officer's order was justified. In his submission, he had the conviction that the officer as the responsible person who gave the order, also has the complete responsibility, especially because this tragedy happened in the so called 'red zone' that is to say in an area without either civil justice or administration, but with full military execution.

Sure of his innocence, relying upon the Higher Court, my uncle insisted on his removal from the American zone to his birth-place, in order to place himself at the disposal of the English Authorities, immediately after arrival.

Sir, we are trying by all means to find the officer Kuhne, who as a captain is completely responsible owing to the severe order he gave my uncle under the threat of death.

My uncle, his wife and the two children, the elder my cousin is still a war prisoner of the Russians, and we all, extremely sorry as we are, beg you most obediently for a delay of the execution at least until you have perused the petitions and until the responsible officer can be called to account for his order.

Sir, we lay a man's life in God's and in your hands.

We thank you in anticipation for your goodness, for we have the firm conviction that in God's and His Majesty the King's name you do the utmost to support a deadly touched wife and two children, until the light of truth and justice has conquered the darkness.

Sir, with full confidence in your goodness and mercy, in the hope that your judgement will be gracious, I remain your obedient servant.

signed *Karl Glamann*

There is a note in the National Archives file against Karl Glamann's letter simply stating: 'There is nothing new in this petition for clemency which affects the legal standpoint.' Hans Renoth was taken to Hameln prison to await execution.

Yorkshireman Albert Pierrepoint was quite meticulous when it came to killing. His father, Henry, had already demonstrated his skill at ending life, as had his uncle Thomas. Henry entered the execution profession at the age of 27, in 1901, and would take part in over 100 executions. He died in 1922, ten years before his son followed in his footsteps. Thomas Pierrepoint surpassed his brother Henry's total; in a career lasting over forty years he put to death over 300 criminals for the British government. Albert had the benefit of his uncle Thomas to act as mentor when he was learning his craft, but Albert would outdo both his seniors in terms of the number of men and women he would put to death, eventually hanging over 400 people.

On 26 September 1932 Albert's name appeared on the List of Assistant Executioners, partly fulfilling his aspiration, decided upon at an early age, to become the Official Executioner. On 29 December 1932 Albert assisted his uncle Thomas in the execution of Patrick McDermott at Mountjoy Prison in Dublin. Albert's first killing as Chief Executioner came on 17 October 1941, when it was reported that Antonio Mancini, a gangster, bade his farewell with a 'cheerio' when he fell through the trapdoor at Pentonville prison. Albert Pierrepoint always sought to avoid publicity in the work he did, and as he continued to ply his trade during the war years, his personal involvement in the process of justice was kept quiet. When the war came to an end, however, his name would feature prominently in the public eye. Press reports, radio commentaries and film footage of the liberation of the concentration camps, such as Bergen-Belsen, had been horrifying and shocking to the British public. Germans who had worked at the camps had been captured and put on trial, and, following conviction, many, such as Belsen camp commandant Josef Kramer, had been sentenced to death. Albert Pierrepoint was called in to finish off the process of justice, at a time when public emotion was running high. In his autobiography Albert Pierrepoint commented: 'Unfortunately for my personal life, that emotion had a painful backlash on me.'

> The announcement that I was to hang the convicted staff of Belsen was made from Field Marshal Montgomery's headquarters in Germany with far fuller publicity that had ever been officially given to executions at home. Because of what people felt about Belsen, and because they saw me as, in a way, their own stand-in avenger, not only for the wrongs of the SS but for all their grief at the deaths in this long war, I became a far too familiar public figure, and in private far too troubled. I had more reporters and photographers camped on my doorstep than a heavily suspected murderer before he is arrested. I was chased to my aircraft in the middle of Northolt airfield by a pack of newspapermen who were to me about as unwelcome as a lynch mob. 'He should avoid attracting public attention . . . He should clearly understand that his conduct and general behaviour must be respectable and discreet . . .' That was how I had been trained to be an executioner, and I could see it all going by the board.[1]

When Pierrepoint arrived in Germany he recalled a 'forty-minute run through dark, devastated country to the storybook Pied Piper town of Hameln'. On arrival at the prison Albert quickly learned that he was tasked with executing eleven prisoners convicted of crimes at Belsen and two other men convicted of the murder of an RAF pilot. 'This was a revolutionary total in modern British criminological history, and the operation demanded careful planning. It was agreed that arrangements should be left entirely in my hands. I had thirty-two hours in which to complete my preparations.' Early on 12 December Albert began preparing, and was introduced to his novice assistant, a Regimental Sergeant Major O'Neil, 'as smart as paint in his freshly pressed uniform'. O'Neil informed Pierrepoint, 'cheerfully', that he had never seen an execution before. 'I was rather startled at being given a novice, but, as it turned out, I could not have hoped for a better man.' Pierrepoint, on his way to inspecting the recently constructed execution chamber, passed the 'smallest cells' he had ever seen. 'I got my first glimpse of the Belsen prisoners, all peering silently through the bars of their cell doors.'

> The first one I saw was Josef Kramer, the former commandant, I recognised him at once . . . I could hear shovelling and scraping in the prison yard outside. It was a jarring and nerve-wracking noise in what would otherwise have been dead silence. I looked through a window and saw a gang of workmen busily digging thirteen graves for the following morning. There was no doubt that the condemned prisoners could also hear this sound. I complained about this to a prison official but was told that nothing could be done to stop it. 'The graves have to be dug and the ground is frozen. It's full of pebbles and flints, and we must do the job today to be ready in time.'[2]

Pierrepoint tested the gallows, and walked back past the cells, once more looking at the prisoners. 'Never in my experience have I seen a more pitiable crowd of condemned prisoners. I knew their crimes were monstrous, but I could not help feeling sorry for them. When I mentioned this to some young British soldiers who were present they said, "If you had been in Belsen under this lot, you wouldn't be able to feel sorry for them."'

Pierrepoint carried on with his preparations for the rest of the day, weighing and measuring the thirteen condemned prisoners, meeting them face to face, including the 'Beast of Belsen' Josef Kramer, Dr Fritz Klein, and three women Irma Grese, Elisabeth Volkenrath and Juana Bormann. In addition to the eleven convicted of crimes at Belsen were Otto Sandrock and Ludwig Schweinberger, who, along with two others, had been put on trial at the Almelo court house, in November 1945, charged with committing war crimes in the killing of Flying Officer Gerald Hood and Bote van der Wal. Both had been found guilty and awaited execution at Hameln.

With his measurements made, Pierrepoint spent the next couple of hours making his calculations. 'It was not a simple task, for I had to allow for the adjustment of the drop after each execution, and this controlled to some extent the order in which I took the prisoners. I was very anxious not to confuse any of the drops. It would have been easy, in this unprecedented multiple execution, to have called for the condemned in the wrong order. But, however it complicated the operation, I had come to the decision that I must take the women first. The condemned cells were so close to the scaffold that the prisoners could not but hear the repeated sounds of the drop. I did not wish to subject the women for too long to this. I determined to carry out the execution of the women, singly, at the start, and follow with double executions for the men.' Having carried out some rehearsals, Pierrepoint completed his preparations, and left. At six o'clock the following morning he was awoken by a batman and made his way back to the prison, to carry out what would be the first of over 200 war criminal executions over the next few years, including that of the Elten gendarme and forester Hans Renoth.

Chapter 19

PUNISHMENT

It was two months after his death that Hans's family found out about his execution. Having not heard anything, Maria Renoth asked the priest in Werl if he had any information. He, in turn, found the information from the priest in Hameln and passed on the news to Anna and Maria.

Werl, 30 May 1946

Dear Miss Renoth,

I cannot really understand why you did not receive any information. At my request the Hameln parish priest sent a reply on 16 April, 'I thought that the relatives had received official notification of the execution, which took place on 8 March in the local prison. Since, according to your letter, this did not happen, I have, by return mail, informed the parishes in question asking them to break it gently to their relatives.'

I am astonished that you did not receive a message from your parish priest. According to the letter mentioned above, your father is already in eternity and surely has found a gracious judge. I pray for peace to his soul; may god console you and your mother in your grief.

You may be sure of my deepest sympathy.

Please, send my regards to your mother. Kind regards to you.

On 1 July 1946 Friedrich Grabowski's wife, Elisabeth, submitted a letter to try and reduce her husband's sentence: 'On the 19 June 1946, one year in punishment has already passed. I request the War Criminal Court to test his judgement and to remit the punishment.' She based her case on his 'peaceful character'. 'My husband was a good family father. In all his actions he showed a deep human feeling. He always tried to mitigate the needs of his fellow men. In his work, [by] his colleagues and all other persons whom he met in his service, without difference, whether they were Germans or foreigners, he was well regarded.' According to Elisabeth he had been ordered to go to the scene: 'I can attest that he had not gone to the scene of this deed based upon his own judgement, but because of the telephone appeals, which had ordered him to this place. These telephone conversations I have accepted. I am also of the conviction that he was there with the best human intentions.' And she finally tried to appeal to common sense: 'As a last proof of his innocence . . . in spite of the great difficulties in the Russian zone, where we were held up during the last year of the war, he came back, and voluntarily gave himself up to the English Police on 19 June 1945.' Frau Grabowski's appeal was turned down.

In 1949 Friedrich was granted leave to travel to Wesel to spend eight days with his children. The following year Friedrich divorced Elisabeth. She had found another man. Arrangements had to be made for the children. Manfred and Ingeborg went to live in an orphanage in Wesel, and Hilmar went to live with an uncle in Westphalia.

With the situation desperate for his children, Friedrich Grabowski made a further appeal to the Zentrale Rechtsschutzstelle[1] in Bonn on 25 January 1951, initially attacking the conduct of his legal defence.

My official defence counsel was an English lieutenant whose name remained unknown to me. I do not possess the case files. All the documents were kept by the defence counsel. I was considerably hampered in my defence by the fact that the case documents were only available in English. In our camp at Recklinghausen there were only three legal advisers available, and they were so busy that only a few individual parts of my indictment were translated into German for me, and those once only and verbally.

Grabowski went on to detail his involvement in the incident, but the appeal adds little to his defence as described earlier in this book. He re-iterates that in his official capacity his responsibility was 'the monitoring of the entire frontier traffic along that area of the Dutch–German border. In particular I also had to supervise military cross-border traffic. That included escaped prisoners of war or members of the former enemy states.' Justifying his presence at the incident, he states that, following a report from the border patrol of a shot-down enemy aircraft, 'according to my standing instructions I had to go immediately to the crash site'. Grabowski stated that the two *Wehrmacht* officers had in fact offered to take him and Nieke to the scene, and that on the way to the car they were joined by Pelgrim and Renoth. 'According to them, the shooting-down had been reported to them as well, which is why they also had to go to the crash site. The two officers offered the gendarmes a ride in their car as well.'

At the crash site it turned out that the pilot must have got out of the aircraft alive. Several aircraft were still circling over the wreckage, shooting at a stopped train and also continually at us, which is why we sought cover in a ditch in the meadow. When the *Jabos* disappeared, it became clear that the pilot had likewise gone to ground in the ditch. Gendarme Renoth thereupon arrested the flier, who was then still un-injured. From the direction of the burning train came four soldiers, two of whom took the flier from the gendarmes and shouted: 'Is this how you treat the bastards who murder our wives and children?!' As we discovered later, there were seventeen dead in the train. One of the soldiers, after punching the flier, grabbed the carbine of one of the gendarmes and beat the flier over the head with it. The second soldier had a truncheon and hit the flier with it so much that the flier started bleeding strongly from several wounds.

Grabowski added that a Hauptmann Kühne ordered Gendarme Renoth to use his carbine to shoot the flier to end his suffering. 'I left the group dur-ing the shooting and went to the car, without having seen the pilot up close. Also, I gave no instructions whatsoever as to the flier's treatment. I was not even in a position to do so, as the flier was in the custody of the *Wehrmacht* and none of us had the authority to issue commands to mem-bers of the *Wehrmacht*.'

Grabowski challenged the court's findings, in particular attacking Johann Bosmann's evidence 'that all those present at the beating-up of the flier were involved'. He claimed that Albertus Konning and Peter Peters, 'both Dutchmen!', refuted this, and stated that he 'took no part at all in the beating-up and killing of the flier'. In fact Peters, at the trial, had testified only seeing men in field grey actually beating; Grabowski was wearing brown. But he had also, in answer to a question by Milman, stated that it was 'quite possible' that there were other men there out of his sight. Peters, who lived close to the rail line, had also claimed that he had not seen a train. At no point in the trial did Konning testify to seeing any of the beating, so he could not say who was or was not involved. After talking with Pelgrim, and before Maloney had been found, Konning, had left the scene, returning later, long after the killing.

Grabowski next sought to find out what had happened to a clemency plea submitted by his brother in May 1950, and whether further points could be made to the review body that might be looking at his case: that it was his 'professional responsibility' to go to the scene, that 'under the wartime regulations' he was not responsibile for a pilot 'in the presence of the gendarmes and the officers of the *Wehrmacht*', that the airman was 'clearly the prisoner of the *Wehrmacht*', that he had in no way 'incited anyone to assault the flier and also had no other influence on the conduct of the members of the *Wehrmacht* with respect to the prisoner', that he personally 'committed no criminal action against the flier', and that 'it has to be taken into account' that, if he had tried to defend a pilot who had attacked non-military targets such as farmers, women and children, who had 'devastated the lives of numerous people', it would have turned the people and the soldiers against him. 'In a situation like that I would have felt in fear of my life.'

Finally Friedrich outlined his family circumstances, which had 'deteriorated catastrophically as a result of my conviction'.

> Because of the annexation of my place of residence to Holland, I have lost my home and nearly all my possessions. I had to accept the ending of my marriage in divorce, for which my wife was to blame, but in fact it was a result of my absence. Meanwhile, of my three unprovided-for children, two had to be accommodated in an orphanage; the third is being brought up with acquaintances.

Finally Friedrich requested that, as he was 'completely without means', and had 'never had a German defence counsel', he should get legal aid. He wanted the lawyer who worked on his divorce case to represent him, as he was 'fully conversant with the details of my "war crime"'.

No documentary evidence has been found to show whether Grabowski's appeal to the Zentrale Rechtsschutzstelle had any effect. As it was, his case came up in front of a Remission Board on 22 February 1952: 'whereas the case has now come before this Board and after due consideration of the recommendation of the Penal Authorities and an allowance made for pre-trial custody served it is hereby ordered that the said Friedrich Grabowski be granted remission of sentence for good conduct and industry in prison and be released on 26 February 1952.' In October 1952 Friedrich, Ingeborg and Manfred took up residence in Düsseldorf, and were subsequently joined by Hilmar. Friedrich always maintained he was subject to an injustice. He died in 1972.

At the end of the trial, following the guilty verdict, Paul Nieke was immediately dismissed from his customs position, and his family was given 20 minutes to vacate the house provided by the customs authorities. Managing to find a single room in Elten, they had to contend with an ever-present atmosphere of ill feeling in the village. When Frau Nieke went to obtain some food parcels, provided in relief by the Allies, she was told that they had all gone. Eventually a local farmer took pity and gave them shelter, and they worked on the farm until Paul had served his time.

On 30 September 1948 Paul Nieke, who was starting to suffer from malnutrition, submitted an application for clemency.

With regard to my family's economic situation, I ask to submit a petition for clemency as follows:

I am married since 22.11.1930 and father of two sons 15 and 9 years of age. Until I was arrested I assisted my family in everything and we were a happy family.

My presence at the place of the offence was committed is explained as follows:

Obeying an order by the superior authority (Administration of the Reich's finances).

Acting in correspondence to an order of my immediate superior (Oberzollsekretär and Abteilungsführer Grabowski).

In October 1944 my family was evacuated to Torgelow near Stettin. I and my family, we were still there at the time of the capitulation. Early in August 1945 I crossed the English–Russian border together with my family risking our lives, and we returned to Elten. Arriving there, I went to the Authority concerned in order to give evidence. If I myself had been concerned in the offence, surely, I should not illegally and voluntarily have left the Russian Zone together with my whole family returning to Elten and at once reporting to the authority concerned. If it had been so I should have remained there, where most of my wife's and my relatives are still alive.

From the day of my conviction my wife has to earn her living and to nourish our two boys. Both of them are now in a stage in which they need the directive hands of their father. In addition, my parents are old and sickly and still living in the Russian sector of Berlin. They lost all their property through the war, and are expecting help and assistance from me. For above mentioned reasons and considering there I have served over three years, I ask you to review my sentence and to remit the balance of sentence as an act of clemency or to commute the sentence to a probationary period. I assure you that I shall never violate any order or instruction of Military Government but loyally fulfil my obligations.

Nieke's appeal was turned down, but, like Grabowski, Paul Nieke would not serve out his full ten-year sentence. On 16 April 1952 Paul Nieke's case came in front of the board, and he was granted remission of sentence, to be released on 27 April that year. Upon his release, the British and German customs authorities reclassified Paul's time in prison as that of a 'prisoner of war', which allowed reinstatement of his pension and salary benefits. The decision concerning his dismissal was rescinded, and he returned to duties as a customs official. Paul Nieke died in 1975.

Agnes Pelgrim kept in regular contact with her father, Hans, often visiting him in Werl prison, taking him food from the bakery, and with her siblings they submitted an appeal for a 'moderation' of their father's sentence in March 1947. Lord Russell of Liverpool, Deputy Judge Advocate General (DJAG) to the British Army of the Rhine, was not interested. 'In view of the fact that this Accused has served little more than a year of his sentence of 15 years imprisonment it seems to me a little premature to consider any remission and I do not propose to send for the proceedings of this trial, which are now with the Judge Advocate General . . . In my opinion the appeal should be dismissed.' On 27 March 1947 Pelgrim's appeal was indeed turned down. But, like Nieke and Grabowski, Pelgrim would serve only about half his sentence.

Hans was released in 1953, and he went to live and work as an electrician in Kranenburg, near Kleve, across the Rhine, staying with his mother-in-law and his wife. He did return to Emmerich early in the 1960s, but died of a heart attack in 1963. He always protested his innocence, maintaining that he had been too far away to do anything and had not even touched the pilot.

Chapter 20

A SMALL DIFFICULTY

Early in May 1947 it became clear that the available burial space at Hameln prison had all but run out. Ninety-one executed war criminals had been interred in the prison grounds, but clearly other arrangements had to be made if the present rate of executions was maintained. On 9 May 1947 a Brigadier G. Ingham, working within a Penal Branch of the BAOR, wrote to a certain 'My Dear McNally' expressing his concerns about 'a small difficulty connected with the burying of German War Criminals whom we hang for you at Hameln Prison in batches once a month. Until the last lot of hangings, we were able to bury them all inside the precincts of the jail, but this accommodation is now quite full.' Ingham informed McNally that the British Governor of the Allied National Prison at Hameln had already arranged locally for a piece of ground adjoining the existing cemetery, 'to be set apart for future burials'.

Our difficulty is getting the bodies from the jail to the cemetery, about two miles I understand, without arousing too much attention and with reasonable security. Of course, it cannot be done by Germans, or by German vehicles. Would it be possible for Provost to provide the transport with a British driver and a military policeman to sit on the front of each vehicle? It would only require two covered-in trucks at the most, possibly only one. We would suggest, if you agree, that so as not to excite any curiosity or interest, the military policemen employed should not wear red cap covers . . . I have also discussed the matter with the local Public Safety Officer at Hameln who will make some unobtrusive arrangements with the German Police on each occasion, but he does not think it will arouse any undue feelings or interest among the German population and if the arrangements are carried out as I have suggested he thought that nobody in the town would know what was happening.[1]

Ingham's suggestion was put into place, and following the next set of executions the corpses were taken to the Friedhof (cemetery) Am Wehl on the outskirts of Hameln, and, as hoped for, there was little public interest. However, a few years later, a decision to move the ninety-one already buried at Hameln did arouse 'undue feelings' on an international scale.

On 4 March 1954 the *Daily Telegraph* reported:

Ninety-one German war criminals executed by the British and buried in unmarked graves in Hamelin prison are being exhumed. They are being buried by the German authorities in the municipal cemetery.

They include Josef Kramer, the 'Beast of Belsen', Irma Grese, 'the woman with the whip and dog', and most of the other notorious Nazi concentration camp officials.

The reburial is the result of years of agitation by Right-wing elements in Lower Saxony. Reports that it was made necessary by structural alterations in the prison grounds are untrue. I have established that there are no such alterations.

The opening of the graves was begun a few days ago on the orders of the Lower Saxony Ministry of Justice. The remains are being put in separate coffins for reburial in separate graves. The Lower Saxony Finance Ministry allocated about £1,700 for the purpose.

The executions were carried out at Hamelin by Pierrepoint, the British hangman, after open trial before British courts in Germany between 1945 and 1948 . . . The prison was handed over to the German authorities in 1950. The names of the buried criminals and the exact position of the graves were not given to the German authorities.

They were eventually discovered and identified by the German prison authorities, who laid out a flower bed to commemorate them.[2]

Included, as one of these buried criminals, was Hans Renoth. The day before the *Daily Telegraph* report, *Allgemeine Zeitung* (Hanover) recorded:

These ninety-one 'war criminals' executed by British military justice by the axe or the rope were consigned to a mass grave in the prison yard. For a long time there was no reminder in the prison yard of this gruesome execution.

Under the conditions then prevailing this leaves open the question whether guilty and innocent were not struck down indiscriminately. On the German side the fact was known, but it was not possible to give the executed persons at least a worthy last resting place.[3]

A. L. Easterman, the Political Director of the World Jewish Congress, was one of the first to weigh in with his protest: 'Men and women of all nations and faiths will share the amazement and horror of the World

Jewish Congress at the news.' Easterman called it 'an act of brazen de-
fiance of the moral principles cherished by decent people', adding that
the 'action of the German authorities mocks the memory of Hitler's
countless murdered victims', that it cast, 'the gravest doubt on repeated
official German professions that the new Germany has purged itself of its
past'. Victor Gollancz, the Jewish British publisher and humanitarian
who had concerned himself with the plight of the defeated Germans in
the aftermath of the war, in a letter to *The Times* of 6 March, gave a
different view.

> Sir, I read that the World Jewish Congress has protested against the
> reburying of certain German war criminals in hallowed ground. As a
> Jew, and one whose detestation of Nazism can hardly be questioned, I
> wish to protest against this protest. To object to the burying of anyone
> whomever in hallowed ground is unseemly and irreligious, for it sug-
> gests that God is as unmerciful and unforgiving as man.[4]

Gollancz's voice was, however, overwhelmed by the din of protest, his
opinion far removed from that of the general public. Lady Russell of
Liverpool wrote to the *Daily Telegraph* on 11 March 1954:

> Sir, You have published a despatch from your Special Correspondent in
> Bonn about the reburial of Josef Kramer, the 'Beast of Belsen', and Irma
> Grese, the head wardress of the same camp, and many other Germans
> convicted of atrocious crimes.
>   So it has come to pass as some of us have oft predicted, as many more
> have feared, and as all might well have expected. These war criminals,
> convicted after long, careful and patient trial – I myself was present at
> one of them – are none other than innocent martyrs, and before long
> Germany's war guilt will once more become a legend.[5]

On 15 March 1954 the Foreign Secretary Anthony Eden had to field
questions in Parliament from a Mr E. Fletcher, asking 'what steps he is
taking to prevent the further recrudescence of Nazism' as demonstrated
by the reburials, and from a Mr Janner, asking whether he was 'aware of
the growth of neo-Nazism and militarism in Germany, which is fostered
by acts such as the exhumation and reburial of German war criminals
and their representation in the German Press as a new myth of martyrdom . . .'.

Mr Eden. Her Majesty's Government have no responsibility for the action of the Lower Saxony Land Government in transferring these bodies to a mass public grave. This did not require British permission, and I do not propose to take any action in the matter.

Mr Fletcher. Whatever the explanation may be, is the Foreign Secretary not aware that this action has caused angry protests, and that there is widespread concern at this action which is contrary to all the official German professions of having repudiated Hitlerism and Nazism. Does not the right hon. Gentleman think that, as an occupying Power, we ought to protest at this action?

Mr Eden. I do not read what the hon. Gentleman does into this event, and I feel more sympathy with the letter which Mr Victor Gollancz wrote to *The Times*. What has actually happened is that the relatives who were anxious to visit the graves could not do so except by visiting the prison, and they asked that the bodies should be removed to some other place where they could visit them and where they were all once more put into a mass grave. I do not think that is a matter about which Her Majesty's Government should protest.

Mr Janner. Surely the right hon. Gentleman is aware that these people were found guilty of the most terrible crimes, that there was unspeakable sadism in their actions prior to the time that they committed the murders of hundreds of thousands of people? Is he really suggesting that a similar thing could happen anywhere else in the world and that if criminals of that nature had been buried within prison grounds they would be exhumed and reburied elsewhere? Will the right hon. Gentleman please make a protest, as so many people are anxious to ensure that this kind of thing does not create in Germany the idea that these acts are tolerated by any other human beings?

Mr Eden. I am certainly not prepared to make a protest about this. I think this was done decently and without provocation. There was no demonstration or anything of the kind at the time, and I am not prepared to pursue hatred beyond the grave.[6]

This was not the end of the matter, as the issue certainly met with general public displeasure. Home Office files at The National Archives contain examples of the vehement objections of numerous other organisations, such as the Association of Jewish Ex-Servicemen and Women (backed up by letters from various branches, such as Stamford Hill, Hammersmith and District, Merseyside and the Polish Jewish Ex-Servicemen's Association). Objections also came in from the National Assembly of Women against UK Government Silence, the Bedford Branch of Electrical Trades Union, the Leeds Peace Committee, and the Newcastle branch of the British Legion. But the British government's standard reply was to refer back to Eden's answer to questions in Parliament. The Friedhof Am Wehl at Hameln would become the final resting place of those executed as war criminals in the town's gaol.

Chapter 21

WITHOUT DELAY

It was September 2008 and I had come to The National Archives at Kew, London, to see if I could find any further details concerning the death of Hans Renoth. Could this be the moment of finishing the cycle of my research? Through the National Archives website I had searched for any files on Hameln prison. There was very little, just a few entries, but one looked promising and I had booked it ahead of my visit.

It was a fairly quiet day at the archives. It was easy to find an empty locker and offload superfluous baggage. I climbed the stairs to the reading room, went through the usual security checks, and retrieved my file from the boxed shelf displaying my seat number. Other researchers sat at their tables; heads were bowed, pencils were poised, fingers tapped at laptops, digital cameras clicked; each person was engrossed in his or her own investigation. The file I had ordered looked quite slim. I hoped it was not going to be a wasted trip. I had the urge to skim through the file, as usual, trying to find quickly the information I was after. But on this occasion I decided to be more meticulous – to start at the beginning and read through. I did feel quite excited. The subject matter was certainly not something to be excited about. But the possibility of a discovery was.

File HO 45/25454, browned and curled at the edges, smelling musty, had been kept from public viewing until 2007. On the first of the collection of loose pages, at the top, it was interesting to note that '21–24 destroyed' was written in red, just above the title 'Judicial Hangings – series of medical researches made at the executions of German War Criminals at Hameln Prison'. At the bottom was a handwritten note made in January 1956:

> This file has been lent to Dr (now Brigadier) Buckland of the Microbiological Research Dept Porton in connection with RAF research into the cause of aircraft accidents. The RAF research people have been told that they must not publish any reference to this report without permission.

Now, of course, the file had been placed in the public domain.

The papers were filed in date order. The first few notes in the files, dated 1956, recorded the movement of the file between RAF Boscombe Down and the Home Office, Scientific Advisers' Branch. Why became clear in a note dated 15 December 1955, from Dr Buckland to Dr J. W. Martin at the Home Office:

> I am proposing to let Wing Commander J. K. Mason of the Pathology Branch, RAF Halton and S/Ldr D. I. Fryer of the Institute of Aviation Medicine, Farnborough have a copy of the report and of the electro-cardiograms. When I send them I will put in a reminder that they must not publish anything in the open literature using this material without Home Office permission.

I sat back. The sense of excitement became mixed with a feeling of un-easiness. I looked out of the window and then round the reading room. Everyone else remained engrossed in their discoveries.

As I went back through the file, and therefore back in time, further documents revealed the nature of the report. On 18 November 1955 a note was made of a telephone request by Brigadier Buckland to Dr Martin, ask-ing for a file to be traced.

> During an official survey made in Germany after the war information was obtained on detailed observations made by medical research work-ers during the war on the detailed reaction of men who were executed in gas chambers.
>
> It is thought that this information, which contains data regarding the time lag which occurs in response to such exposure would be of considerable value in an important study now being carried out by Royal Air Force pathologists in another connection.
>
> It appears that the file containing the case histories and electro-cardiographs of eight cases was referred by the War Office to the Home Office in the Autumn of 1946. There is no further trace of what happened to these records.
>
> Can Home Office assist in tracing the file?

Two weeks later Buckland received a note from Martin telling him that the file had been located and that the report had been referred to the Home Office by Brigadier Paton Walsh from the Prison Commission. Buckland received an apology for the delay, 'due to the fact that owing to the necessarily guarded terms of our telephone conversation I thought you were referring to executions which had been carried out in gas chambers in Germany during the war and were subsequently investigated by Allied investigators. There is, however, no record of this in the Home Office.' In fact they were looking for a file with medical research information obtained from men who had been hanged.

There was then a jump of over eight years to the next item of correspondence. On 27 April 1947 Brigadier E. J. Paton Walsh had written to a Mr Hoare at the Home Office.

Since my return from Germany I have received the enclosed report on certain medical researches in regard to the moment when death can be safely presumed, which was carried out at my request by Dr F. E. Buckland, an Asst Director of Pathology with the HQ of BAOR, during a series of executions by judicial hanging at Hameln Prison.

I thought that Dr Buckland's paper might be of some interest to certain advisers at the HO and with his agreement I requested and obtained the consent of the Control Office to my passing of a copy to you for such further action as you may deem suitable.

The circumstances which led to the research were a little unusual and the results are not as conclusive as would have been possible had we been able to hold post-mortem examinations. Such examinations are not usual however in the case of executions in Germany, and it was undesirable that we should inaugurate them, as such action might have been misinterpreted. For the same reason you will appreciate that it would be undesirable to give any publicity to the early part of the enquiry, including the first series of executions . . .

I enclose the five original electrocardiographic records – Appx D – of which there are no duplicates. The only other copies of the typescript are single copies held by the General Department of the Control Office, by Dr Buckland and by myself.

I return to my old work with the Prison Commission with the 1st of May, and will be glad to be working in this country again. The work in Germany was intensely interesting and a remarkable experience that I am very glad to have had; but the prisons in our Zone are now re-established, and the whole penal system from probation to penal servitude operating as an integrated whole, so with the handing over to the Germans of responsibility for future policy, I felt that my task was done, and that I need not remain in exile merely for the negative work of guarding against a misuse of power.

Dr Martin had commented on Paton Walsh's letter almost a month later, stating that: 'There is nothing in it which was not already known to experienced medical officers who have for many years reported the fact that the heart continues to beat for varying periods of time after the execution has taken place. Unconsciousness is immediate, and there is no possibility of life continuing after a fracture dislocation of the vertebrae.'

In the Home Office file, following Paton Walsh's letter, there is a thin set of white papers, typed in blue, headed 'An Account of Observations Made at Judicial Hangings in BAOR'.

In the autumn of 1945 a number of Germans found guilty of War Crimes and sentenced to death were awaiting executions. A gallows had been constructed to the standard English design and the official executioner, Pierrepoint, detailed for the task.

Because there were as many as 13 persons awaiting execution on the first occasion the Director of the Penal Branch, Control Commission for Germany felt that there would be inordinate delay if the bodies were left hanging for an hour or more which, it is understood, is the customary practice in England.

The Assistant Director of Pathology BAOR who was to be the Medical Officer present at the executions was asked by the Director of Medical Services BAOR whether he considered that there was any objection to injecting the body immediately after execution with a lethal dose of some chemical substance in order to ensure the body could be taken down without delay.

The Assistant Director of Pathology felt that there was no ethical objection to such a course and that an injection of 10cc of chloroform would be appropriate.

This use of chloroform, to speed death, is not mentioned in Albert Pierrepoint's biography.

The report went on to describe the arrangements for the first set of executions on 13 December 1945, when, following a trial drop using a dummy, 'three women were executed one by one, ten men then followed in pairs'. Immediately after the trap had been sprung, the medical officer left the execution chamber and went down some stairs to a room below, climbing a step ladder to listen to the beat of the heart for half a minute, then injecting 10cc of chloroform. Notes were taken of 'the tachycardia which was assumed to be due to vagus escape' for seven of those executed. Irma Grese (convicted in the Belsen trial) – 160 per minute, Juana Bormann (Belsen) 170 per minute. The number against Dr Fritz Klein (Belsen) had faded somewhat, making it difficult to read, but it was possibly 150 per minute, 'with some missed beats'. Josef Kramer (Belsen) – 160 per minute, Karl Franchosch (or Flrazich (Francioh) – Belsen) – 150 per minute, Peter Weingartner (Belsen) – 150 per minute, Otto Sandrock (who had been found responsible for the deaths of Flying Officer Gerald Hood and Bote van der Wal in the Almelo case) – 140 per minute. The report went on to describe the effect of the injection of chloroform.

(a) 10cc chloroform intracardially as proved by withdrawal of blood on suction – instant stoppage of heart.

(b) 10cc chloroform intravenously in arm, as soon as needle was withdrawn a stethoscope was applied to chest just in time to hear heart sound dying away.

(c) 10cc injected into area of cardiac dullness but no blood seen on suction – heartbeat was inaudible at the end of four minutes.

In this series of 13 cases slight momentary flexion of the knees in the case of Kramer and Klein was the only movement following the drop; it appeared that complete unconsciousness was achieved instantaneously.

In the second series of executions carried out on 8 March 1946 it had been decided not to use chloroform, and the heart rate was measured at various times until an apex beat was no longer audible, the report stating, 'after fifteen minutes it is unusual for the heartbeat to be audible at the apex'.

For the executions of 15 May 1946, electrocardiography was used to see how long cardiac impulses were produced after the heartbeat had become inaudible in four of the prisoners executed that day. To carry out the procedure the bodies were lifted by block and tackle, the noose taken off and the body placed on a table.

In the first case which a reading was being taken of Lead 1, 7½ minutes after execution respiratory excursions suddenly started – an injection of 10cc chloroform in the area of cardiac dullnesss was made resulting in disturbance of rhythms [next word illegible] at the end of the recording in Lead 1. Subsequent readings were obtained but this time the picture was vitiated owing to the circulating chloroform.

A similar situation would arise in the second case, 'respiratory excursions started while the ECG leads were being adjusted', resulting in the injection of chloroform, and in the next case the prisoner was left 'hanging until the heart sounds could no longer be heard'. For the fourth case, although it is not clear, it appears that the same procedure as for the third case was adopted. 'In none of the series was there the slightest movement of the bodies after execution hence there was nothing to show whether there was complete or incomplete severance of the cord while remaining suspended.'

In the fourth series of executions the electrocardiograph equipment was not available. The bodies were allowed to hang until the apex beat was inaudible, an average of 12 minutes, and none of the bodies was seen to make any movements. In the fifth series it was decided to examine the state of the knee and ankle jerks. In some there were no jerks, in others there were, and in one 'ankle jerks could be elicited at 10 but not at 11 minutes'. 'Without a post-mortem examination of the cervical cord it does not appear possible to correlate these findings with the degree of damage done to the cord.' The fifth series brought the tests to a close, with fifty-three executions having been scrutinised. The report went on to summarise the findings including:

Fifteen minutes are usually sufficient to allow heartbeats audible at the apex to cease. Electrocardiograms show that inaudible impulses may be produced for a further ten minutes. For practical purposes it appears safe to declare life extinct when the apex beat can no longer be heard. Allowing this period of hanging it has been possible in this series to effect dual execution at half hourly intervals.

Appendix 'A' then went on to list the results of the tests conducted at the executions carried out on 8 March 1946. First in the column title 'Name' was Renoth. 'Age' – 49. 'Weight in Lbs' – 154. 'Height' – 5 foot 7 inches. 'Drop' – 7 foot 3 inches. Hans Renoth's heart rate was then shown in a table; after 2 minutes it was 140 beats per minute, after 10 minutes it was 120 beats. There were no further entries.

So there it was. I was actually overcome with a sense of sadness. It was a strange feeling. I did not necessarily like the feeling that I had. Here was the conclusion to the case. A man had been murdered. A man, in return, had paid in full with his life. Bill Maloney's loss was awful and unnecessary; now the tragic circle was complete. Two men dead, two families grieving.

EPILOGUE

Legend has it that the Pied Piper of Hamelin (or Hameln) cured the town of rat infestation with his music, enticing the rodents to a watery death in the Weser River. When the town's people refused to pay the rat catcher, he acted out his revenge, luring away the children while their parents were in church celebrating a Catholic feastday, never to be seen again. Across the centuries many versions of the infanticide developed. Some accounts say he took them to a cave, some say they were drowned like the rats in the river. And theories abound on the origins of the story. The Pied Piper has been described as a 'psychopath pederast', while the children were victims of natural calamities, accidents or disease, or became part of a pilgrimage. Or they left to start their own villages during the colonisation of Eastern Europe in the thirteenth century, with the man in pied garments as their leader, just as a Nazi leader in the twentieth century sought out *Lebensraum* in the east for the people who had fallen under the spell of his particular music.

Over the years eminent writers took up the Pied Piper legend. Johann Wolfgang Goethe, at the centre of German literature, penned a poem, the Brothers Grimm included their version of the tale in a collection of stories, and English poet and playwright Robert Browning described the exploits of the piper in verse, in which he described the fate of the naive followers.

> When, lo, as they reached the mountain's side,
> A wondrous portal opened wide,
> As if a cavern was suddenly hollowed;
> And the Piper advanced and the children followed,
> And when all were in to the very last,
> The door in the mountain-side shut fast.

Despite the fact that the modern-day legend of the Pied Piper, as it has developed, is based upon a mass murder, it is now exploited in the interests of commerce. Atop a bridge spanning the Weser, which joins the river-divided town, sits a large shining golden rat. It is the story of the rat catcher that drives tourism to the town of Hameln. The town needs this particular legendary killer.

I had a strange feeling as I drove towards Hameln, aside the banks of the Weser, flanked by the Weserbergland mountains, shrouded in low cloud – a sense of anticipation bordering on excitement, even though it was the culmination of a disturbing journey. My research in Germany had come full circle, from the grave of the man who had been murdered to the grave of the man executed for that murder. But I felt uneasy. I was visiting the place where some of the most infamous criminals, and most notorious psychopaths, who had embraced Nazi doctrine now lay buried.

On the outskirts of the historic town I followed the signs to the Friedhof Am Wehl, the road climbing through an avenue of trees, cut along the side of the densely wooded hill. Having parked my car, I walked across to the iron gates. I was due to meet local historian Bernhard Gelderblom, but I was early, so I passed through into the cemetery. The misty air was very still. Those leaves still on the trees remained unagitated.

Near the entrance a grassed area sloped upwards to the left, through an avenue of trees and shrubs. At the crest, three large red sandstone crosses stood prominent, with mass graves either side of the quarried monuments. On that particular day the areas were covered in leaf litter: yellows, browns, reds, oranges, purples. Now used as a municipal cemetery, the Friedhof Am Wehl was originally designed as a place to bury the war dead, a place for German war heroes. Here was a place where death recorded the history of Germany's twentieth-century conflict.

I walked along a foliage-sheltered pathway beside the main avenue; to the left and right, enclosed wooded shrines, with heavy dark headstones, memorialised local civilians. At the top of the incline I came across a vertical plinth marked 'Bomber Opfer 1939–1945' (bombing victims). As Bernhard would explain later, here were the graves of Hameln civilians killed by Allied bombing, each marked by horizontal slabs of stone. Rows upon rows. Included were seven slabs naming members of the Klecha family, who had been killed during a bombing raid by twelve Flying Fortresses of the American Eighth Air Force on 14 March 1945: Bärbel aged 11, Dietmar aged 5, Else aged 26, Harald aged 3, Karin aged 10, Otto aged 13 and Wolfgang aged 8. Instead of taking cover in a bomb shelter, the Klechas cowered in a ditch, which failed to protect them against a direct hit. There were also some red sandstone slabs with 'unbekannt' inscribed. Then, in another area were the graves of German soldiers, marked by small and vertical thick stone crosses, including a few informing of the resting place of an 'unbekannt soldaten'. A further separate mass grave held the remains of foreign workers – Dutch, Poles, Russians, Serbs, Belgians – each identified, where possible, on a slab. Some were 'unbekannt'. It had been deemed unacceptable for them to share the same burial area as German civilians. Some were children. At one of the stones I swept away some leaves to reveal the name of the person below. In May 1943 Marianna Smus and her Polish family had been deported to the Hameln area as slave workers. She gave birth to Stefan on 1 August 1943, but Marianna died on 7 September 1943 in a hospital at Hameln, officially from tuberculosis, although reports are that she had also been beaten by some German soldiers. Stefan died the following day, aged 5 weeks. Both lay interred at the Friedhof Am Wehl.

Further into the cemetery I came across the burial ground of those who lost their lives while detained in the local prisoner-of-war camp during the First World War. Nobody knew the exact whereabouts of individual remains, so isolated carved stones identified the general area. A large monument memorialised the 'englischen, belgischen, französischen, italienischen, rumänischen, russischen und serbischen kriegsgefangenen' who had died. Next to this were the graves of the German dead from the First World War. The servicemen from the Western countries, such as the British, who had lost their lives in the twentieth-century wars and had originally been buried at the Friedhof Am Wehl had all been exhumed and laid to rest elsewhere.

I returned to the entrance and met Bernhard Gelderblom. We walked straight on, with the avenue to the war graves to our left, up a slight incline, past some men working on their family grave and then down to some isolated ground at the edge of the cemetery, and to the boundary with the forest. We initially came to a simple grassed area with a short path to a memorial stone dedicated to the people who had lost their lives while imprisoned at the Hameln Zuchthaus during the war. Within this mass grave was Paul Jost, who had been sent to the Zuchthaus in 1943 for listening to foreign radio stations. Jost, born in 1892 in Witten, worked for the railways and was a member of the Social Democratic Party (the *SPD*) – a socialist party banned by the Nazis. Under suspicion of providing food to slave workers and distributing anti-Nazi leaflets, he regularly had to report to the Gestapo. On 28 June 1943 Paul was arrested and sentenced to two years in the Zuchthaus. Days before the war ended, with the American army having recently seized Hameln, Paul Jost died in the Zuchthaus hospital; the official record shows he succumbed to diarrhoea and heart failure.

Bernhard and I walked on to a further levelled area, which was clearly not tended. Beneath a blanket of leaves, nettles were abundant. There was nothing to identify who lay in this mass grave. No memorials, no headstones, no crosses, nothing. It was neglected and seemingly forgotten, and nature was recovering the ground. There was a chill in the still air. The trees hardly moved. It was a very quiet moment. But those buried had not always been left in peace. In 1975, after a statutory thirty years, the Hameln authorities had wanted to 'level', 'smooth out', the area. The graves did not come under the law that provided memorialisation in perpetuity to war graves. But to some local people this ground held many victims who had been 'arbitrarily condemned' by British 'victors' justice', and it represented a 'piece of post-war history'. A decision was made, allowing a group of local people to maintain the area, and wooden crosses were erected, although representations made to the town council for the erection of a memorial were turned down.

In 1985 Grabfeld III, the area in the cemetery where the executed war criminals were buried, became the scene of a clash between right-wing radicals and their opponents, culminating on Saturday, 16 November, just before national memorial day. Neo-Nazi and white nationalist groups marched through Hameln, performing Nazi salutes, to the Friedhof Am Wehl. Watched by hundreds of policemen, they held a commemorative service at the mass grave; wreaths were laid and speeches made. Many who had come to protest against the commemoration took exception, violence erupted and blood was spilled. Television cameras brought the clashes to the attention of the nation, and lengthy debate followed at the town council. On 5 March 1986, overnight, the graves were cleared, and 200 iron crosses were removed from the frozen ground, along with some named grave plates. A few days later neo-Nazis again flocked to Hameln to demonstrate. Their political opponents did likewise. The cemetery was closed, and over a thousand police were called in to keep the two factions apart.

In the years following there were further 'commemorations', small gatherings to lay wreaths, and in 2001 the Hameln authorities turned down a request for an official ceremony. But in 2008 the grave area that caused such controversy was simply overgrown with weeds. For now this 'mountain-side' was 'shut fast'. Within this soil lay the remains of the people executed as war criminals at Hameln prison. Some of the most notorious perpetrators of Nazi horror were buried here, including those put to death by Albert Pierrepoint for their involvement in the crime and the horror that was Bergen Belsen. Also, somewhere in front of me, as my eyes swept the area, lay the remains of Hans Renoth, the exact location 'unbekannt'.

COMMENT

Hans Renoth, Hans Pelgrim, Friedrich Grabowski and Paul Nieke did, in the main, in this author's opinion, receive a fair trial. One flaw was the joint representation of Pelgrim, Grabowski and Nieke. They would have been served better by separate counsel, particularly Nieke. A 'cut-throat' defence could have emphasised that, apart from a suggestion in Renoth's statement, he was not specifically named during the trial as participating in the beating, and the eyes of the witnesses would have been focused on the attack on Maloney. However, there is a document in the National Archives files that definitely implicates Nieke in the beating. A document dated 1 June 1945 outlines the prima facie case against Hans Renoth, and included is a brief outline, provided by Renoth, of what happened on the fateful day.

> I found pilot hiding in ditch and wanted to turn him over to *Wehrmacht* and I took him towards the plane with two new German soldiers. I was threatened by everybody present as friend of enemy. I went away and everybody beat the prisoner . . . The two political leaders [Grabowski and Nieke], the *Oberwachtmeister* [Pelgrim] and the two soldiers beat the prisoner.

When Bill Maloney was found in Franken's field on that fateful day in September 1944, he fell into the hands of a group of men who had sworn the oath of allegiance to Adolf Hitler, who were at the lower end of the political hierarchy, and who had been brutalised to some extent by five years of war. Moreover, even if they had not had direct experience of the harshness of war, such as the Allied bombing, Joseph Goebbels had ensured they knew about it. We know that Hans Pelgrim's daughter had experienced the horrors of Allied bombing in Essen and Friedrich Grabowski's son had survived a strafing attack by an Allied fighter-bomber. And Goebbels' Nazi propaganda carried the 'spirit of the regime' to people like Nieke, Grabowski, Pelgrim and Renoth. When Renoth shot Bill Maloney, was he 'working towards the Führer'?

Even so, there was clearly a sense among those concerned that the act was in some way wrong, because Renoth, if we believe his story – and there is a lot of corroborative testimony – was advised to obtain, and indeed sought out, a certificate stating he was ordered to shoot. By obtaining the certificate, he clearly shows his concern that the shooting of Maloney was in some way wrong. Because the certificate was never found and put into evidence, the authenticity could not be checked. Anyone could have written the certificate.

There is no doubt in my mind that Justice and the Law, as defined at the time, were applied properly. Hans Renoth had committed a war crime and was therefore a war criminal. He received the punishment deemed applicable. Bill Maloney had been 'executed', by a group of men who had been brutalised by over five years of war and propaganda, and at that time and at that place Bill Maloney represented to them a hated enemy air force that had been devastating their country. He was not a brother and a son, from a faraway country, who had enjoyed his sport and wanted to fly. Unlike Renoth, Pelgrim, Grabowski and Nieke, Bill Maloney was not granted his day in court. And I do believe that there are men who got away with Bill Maloney's murder. A preponderance of testimony does suggest that there were soldiers present at the time of the beating, and if you accept that Renoth was ordered to carry out the *coup de grâce*, then the man who gave that order is also guilty of Maloney's murder.

When Renoth, Pelgrim and Grabowski were arrested, they described in their statements the involvement of 'two captains' in the incident. The investigators did pursue some lines of enquiry, in particular trying to find a 'Hauptmann Kuehne' (also listed in the investigation files as possibly being called Krause). His name became one of thousands swelling the CROWCASS lists. But to find anything about Kuehne proved nigh on impossible. One witness had stated that she believed he was a barrister in Hamburg in civil life, and the Field Security police in Hamburg were asked in November 1945 to make a special search. But nothing came of it, and a decision was made to progress the trial of the four other accused in Kuehne's absence. Following the trial there appears to have been little follow-up on the enquiries concerning Kuehne. When the British government recently allowed the publication of the CROWCASS list, his name was still on it. In post-war Germany it was simply impossible fully to investigate each case; a decision had to made based on resources available, and in the Elten case people had been brought to account.

What dismays me is that the forces of war brought an Australian and a German together in a field in Germany to enact a tragedy. To quote Aldous Huxley, 'What is absurd and monstrous about war is that men who have no personal quarrel should be trained to murder one another in cold blood.' Within the context of the brutalisation of war, the 'simple-minded' Renoth murdered Maloney in cold blood. As Prosecuting Counsel Captain Diamond said in his summation at the trial: 'He fired and he hit the pilot. The pilot was still alive at the time he fired.' Yet I am still uneasy about the fact that, at the exhumation, the pathologist, Balfour, found no evidence of a gunshot wound. Balfour claimed that the skull was terribly decomposed, and the photographs back this up. But the rest of the body is fairly intact, and surely a bullet wound to the body would have been evident. Possibly this was overlooked because of the clearly extensive fatal wounds to the skull.

I find it very hard to believe that the men who sat in judgment of the Elten case were completely impartial. And it is the word 'completely' that is important here. These men cannot now answer back to such a claim. Certainly the defendants were given the opportunity to defend themselves. But surely what Sigwick, McNeill, Kington-Blair-Oliphant and Leicester-Warren had witnessed and heard about during the fighting of the war, and what they had witnessed and heard about during the liberation of Germany and the fight for post-war order, affected them. McLauchlan's war had been different, but could he really find the man who had shot an Australian airman innocent. Not that Renoth was innocent: he was, as I have stated, clearly guilty of a war crime, as it was then defined. Could the fact that he had acted under orders be seen as a mitigating circumstance when it came to sentencing? An Australian airman was unlikely to think so.

If you accept the application of military law and that the defendants in the Elten case received a fair trial, then Pelgrim quite literally got away with murder. There is firm testimony of his involvement in the 'fatal' beating, and his attempts at explaining how his rifle came to be in the hands of a soldier are, on the face of it, implausible. It is not documented anywhere whether Kington-Blair-Oliphant and Leicester-Warren knew that those convicted could be released before serving out their full term. If they did, then Pelgrim's sentence was very lenient, if it was known he might only have to serve half of his fifteen-year term. It is one of the great ironies of this case that Renoth's actions saved his fellow policeman's life. Bill Maloney, who suffered a horrific and vicious assault, was going to die from the beating. Renoth shortened his life by a matter of seconds. As a result, he saved Pelgrim and condemned himself.

ACKNOWLEDGEMENTS

Thanks to my mother and father for their support. And thanks to Mags, Michael and Adam, who had to put up with my moods as my mind took me to some very dark places.

Bill Maloney's family, his sisters, nieces and nephews, provided invaluable support. They really did not know the details surrounding Bill's death; they had simply been told that he had been shot. They knew nothing of a post-war trial. It was one of my major concerns that I was bringing to light the brutal circumstances in which Bill had been killed. I did not want to distress some old ladies who had fond memories of growing up with their energetic brother Bill. However, the Maloney family was extremely supportive. Special thanks to Shane Maloney, Greg and Marie Keen, Peter Maloney and Frances Rohde (Maloney).

A special thank you extends to Dr Hado Ebben for his help with the German side of the story. Hado, as a young boy, along with his family, had suffered beneath the Allied bombers; their house in Kleve was destroyed during the war. Hado's wife Gertrud still has vivid memories of the bombing of her home town, Cologne. Without Hado, much of the German side of this story could not have been told. Hado, sometimes accompanied by his son Jan, sat with me, the grandson of an Allied bomber pilot, and with impartiality translated tragic tales from senior residents of Emmerich into English words. You have my sincerest thanks, Hado, as do Gertrud and Jan, for their time, and your grandson Marc Buckermann.

The people of Elten and Emmerich were most welcoming. I was delving into a story that had divided a community all those years ago. Yet they invited me into their homes and were warm hosts. Even the relatives of the men accused and convicted were most welcoming and of great assistance.

So my appreciation extends to Herbert Kleipass of the Rheinmuseum/Stadtarchiv, Willi Bosmann (son of witness Johann Bosmann), Gerd Dörning (son of the former funeral undertaker), Willi Franken (son of witness Hubert Franken), Theo Meenen, Fritz Leinung, Hubert Meenen, Herbert Schüürman, Herta Schieck, Irmgard Renoth (daughter-in-law of Hans Renoth), Monika Kersjes (granddaughter of Hans Renoth), Frau A. Janssen (daughter of Hans Pelgrim) and her daughter Sylvia van Alst, Claudia Paul, Manfred and Hilmar Grabowski (sons of Friedrich

Grabowski) and Reimar Grabowski (Friedrich's grandson) and Jörg-Ulrich Nieke (Paul Nieke's grandson).

Barrister Stephen Vullo, a leading criminal defence expert, of 2 Bedford Row, was kind enough to cast his eye over the transcript of the trial and assisted with matters of law and some of the nuances of advocacy.

I was extremely fortunate to make contact with one of the key investigators in the Elten case, Wady Lehmann. Wady's notes, recollections and photographs provide further depth to the story. Thank you also to Susan Lehmann.

Thank you to Hugh Ross, a veteran of 80 Squadron, and to Stuart Eastwood, Rex Cannon, Mark Barraclough, Roy Hemington (CWGC), Leonora Klein, Ian Whisker, Don Wills, Mark Eaton, the Historical Section of the RCMP, Gordon Caley, Ryan Helly, Patrick Brode, John Baines, Paul Evans, Paul Brandon, Donald McLeod, Ian Jewison, Jean Hammond and Marionne Diggles of the Toowoomba & Darling Downs Family History Soc. Inc., Mervin Burgard, Edith Nicol, Daniel J. McNamara, Ryan Kelly, Lindsey Scott, Marilyn Hill, Jane Marie Stock, Anita M. (Deane) Abdullah, Moe Skinner, Brian Aziz, Mitchell Aziz, George Cole, John Baines, Andrew Lownie, S. Weston, Geoffrey Crump (Cheshire Military Museum), Sir Michael Leighton, Marion Roberts, Mrs Florence Wilkie, C. K. Pfeffer (Boonah Shire Archives), Paul Evans (Royal Artillery Museum), Dr Peter Stanley (Director of the Centre for Historical Research – National Museum of Australia), Rachel Dohme, Randall Bytwerk and Bernhard Gelderblom (http://www.gelderblom-hameln.de).

I also want to express my gratitude to Hilary Walford for the diligence of her editing. And finally a thank you to Jonathan Falconer and all at Haynes Publishing who put their faith into this project and were most supportive.

NOTES

Prologue

1.   O. Clutton-Brock, *Footprints on the Sands of Time: RAF Bomber Command Prisoners of War in Germany 1939–45* (Grub Street, 2003), p. 327.

2.   Figures of raid damage and German lives lost are from Martin Middlebrook and Chris Everitt, *The Bomber Command War Diaries* (Midland Publishing, 1995).

Chapter 1. 'Unbekannt'

1.   Quoted in P. Brode, *Casual Slaughters and Accidental Judgements: Canadian War Crimes Prosecutions 1944–1948* (published for the Osgoode Society for Canadian Legal History by University of Toronto Press, 1997), p. 37.

Chapter 2. Beginner's Luck

1.   The state formed by the British Military in 1946.

2.   http://saintvitus.com/SaintVitus/#Saint.

3.   W. Shirer, *The Rise and Fall of the Third Reich* (Mandarin, 1996), pp. 256–8.

Chapter 3. Spike – the Boy from Australia

1.   Dr Peter Stanley, Principal Historian at the Australian War Memorial, 'The Roundel: Concentric Identities among Australian Airmen in Bomber Command', presented at the 2003 History Conference – Air War Europe. Stanley's paper drew upon contemporary material, mainly letters and diaries, on oral history interviews compiled as part of the Keith Murdoch Sound Archive of Australia in the War of 1939–45, and on memoirs written by Australians who flew as part of Bomber Command.

Chapter 4. Death of a Pilot Officer

1.   TNA: PRO AIR 37/564.

2.   Figures of raid damage and German lives lost are from Martin Middlebrook and Chris Everitt, *The Bomber Command War Diaries* (Midland Publishing, 1995).

3.   Bob Spurdle's details from C. Shores and C. Williams, *Aces High* (Grub Street, 1994).

4.   Bob Spurdle quotes from *The Blue Arena* (Kimber, 1986).

5.   Author's interview with Hugh Ross.

Chapter 5. Witnesses to Murder

1.   We cannot be sure, but this could have been Canadian Pilot Officer P. E. Hurtubise of 412 Squadron. Commonwealth War Graves Commission records show that an unidentified airman was removed from a lone grave at the rear of Elten cemetery chapel in April 1947. The remains were reburied in grave 2.B.12. of Reichswald Forest War Cemetery and, following an investigation, identified as Hurtubise, who was killed on 27 Sept. 1944 during a combat with enemy aircraft. If it is Hurtubise, then it does raise the question as to why his body was allowed to remain in Elten whereas Maloney's body was taken away.

Chapter 6. Rise of the *Terrorflieger*

1.   L. Rees, *The Nazis: A Warning from History* (BBC Books, 2005).

2.   The German Propaganda Archive, Calvin College, Randall Bytwerk www.calvin.edu/academic/cas/gpa/ww2era.htm.

3.   Ibid.

4.   Ibid.

5.   Ibid.

6.   Ibid.

7.   Lord Russell of Liverpool, *The Scourge of the Swastika: A Short History of Nazi War Crimes* (Macmillan Publishing, 1989)

8.   Ibid.

9.   Joachim von Ribbentrop, *Nazi Conspiracy & Aggression, Individual Responsibility of Defendants*, vol. II, ch. XVI, at www.nizkor.org/hweb/imt/nca/nca-02/nca-02-16-03-index.html.

10.   Oliver Clutton-Brock, *Footprints on the Sands of Time: RAF Bomber Command Prisoners-of-War 1939–1945* (Grub Street, 2003), p. 473.

11.   Lord Tedder, *With Prejudice: The War Memoirs of Marshal of the Royal Air Force Lord Tedder G.C.B.* (Cassell and Company, 1966).

Chapter 7. Blowing the Hell Out

1.   IWM sound archive, 28676, Jack Ball.

Chapter 8. Death of Nazism

1.   IWM sound archive, 21561, John Hayes.
2.   IWM sound archive, 20008, Denis Whybro.
3.   Alexander McKee, *Dresden 1945: The Devil's Tinderbox* (Souvenir Press, 1982).
4.   Ibid.
5.   This appears to be a misspelling and probably refers to an SS Nachrichten Abteilung.

Chapter 9. Condemnation

1.   Eden's statement as reported in *The Times*, 23 June 1944, 'Shooting of RAF Officer "Cold-Blooded Butchery"'.
2.   TNA: PRO PREM 4/100/10, note by Prime Minister, 1 Nov. 1943, quoted in R. Overy, *Interrogations: Inside the Minds of the Nazi Elite* (Penguin, 2002).
3.   TNA: PRO PREM 4/100/10, minute by Foreign Secretary, 'Treatment of War Criminals', 22 June 1942, quoted in Overy, *Interrogations.*
4.   Quoted in M. R. Marrus, *The Nuremberg War Crimes Trial 1945–46: A Documentary History* (Bedford Books, 1997), pp. 24–5.
5.   Ibid., p. 29.

Chapter 10. The Drive for Justice

1.   *The Times*, 15 June 1945.
2.   P. Brode, *Casual Slaughters and Accidental Judgements: Canadian War Crimes Prosecutions 1944–1948* (published for the Osgoode Society for Canadian Legal History by University of Toronto Press, 1997).
3.   The testimony of Lance Sergeant Stanley Dudka, quoted in ibid., p. 15.
4.   Correspondence with Wady Lehmann.

Chapter 11. Violating the Laws and the Usages of War

1.   The United Nations War Crimes Commission, *Law-Reports of Trials of War Criminals*, vol. I (London, HMSO, 1947), and www.ess.uwe.ac.uk/genocide/.
2.   Transcripts made from the sound archives held on the CBC digital archives website http://archives.cbc.ca/war_conflict/second_world_war.

Chapter 12. Judges

1. *Daily Telegraph*, obituary, 21 June 2005.
2. www.thepeerage.com.
3. TNA: PRO WO 171 5218, WO 171 9250.
4. The war diary of the 111th HAA Regiment, held at the Royal Artillery Museum.
5. The war diary of the 62nd A/Tk Regiment, held at the Royal Artillery Museum.
6. Lt-Col. Sir Richard Verdin, OBE, TD, *The Cheshire (Earl of Chester's) Yeomanry 1898–1967* (published by the author, 1971).

Chapter 13. Trial

1. The correct spelling is Göbel, but Gobbels was used in the transcript.

Chapter 14. Free Hunting

1. Oliver Durdin's obituary, *London Free Press*, 12 Dec. 2004.

Chapter 17. 'To be or not to be'

1. This is an English translation, made at the trial, of his summation (which was given in German). The grammar has not been corrected.

Chapter 18. Death of a Police Officer

1. A. Pierrepoint, *Executioner Pierrepoint* (Eric Dobby, 2005).
2. Ibid.

Chapter 19. Punishment

1. The Zentrale Rechtsschutzstelle (literally the Central Legal Rights Protection Authority) was set up by the Bundestag (Federal Parliament) on 1 Dec. 1949 to provide for the protection of the legal rights of those Germans imprisoned abroad as a result of the war (www.bundesarchiv.de/bestaende_findmittel/bestaendeuebersicht/body.htm).

Chapter 20. A Small Difficulty

1. TNA: PRO HO 45/25454.
2. TNA: PRO FO 371/109722.
3. TNA: PRO FO 371/109722.
4. TNA: PRO FO 371/109722.
5. TNA: PRO FO 371/109722.
6. TNA: PRO FO 371/109722.

BIBLIOGRAPHY AND SOURCES

The major source of information concerning the investigation into the case and the trial itself come from the following National Archives files: TNA: PRO WO 235/55, WO 309/45, WO 309/629 and WO 309/1493. Bill Maloney's background comes from correspondence with his family, his flying logbook and his letters. Details of other sources can be found in the endnotes and acknowledgements.

Axmacher, W., *Elten die letzten 100 Jahre* (1997).

Brode, P., *Casual Slaughters and Accidental Judgements: Canadian War Crimes Prosecutions 1944–1948* (published for the Osgoode Society for Canadian Legal History by University of Toronto Press, 1997).

Clutton-Brock, O., *Footprints on the Sands of Time: RAF Bomber Command Prisoners of War in Germany 1939–45* (Grub Street, 2003).

Darlow, S., *Victory Fighters* (Grub Street, 2005).

Gilbert, M., *Second World War* (Orion Books, 1995).

McKee, A., *Dresden 1945: The Devil's Tinderbox* (Souvenir Press, 1982).

Marrus, M. R., *The Nuremberg War Crimes Trial 1945–46: A Documentary History* (Bedford Books, 1997).

Middlebrook, M., and Everitt, C., *The Bomber Command War Diaries* (Midland Publishing, 1995).

Overy, R., *Interrogations: Inside the Minds of the Nazi Elite* (Penguin, 2002).

Pierrepoint, A., *Executioner Pierrepoint* (Eric Dobby, 2005).

Rees, L., *The Nazis: A Warning from History* (BBC Books, 2005).

Russell, Lord, of Liverpool, *The Scourge of the Swastika: A Short History of Nazi War Crimes* (Macmillan, 1989).

Shirer, W., *The Rise and Fall of the Third Reich* (Mandarin, 1996).

Shores, C., and Williams, C., *Aces High* (Grub Street, 1994).

Spurdle, R. *The Blue Arena* (Kimber, 1986).

Tedder, Lord, *With Prejudice: The War Memoirs of Marshal of the Royal Air Force Lord Tedder G.C.B.* (Cassell and Company, 1966).

Verdin, Lt-Col. Sir Richard, OBE, TD, *The Cheshire (Earl of Chester's) Yeomanry 1898–1967* (published by the author, 1971).

Details of other books by Steve Darlow can be found on the author's website, www.stevedarlow.co.uk

INDEX